Wittgenstein and Artificial Intelligence, Volume I: Mind and Language

ANTHEM STUDIES IN WITTGENSTEIN

Anthem Studies in Wittgenstein publishes new and classic works on Wittgenstein and Wittgensteinian philosophy. This book series aims to bring Wittgenstein's thought into the mainstream by highlighting its relevance to 21st century concerns. Titles include original monographs, themed edited volumes, forgotten classics, biographical works and books intended to introduce Wittgenstein to the general public. The series is published in association with the British Wittgenstein Society.

Anthem Studies in Wittgenstein sets out to put in place whatever measures may emerge as necessary in order to carry out the editorial selection process purely on merit and to counter bias on the basis of gender, race, ethnicity, religion, sexual orientation and other characteristics protected by law. These measures include subscribing to the British Philosophical Association/ Society for Women in Philosophy (UK) Good Practice Scheme.

Series Editor
Constantine Sandis – University of Hertfordshire, UK

Forthcoming Titles in the Series
Extending Hinge Epistemology
Normativity, Meaning and Philosophy: Essays on Wittgenstein
Practical Rationality, Learning and Convention: Essays in the Philosophy of Education
Wittgenstein and Modernist Fiction: The Language of Acknowledgment
Wittgenstein and the Life We Live with Language
Wittgenstein, Human Beings and Conversation
Wittgenstein on Other Minds
Wittgenstein Rehinged
Wittgenstein, Scepticism and Naturalism: Essays on the Later Philosophy

Wittgenstein and Artificial Intelligence, Volume I: Mind and Language

Brian Ball, Alice C. Helliwell and Alessandro Rossi

ANTHEM PRESS

Anthem Press
An imprint of Wimbledon Publishing Company
www.anthempress.com

This edition first published in UK and USA 2024
by ANTHEM PRESS
75–76 Blackfriars Road, London SE1 8HA, UK
or PO Box 9779, London SW19 7ZG, UK
and
244 Madison Ave #116, New York, NY 10016, USA

© 2024 Brian Ball, Alice C. Helliwell, Alessandro Rossi, editorial matter and selection; individual chapters © individual contributors

The moral right of the authors has been asserted.

All rights reserved. Without limiting the rights under copyright reserved above, no part of this publication may be reproduced, stored or introduced into a retrieval system, or transmitted, in any form or by any means (electronic, mechanical, photocopying, recording or otherwise), without the prior written permission of both the copyright owner and the above publisher of this book.

British Library Cataloguing-in-Publication Data
A catalogue record for this book is available from the British Library.

Library of Congress Cataloging-in-Publication Data: 2024933808
A catalog record for this book has been requested.

ISBN-13: 978-1-83999-136-3 (Hbk)
ISBN-10: 1-83999-136-4 (Hbk)

Cover Credit: DreamStudio

This title is also available as an e-book.

CONTENTS

Introduction 1
Brian Ball, Alice C. Helliwell and Alessandro Rossi

Chapter 1. Wittgenstein and Turing on AI: Myth Versus Reality 17
Diane Proudfoot

Chapter 2. Between Wittgenstein and Turing: Enactive Embodied Thinking Machines 39
Tomi Kokkonen and Ilmari Hirvonen

Chapter 3. Wittgenstein, Psychological Language and AI 61
Arturo Vázquez Hernández

Chapter 4. The Metonymical Trap 85
Éloïse Boisseau

Chapter 5. The Forms of Artificially Intelligent Life: Brandom, Chomsky and Wittgenstein on the Possibility of Strong-AI 105
Laith Abdel-Rahman

Chapter 6. Black Boxes, Beetles and Beasts 123
Ian Ground

Chapter 7. Language Models and the Private Language Argument: A Wittgensteinian Guide to Machine Learning 145
Giovanni Galli

Chapter 8. Simplification without Falsification: The Problem of Relevance in Logic and AI 165
Oskari Kuusela

Chapter 9. Modelling Analogical Reasoning: One-Size-Fits-All? 183
Ioannis Votsis

Notes on Contributors 205
Index 207

INTRODUCTION

Brian Ball, Alice C. Helliwell and Alessandro Rossi

Why Wittgenstein and Artificial Intelligence?

Ludwig Wittgenstein (1889–1951) is widely regarded as one of the most significant philosophers of the twentieth century.[1] His influence has been deep and wide-ranging, extending well beyond philosophy. Alongside a lasting impact in areas where he wrote extensively (the philosophies of language, logic, mathematics, mind and psychology, as well as metaphysics, and the theory of knowledge), Wittgenstein's philosophy has continued to influence areas beyond his focus (e.g. aesthetics, ethics and jurisprudence).[2] Many

---

1 The results of the 2009 poll conducted by the philosophers-led blog *Leiter Reports* placed him at the top of the list of most influential philosophers of the twentieth century (https://leiterreports.typepad.com/blog/2009/03/lets-settle-this-once-and-for-all-who-really-was-the-greatest-philosopher-of-the-20thcentury.html), and the *New York Times* article that prompted it had already articulated this view, which may reflect wider public opinion on the matter (https://www.nytimes.com/2009/03/01/books/review/Holt-t.html?_r=1&ref=review). The *Internet Encyclopedia of Philosophy* entry on *Ludwig Wittgenstein* by Duncan Richter suggests he may be the most important philosopher since Kant. Or again, from Hyman and Glock (2017, 1): 'He is recognized today as one of the most original and powerful thinkers of the twentieth century.'

2 Arrington (2017, 605) begins: 'Wittgenstein wrote very little about ethics. [...] Nevertheless, [...] [his] works exerted an enormous influence on ethical thinkers'. Similarly, Schroeder (2017, 612) remarks, 'in Wittgenstein's philosophical writings aesthetics is only ever touched upon in passing'. *A Companion to Wittgenstein*, the edited collection from which these comments are extracted, contains no article on Wittgenstein and law – presumably because Wittgenstein 'wrote nothing in political philosophy or jurisprudence' (Hyman and Glock, 2017, 1). (They also note that he wrote 'very little in ethics, and the only sustained record of his philosophical ideas about religion and art consists in notes taken by students at his lectures' [2017, 1]). The IEP article cited in the previous note points out that 'his later philosophy is influential in a growing number of fields outside philosophy'.

of the themes of his work[3] bear – either directly, or indirectly – on issues that arise in (both scientific and commercial) attempts to produce artificial intelligence (AI).

The link between Wittgenstein and AI should perhaps not be a surprising one. During his life, Wittgenstein interacted with Alan Turing (1912–1954), considered by many to be the founder of AI as an area of inquiry:[4] Turing attended Wittgenstein's 1939 lectures in Cambridge on the foundations of mathematics (Wittgenstein 1976: LFM; see also Copeland 2012, 32–34; and see Floyd 2019 for an account of what their mutual intellectual influence may have been). And years earlier, in the Blue Book of 1933, Wittgenstein had even discussed the central animating question of AI, 'Is it possible for a machine to think?' (Wittgenstein 1958: BB, 47).

There is therefore ample reason to suspect both that historical investigations of Wittgenstein's work and the context in which it was situated can reveal the intellectual landscape at the dawn of AI, and that philosophical engagement with his work might shed light on important issues in the theory and application of AI.[5] The present collection touches on the former, historical variety of inquiry (see especially Proudfoot's contribution), but it focuses primarily on the latter, more philosophical project.

Why Now?

This collection is not the first work to explore the interaction between Wittgenstein and AI. However, the last concentrated look at the topic was published over a quarter of a century ago: Shanker's (1998) single-authored monograph, *Wittgenstein's Remarks on the Foundations of AI*. Since then, there have been significant advances in AI – most notably, the advent of big data and the use of deep neural networks for machine learning (ML), which underpin recent generative AI systems (such as ChatGPT, Dall-E and Midjourney) – as well as changes in Wittgenstein scholarship. So the time is ripe for bringing the two together afresh.

The scholarly literature on Wittgenstein's philosophy is, of course, vast, and we cannot hope to do justice to it here. But the following sketch can

---

3 Biletzki and Matar's (2023) *Stanford Encyclopedia of Philosophy* entry on *Wittgenstein*, for instance, has sections on the nature of philosophy, sense and nonsense, meaning as use, language games and family resemblance, rule-following and private language, and grammar and form of life.
4 See e.g. Hodges (2019).
5 It is also possible that recent developments in AI might provide evidence that enables us to assess and/or evaluate certain aspects of Wittgenstein's philosophy, or to illuminate aspects of its evolution over time. This more scholarly prospect is not much explored here.

perhaps help to orient our readers, without doing too much violence to its details and nuance.

The orthodox view within Wittgenstein scholarship has presented his work as falling into two stages, early and late, with the former epitomized by the *Tractatus Logico-Philosophicus* (*TLP*) (Wittgenstein 1922 [Ogden/Ramsey translation]; 1961 [Pears/McGuinness]; 2021 [Bazzocchi/Hacker]; 2023 [Beaney]), and the latter by the *Philosophical Investigations* (*PI*) (Wittgenstein 1953 [Anscombe translation]; 2009 [Ancombe/Hacker/Schulte]). On this style of interpretation, the early Wittgenstein was sympathetic to an atomistic metaphysics, and a representationalist 'picture theory' of mind and language, but deployed a distinction between saying and showing to indicate that some important (e.g. metaphysical, semantic or ethical) truths could not be articulated, but must be 'pass[ed] over in silence' (Wittgenstein 1961: TLP 7). The later Wittgenstein, however, rejected these views, pursuing anti-essentialism in metaphysics, and the doctrine that meaning is best understood in terms of use, rather than representation.

More recently, however, there have been alternative readings of the Wittgenstein corpus, with some scholars suggesting a 'middle Wittgenstein' and/or further stages (e.g. post-*Investigations*), while others propose continuity of thought.[6] One significant development in this trend has been the articulation of a so-called resolute reading of the *Tractatus* – a term only officially introduced into the secondary literature by Goldfarb (1997), and embraced by its original advocates in Conant and Diamond (2004).[7] On this reading, we must take very seriously Wittgenstein's claim that his own propositions (including the articulations of atomism and the picture theory of meaning) are nonsense,[8] and not – as Frank Ramsey famously joked – try to 'whistle' (or show) them. In any case, whatever the scholarly upshot of this debate may be, neither Diamond nor Conant is referenced in Shanker's (1998) book, and the term 'resolute' does not occur within it. Perhaps some fresh insights on AI can

---

6 The *Investigations* comprises two parts. The first of these was ready for publication already in 1946, while the second was added posthumously. Thus, post-*Investigations* is the period comprising the last five years of Wittgenstein's life, from 1946 to 1951. See Biletzki and Matar (2023).

7 See Bronzo (2012) and Conant and Bronzo (2017) for this history of the scholarship. The resolute reading itself was introduced by Diamond (1988) and Conant (1989), and the term was coined in an unpublished manuscript by Ricketts – see e.g. Koethe (2003).

8 'My propositions are elucidatory in this way: he who understands me finally recognizes them as senseless, when he has climbed out through them, on them, over them. (He must so to speak throw away the ladder, after he has climbed up on it.) He must transcend these propositions, and then he will see the world aright' (Wittgenstein 1961: TLP 6.54).

be gleaned from Wittgenstein's work in light of this more recent scholarship (see e.g. Rossi's contribution to Volume 2 of this collection).

According to some, AI research and development has likewise come in two stages, or 'waves' (Cantwell-Smith 2019) – arguably mirroring the two stages of Wittgenstein's philosophy.[9] During the period of 'Good Old Fashioned AI' (Haugeland 1985), or GOFAI, a symbolic approach was taken, with both representations (of key notions) and rules (for their manipulation) explicit. This made AI systems readily interpretable (by those who understand the relevant programming languages). But more recently, since the advent of big data (thanks, in large part, to the Internet) and increases in computing power (in the form of graphical processing units, or GPUs), sub-symbolic approaches have been more common, with deep neural networks employed to enable ML. The operations of such systems are not always transparent (even to AI engineers),[10] but the statistical engines which lie at their cores have enabled significant improvements in everything from computer vision to machine translation, and even text, audio, and image generation. This two-stage account of the history of AI might be challenged, however, by pointing to the mid-century 'cybernetics' (Wiener 1948) movement and the 'connectionism' of the 1980s (Rumelhart and McClelland 1986; McClelland and Rumelhart 1987) to suggest continuity with contemporary ML; and some (e.g. Boden 2018) suggest the need for hybrid, 'neuro-symbolic' architectures, highlighting the ongoing need for good old fashioned methods. Unfortunately, we cannot give an extended discussion of the history of AI here – but see for example Wooldridge (2020) for some further details.[11]

There is also a third reason for engaging with this topic again, a quarter of a century after its last book-length treatment: Shanker (1998) only really engages with the question of whether intelligent machines are possible, and how this interacts with Wittgenstein's philosophy. Indeed, Xu (2016) identifies five arguments Shannker articulates against the possibility of what Searle (1980) called 'strong AI' – roughly, the possession (rather than mere simulation) of intentional mental states such as understanding by a machine – from a Wittgensteinian perspective. And yet, in light of the development – and deployment – of myriad and various narrow AI applications in recent years,

---

9 Thanks to Anthony Grayling for this suggestion.
10 See e.g. Ball and Koliousis (2022) for two sources of opacity in AI systems: technical and commercial.
11 See also the 2023 version of Williams's poster, available at https://www.daniellejwilliams.com/.

there is a need to take a look at a more encompassing set of issues in the philosophy of AI on which Wittgenstein's view may yield insights.

Nevertheless, it will be worth briefly recapping the five arguments identified by Xu in Shanker's book. The first is an argument from Wittgenstein's own remarks on the question noted above about thinking machines: very roughly, it is said to be a contradiction in terms to say that a machine thinks, so that this claim can be known a priori to be false, whereas AI presupposes it to be an open empirical question. This argument is addressed in a number of chapters in this first volume of our collection. Two chapters – one by Proudfoot, the other by Kokkonen and Hirvonen – discuss the argument in light of Wittgenstein's apparent disagreement with Turing; while those by Abdel-Rahman, Vázquez and Boisseau engage with the Wittgensteinian point of view alone.[12]

A second argument concerns rule-following. According to Shanker's Wittgenstein, intelligent agents follow mechanical rules (flexibly): but machines can only (inflexibly, or) mechanically follow a rule; thus, machines cannot be intelligent agents. Xu responds that the neural nets of connectionist AI systems admit of flexibility (so that the second premise is false).[13] In any case, Wittgenstein's rule-following considerations in the *Investigations*,[14] and their relationship to AI, are central to many of the chapters in our volumes – for example, the chapters by Ground and Galli.[15]

A third argument concerns psychologism – roughly, the doctrine that logical validity is grounded in psychological facts: Shanker (1998, 102) holds that AI is psychologistic, while Wittgenstein is (rightly) opposed to psychologism, so that AI cannot succeed. Interestingly, Shanker cites Newell and Simon (1976) in favour of the first premise, and they do engage in what Russell and Norvig (2022) call 'cognitive modelling' – roughly, the attempt to replicate human modes of reasoning in AI systems. Xu responds to this argument by denying the first premise, that AI is committed to psychologism. And rightly

---

12 And, interestingly, reaching not always convergent conclusions.
13 In a similar spirit, Lowney et al. (2020) provide details (in terms of a 'vector symbolic architecture') on how twenty-first century connectionism might dovetail, rather than conflict, with Wittgenstein's philosophy.
14 There are slight divergences amongst commentators as to the exact location of Wittgenstein's remarks on rule-following in the *Philosophical Investigations*. Thus, for example: for Kripke (1982, 3), these are found in the sections preceding §243, with §202 already containing the key conclusion reached by Wittgenstein about rule-following; Boghossian (1989, 507) traces Wittgenstein's reflection on rule-following to §§138–242; whereas for Miller and Sultanescu (2022) it stretches from §135 to §242.
15 In the companion volume to this one, the chapters by Gori, Rappuoli and Pelland, Trächtler, and Love also engage with this topic and may provide interesting comparisons.

so: using symbolic logic for cognitive modelling does not imply validating logic through psychology. Moreover, not all AI is concerned with cognitive modelling – the 'modern approach' advocated by Russell and Norvig (2022) consists (at least in part) in the abandonment of this objective.[16] Kuusela's contribution in this volume might also be particularly relevant here, as it suggests that Wittgenstein's opposition to psychologism may be more nuanced than it is usually thought.

The final two arguments – mentioned, but not discussed, by Xu – concern the role of metaphor within scientific discovery (see Shanker 1998, Chapter 4), and the vagueness and even indeterminacy involved in the application of concepts, due to the fact that the various particulars in their extensions bear mere 'family resemblances' to one another (see Shanker 1998, Chapter 5). Votsis' contribution to the present volume replies indirectly to the first of these arguments. Finally, a number of chapters in the second volume engage in one way or another with the final argument – in both the aesthetic and legal contexts (see the introduction to that volume for some further details).

As already indicated, these various arguments do not exhaust the ways in which Wittgenstein's philosophy interacts with the theory and practice of AI, even within the realm of mind and language (that is the focus of the present volume). But they do perhaps provide enough by way of overview, and thereby orientation, as we begin to re-examine the insights – and perhaps pitfalls – of drawing on Wittgenstein's work to navigate the various questions posed by recent developments in AI.

The Conference

It was against the above intellectual backdrop – and a perhaps somewhat inchoate awareness of certain aspects of it – that two of the present editors (Ball and Rossi) organized the 11th Conference of the British Wittgenstein Society (BWS) on the theme of Wittgenstein and AI in London, at what was then the New College of the Humanities at Northeastern, from 29 to

---

16 Russell and Norvig (2022,19 ff) note that, historically, researchers in Artificial Intelligence have differed over both the sense of intelligence which AI was to model (human intelligence or rational intelligence), and the actual subject matter of the discipline – with some theorists seeing AI as essentially focusing on reasoning and others on behaviour. For Russell and Norvig, four broad research programmes in Artificial Intelligence have emerged as a consequence of this double dichotomy, which they call: the Turing Test approach; the cognitive modelling approach; the 'laws of thought' approach; the rational agent approach.

31 July 2022.[17] It was decided that this theme would further the Society's aim of bringing Wittgenstein's work to new audiences (beyond philosophy), and it would provide a wonderful opportunity to showcase the value of interdisciplinary interactions on a topic of present interest and concern (AI). We are grateful to the BWS – especially, Danièle Moyal-Sharrock, Constantine Sandis and (contributor to this volume) Ian Ground – and to a number of sponsors,[18] as well as the (now) University itself,[19] for their support in making the conference a success – at least on the above metrics. There were talks by historians, lawyers, philosophers, digital humanists, artists, computational linguists, roboticists and AI researchers and practitioners. And there was even something new for the seasoned Wittgensteinian philosophers – namely, a hackathon.[20,21]

The present collection of two volumes cannot be readily regarded as conference proceedings: many of the talks given are not included as chapters in either volume; and some of the chapters were not presented at the conference (while others, of course, have undergone very significant revisions). Nevertheless, all of the contributions are by at least one co-author who was involved in the conference, and in this sense, the two volumes are its products.

We have divided the contributions into two volumes: the present volume, on Mind and Language; and a companion volume, on Value(s) and Governance. We will introduce that second volume, and its various chapters, separately (see Ball, Helliwell and Rossi 2024). In what follows we briefly summarize the chapters of the present volume.

---

17 The institution was subsequently awarded University title, and expanded its disciplinary offerings: it is now known as Northeastern University – London.

18 We gratefully acknowledge financial support from the Analysis Trust, the Mind Association, and the Society for Applied Philosophy, as well as the GB Colour Group.

19 Not only the college (now University) in London, but also the Institute for Experiential AI at Northeastern University in Boston should be mentioned here for recognition and thanks. We were delighted to have the Institute's Director of Research, Ricardo Baeza-Yates, present at the conference.

20 The hackathon, devoted to a textual analysis of the *Remarks on Colour* (Wittgenstein 1976: LFM), was led by Dimitris Mylonas, who has made the code available open access in a Jupyter notebook available at https://github.com/dmylonas/colourHackathon.

21 A further digital Wittgenstein resource should also be mentioned in the present context – namely, the Bergen Electronic Edition of the Wittgenstein Nachlass, available at https://wab.uib.no/wab_BEE.page. Attendees were given an orientation to the digital humanities considerations underpinning these by Alois Pichler at the conference.

Language and Meaning

Diane Proudfoot, Wittgenstein and Turing on AI: Myth Versus Reality

Proudfoot's chapter criticizes what she calls the *orthodox* and *alternative* accounts of the relationships between Wittgenstein's and Turing's thoughts on AI: on the orthodox view, both are behaviourists; on the alternative account, Wittgenstein is highly critical of Turing, denying the conceptual possibility that machines can think, while Turing treats this as an empirical question.

Proudfoot addresses the question whether it is an anachronism to regard Wittgenstein as engaging with the question of whether AI is possible, as he was dead before the term was coined in 1956. Pointing to relevant material prior to the publication of Turing's landmark 1936 paper, Proudfoot notes that Wittgenstein was already exploring the abilities of 'reading-machines' such as player pianos; and suggests that he was likely aware of a highly public debate on the possibility of an 'electronic brain' displaying intelligence in the late 1940s.

Against the orthodox interpretation, Proudfoot notes that Turing was not a behaviourist: he took the attribution of intelligence to be based in part on emotional considerations. This (but not the behaviourist reading of his work) explains the three-player form of the imitation game that lies at the basis of the Turing Test. Against the alternative account, Proudfoot argues that Wittgenstein's various remarks are consistent with the conceptual possibility of AI: he distinguished a 'machine' from an 'automaton'; where the latter is incapable of thought as a matter of logical necessity. Nothing he says precludes the possibility that computing machinery of the sort envisioned by Turing should have such a capacity.

Moreover, the paper argues (against the alternative view) that Wittgenstein and Turing agreed on a number of key points: that regarding an entity as having a mind has both a cognitive and an affective side, involving emotion (Turing) or attitude (as opposed to opinion – Wittgenstein); that human beings are the paradigms of intelligence – a view, it is argued, that can answer the charge of speciesism; and that we should remain open about the cognitive architecture(s) that might underlie intelligence. All of this serves to counter the idea that Turing's and Wittgenstein's views are now little more than historical curiosities – rather, they may continue to shed light on intelligence (artificial and otherwise) even now.

Tomi Kokkonen and Ilmari Hirvonen, Between Wittgenstein and Turing: Enactive Embodied Thinking Machines

Tomi Kokkonen and Ilmari Hirvonen's contribution explores the issue of whether it is in principle possible for machines to think, and whether there *might* be a common ground between Wittgenstein and Turing's views on this issue. The philosophical backdrop of Kokkonen and Hirvonen's discussion is an anti-internalist one; more specifically, underlying the discussion is enactivism, the view, roughly, that cognition arises from the interaction of an organism with its surrounding environment. Within such an enactivist framework, Kokkonen and Hirvonen argue for positive answers to each one of the questions their paper intends to address.

With regard to the first question – whether it is possible for machines to think – Kokkonen and Hirvonen distinguish between two senses of *enactivism*: as an anti-internalist theory of cognition; and as a theory of robotic design. Kokkonen and Hirvonen remain neutral about enactivism understood in the former sense, but express optimism about the prospect brought about by enactivism understood in the latter sense. The reason is that we will likely attribute thought to an agent consistently manifesting intentional behaviour, and enactivism *qua* theory of robotic design might enable robots to achieve this form of behaviour.

With regard to the second question – whether there might be a common ground between Wittgenstein and Turing about the possibility of thinking machines – Kokkonen and Hirvonen contend that enactivism might allow us to resolve at least in part the apparent tension between the two thinkers. Kokkonen and Hirvonen argue that, not only would enactive robots qualify as thinking machines for Turing; if they could exhibit a kind of behaviour that is sensitive to norms, then they may qualify as thinking machines for Wittgenstein too. Kokkonen and Hirvonen note that it is an open question whether there will ever be machines exhibiting the required level of sensitivity to norms to count as thinking; future enactive robots, they suggest, are nonetheless plausible candidates.

Arturo Vázquez, **Wittgenstein, Psychological Language and AI**

Arturo Vázquez's contribution addresses, from a Wittgensteinian perspective, what he calls *the fundamental problem in the philosophy of AI*; namely, *can machines think?* In particular, it introduces Searle's (1980) distinction between weak and strong AI – roughly, the simulation versus possession of intelligence by machines – and maps it to the distinction between figurative (especially metaphorical) as opposed to literal use of psychological language in connection with AI systems. Thus, a system exhibits weak AI if expressions such as 'understands' can be said only metaphorically of it, whereas it manifests strong AI if they apply to it quite literally.

The backdrop of Vázquez's discussion is the distinction, in Wittgenstein's thought, between conceptual and empirical problems, the difference residing in the method by which a proposition resolving it can be verified. Vázquez argues that the question whether machines can think is not an empirical one, and that much (non-Wittgensteinian) discussion of it treats it as admitting only two answers – yes, and no – because of a failure to recognize this. It is said that the problem is *metaphysical* or *philosophical* in Wittgenstein's sense – that is, something akin to a conceptual problem.

Two traditional Wittgensteinian approaches to the fundamental problem are then compared: on an orthodox view, taken by Hacker (2019) amongst others, machines are said to be unable to think, so that at most only weak AI can be achieved. The reason is that, for human beings, the relationship between mind and body is not contingent, or open to empirical investigation, whereas the relationship between a machine's hardware and software is. By contrast, on an alternative Wittgensteinian approach, due to Neumaier (1986), the reason for this verdict is that our knowledge of machines does not display the uncertainty associated with our knowledge of other minds.

Vázquez criticizes both of these approaches on the grounds that they display dichotomous thinking. He argues that psychological language is used to describe AI systems in ways that are neither metaphorical (weak) nor literal (strong) – rather the terms in question are used in what Wittgenstein calls a *secondary sense*. Thus, a Wittgensteinian analysis of the psychological language applied to AI can help us to move beyond the false dichotomy of strong versus weak AI, which arises from the question, 'Can machines think?'

Éloïse Boisseau, *The Metonymical Trap*

Éloïse Boisseau's contribution addresses, and critically examines, the common practice of extending to machines certain attributes, typically (and unproblematically) attributed to humans. In particular, Boisseau's discussion focuses on the class of so-called intellectual attributes, which comprise predicates describing psychological states and intentional relations. Is it correct, for example, to say that a machine calculates?

Boisseau's view is that, taken literally, a similar assertion falls into what can be dubbed *metonymical trap*; that is, roughly, a failure to appreciate that the sentence is used metonymically. More precisely, for Boisseau metonymical sentences involve reference to a twofold subject: the primary one, corresponding to the grammatical subject of the sentence (the machine); and the secondary or intended subject (the human agent who actioned the machine's calculation).

The question then arises as to whether there is any sense to be made of such metonymical statements. Boisseau's position, drawing from a distinction revitalized by Hacker, is that we might want to distinguish between one-way agents (who cannot but bring about an action when the appropriate circumstances obtain) and two-way agents (who might refrain from performing such an action). Machines, unlike human agents, are canonical examples of one-way agents. Further, building on the Geachean distinction between intrinsic and so-called *Cambridge* properties, Boisseau proceeds to define the notions of real and Cambridge *actions*. Whilst the former involve a change in an object's intrinsic properties, the latter do not. Machines, again, can at least be understood as capable of bringing about Cambridge actions. But such senses of attributing intellectual properties to machines do not take away from the main thesis of the chapter, to the effect that interpreting similar attributions literally is something in the vicinity of a category mistake.

Laith Abdel-Rahman, The Forms of Artificially Intelligent Life: Brandom, Chomsky and Wittgenstein on the Possibility of Strong-AI

Laith Abdel-Rahman's chapter is concerned with the question of so-called *strong AI* – the possession (rather than simulation) by machines of the mental states that are characteristic of intelligence. The chapter engages with the state of the art in computer science, emphasizing the role of the Transformer architecture in underpinning recent advances in 'statistical AI' and its flagship large language models (LLMs) such as GPT and BERT – and it notes/explores recent speculation surrounding machine consciousness. The chapter considers two philosophical lines of argument against the possibility of strong AI: an Internalist one due to Chomsky (2023); and an externalist critique developed by Brandom (2006, 2008). Abdel-Rahman offers a Wittgensteinian response: effectively, both criticisms are held to be guilty of anthropocentrism; thinkers engaging with the possibility of strong AI should be open to genuinely alternative, non-human forms of life – and intelligence.

The Chomskyan attack holds that a real understanding of natural language, for instance, would be underpinned by innate grammatical knowledge in the form of rules such as 'merge', which takes two (relatively simple) expressions and outputs a single (more complex) expression. As current Statistical AI models are not underpinned by such rules, they at best simulate understanding. Brandom's critique, on the other hand, holds that an understanding of language must be underpinned by engagement in an autonomous discursive practice. Once again, LLMs are not so engaged, and thus do not qualify as genuinely intelligent, as required for strong AI.

Abdel-Rahman responds, in each case, that the requirements imposed by the philosophers embed assumptions that are unduly anthropocentric. Wittgenstein can be read as suggesting a descriptive approach, and when we look at what these AI systems can do and how they operate, we may see signs of a non-human intelligence.

Ian Ground, Black Boxes, Beetles and Beasts

Ian Ground's contribution seeks to tackle some issues that face philosophers sympathetic to Wittgenstein's work when thinking about the so-called *Black Box* problem. Historically, the main line of Wittgensteinian critique redeployed arguments against the idea of intrinsic intentionality in the human case – which are so frequent in the *Investigations* – against claims about the intrinsic meaningfulness of symbols in software. Ground argues that these arguments (and their descendants, e.g. in Searle's Chinese Room Argument) are effective against GOFAI systems but lack traction in the case of contemporary AI systems precisely because they are black boxes.

Ground then argues that rather than treating the phrase 'thinking machine' as an oxymoron, Wittgensteinians should be more philosophically 'relaxed' about contemporary AI. The conceptions of cognition and judgement that underlie AI can be seen as Aristotelian and anti-Platonic in a way that runs parallel with Wittgenstein's approach. Moreover, AI systems can be understood as historically conditioned paths laid down in pattern finding and making. This invites a comparison with claims made about cognition by an heir to Wittgenstein's thinking: Radical Enactivism.

Underlying Ground's account is a reading of Wittgenstein's view of cognition and its associated concepts as more radically anti-essentialist, more dynamic and more open to empirical surprise than other interpretations of Wittgenstein's approach. Via a comparison between our thinking about AI and our response to ethological discoveries about the cognition of other animals, Ground argues that, one day, perhaps far off, we might come to see AI systems as primitive digital animals. In the meantime, progress – and failures – in the development of AI are likely to be philosophically instructive.

Giovanni Galli, Language Models and the Private Language Argument: A Wittgensteinian Guide to Machine Learning

As this contribution's title suggests, Giovanni Galli intends to offer a Wittgensteinian guide to ML. More precisely, Galli offers a discussion of Wittgenstein's celebrated Private Language Argument against the backdrop of a connectionist account of cognition, on which cognition is explained in terms of neural networks. In particular, Galli's discussion mainly focuses on two connectionist models designed for Natural Language Processing: Word2Vec and Vector Symbolic Architecture (VSA).

Galli puts forward a twofold thesis. First, the above connectionist models are in essence computational analogues of Wittgensteinian language games, formalizing in their own distinctive ways the notion of context – which as is known played a central role in Wittgenstein's later philosophy. One of the key movements in AI thus originates, according to Galli, from Wittgensteinian reflections on language.

Galli then moves on to discussing the attempt by Lowney et al. (2020) to capture the meaning of private words using their VSA, in a context simulating Wittgenstein's beetle in the black box case. If Lowney et al.'s attempt turned out to be successful, we should presumably regard one of Wittgenstein's most famous and widely accepted arguments – namely the Private Language Argument – as incurring a counterexample. Galli's thesis, however, is that whilst the meaning of 'beetle' as occurring in Wittgenstein's example is impossible to capture, 'beetle' as occurring in the experiment by Lowney et al. has an accessible meaning. Galli thus concludes that we ought to be suspicious about the fact that the model successfully captured the essence of Wittgenstein's case: indeed, the private word whose meaning we were meant to determine is arguably not treated as such in the model.

Oskari Kuusela, Simplification Without Falsification: the Problem of Relevance in Logic and AI

Oskari Kuusela's chapter discusses the problem of relevance in logic and AI, and the contribution which Wittgenstein's philosophy of logic might offer to address it. According to Kuusela, the problem of relevance arises in the process of simplifying complex, true information. Over the course of a similar process, indeed, one is open to the risk of producing falsehoods. A safety requirement thus appears very much needed, and Kuusela identifies in Wittgenstein's philosophy of logic some ideas which may deliver it.

Kuusela's discussion encompasses Wittgenstein's early and late conceptions of logic and language, with a focus on Wittgenstein's early (and later abandoned) view that it is possible to describe the essence of language and the general form of all propositions. Kuusela argues that the reasons underlying Wittgenstein's departure from this irenic view of language may provide us with the desired safety requirement to address the aforementioned problem of relevance. What led Wittgenstein to abandon the Tractarian conception of language, on Kuusela's account, is in essence the realization that logic is neither context nor topic-neutral. That is to say, the laws of logic hold or fail depending either on the topic at hand, or the purpose for which we are using language (or both). In particular, Kuusela finds in the fact that speakers may use language for different purposes the key to providing the safety mechanism needed to address the problem of relevance. An AI able to simplify complex information without producing falsehood requires, one may say, a teleological thrust. Its success at producing relevant outputs, in other words, is importantly tied to its capacity of being informed by the purpose for which – the reason why – it is used to simplify information in the first place.

Ioannis Votsis, Modelling Analogical Reasoning: One-Size-Fits-All?

Votsis's chapter is concerned with analogical reasoning – that is, transposing solutions from one domain to another on the basis of certain feature similarities. Central to both ordinary and scientific thought, such reasoning must be modelled if it is to be automated. Local and universal models exist. Votsis defends the latter, proposing a novel 'relevant conceptual uniformity' condition to avoid problems encountered by existing models; and he defends this proposal against an objection based on the Wittgensteinian notion of family resemblance.

Various models of analogical reasoning are reviewed. According to 'the simple schema' (TSS), for instance, a piece of analogical reasoning is admissible if and only if the source domain is similar to the target in certain known respects, and has some further feature as well (a feature similar to) which is inferred to be possessed by the target. TSS is said to be too liberal, treating problematic inferences as admissible. Various refinements that have been proposed in the philosophical literature are also considered, involving additional causal and/or correlational conditions – but all are taken to succumb to counterexamples. Suggestions from the AI literature – whether of symbolic or of neural models – fare no better.

Votsis also considers a challenge (due to Norton [2003, 2011, 2021]), according to which different fields, or different research questions within a field, require different models. He replies by proposing a condition that may be added to any of the universal models considered that have faced counterexamples: relevant conceptual uniformity. The more uniform the relevant concepts are, the more admissible the analogical inference involving them will be.

Wittgenstein, of course, held that many terms, or concepts, bind together individuals that bear only family resemblances to one another. This might be thought to invalidate Votsis's proposed (computationally and empirically testable) solution. But Votsis denies that all concepts are like this – and he suggests that in science especially there is pressure towards greater uniformity. Why, then, does analogical reasoning work? Ultimately, according to Votsis, because nature is uniform (to some degree).

References

Arrington, R.L. (2017). Wittgenstein and Ethics. In Hyman, J. and Glock, H-J. eds, *A Companion to Wittgenstein* (pp. 603–611). Oxford: Wiley Blackwell.

Ball, B., Helliwell, A. and Rossi, A. (2024). Introduction. In Ball, B., Helliwell, A., and Rossi, A., eds, *Wittgenstein and Artificial Intelligence, volume* 2. London: Anthem.

Ball, B. and Koliousis, A. (2022). Training Philosopher Engineers for Better AI. *AI and Society*, 38: 1–8.

Biletzki, A. and Matar, A. (2023). Ludwig Wittgenstein. In Zalta, E.N. and Nodelman, U. eds, *The Stanford Encyclopedia of Philosophy* (Fall 2023 Edn). https://plato.stanford.edu/archives/fall2023/entries/wittgenstein/.

Boden, M.A. (2018). *Artificial Intelligence. A Very Short Introduction*. Oxford: Oxford University Press.

Boghossian, P.A. (1989). The Rule-Following Considerations. *Mind*, 98(392): 507–549.

Brandom, R.B. (2006). Between Saying and Doing: Towards an Analytic Pragmatism Lecture One – Extending the Project of Analysis. Lecture presented at the *John Locke Lectures*. University of Oxford. http://media.philosophy.ox.ac.uk/assets/pdf_file/0011/902/LL1_Text.pdf.

Brandom, R.B. (2008). *Between Saying and Doing: Towards and Analytic Pragmatism*. Oxford: Oxford University Press.

Bronzo, S. (2012). The Resolute Reading and its Critics: An Introduction to the Literature. *Wittgenstein-Studien*, 3(1): 45–80.

Cantwell Smith, B. (2019). *The Promise of Artificial Intelligence: Reckoning and Judgement*. Cambridge, MA: The MIT Press.

Chomsky, N. (2023). Genuine Explanation and the Strong Minimalist Thesis. *Cognitive Semantics*, 8(3): 347–365.

Conant, J. (1989). Must We Show What We Cannot Say? In Fleming, R. and Payne, M. eds, *The Senses of Stanley Cavell* (pp. 242–283). Lewisburg, PA: Bucknell University Press.

Conant, J. and Bronzo, S. (2017). Resolute Readings of the *Tractatus*. In Hyman, J. and Glock, H.-J. eds, *A Companion to Wittgenstein* (pp. 175–194). Oxford: Wiley Blackwell.

Conant, J. and Diamond, C. (2004). On Reading the *Tractatus* Resolutely. Reply to Meredith Williams and Peter Sullivan. In Kölbe, M. l. and Weiss, B. eds, *Wittgenstein's Lasting Significance* (pp. 42–97). London; New York: Routledge.

Copeland, B.J. (2012). *Turing: Pioneer of the Information Age*. Oxford: Oxford University Press.

Diamond, C. (1988). Throwing Away the Ladder. *Philosophy*, 63(243): 5–27.

Floyd, J. (2019). Wittgenstein and Turing. In Mras, G.M., Weingartner, P. and Ritter, B. eds, *Philosophy of Logic and Mathematics: Proceedings of the 41st International Ludwig Wittgenstein Symposium* (pp. 263–296). Berlin: ;De Gruyter.

Goldfarb, W. (1997). Metaphysics and Nonsense. *Journal of Philosophical Research*, 22: 57–73.

Hacker, P.M.S. (2019). *Wittgenstein: Meaning and Mind*. Oxford: Wiley Blackwell.

Haugeland, J. (1985). *Artificial Intelligence: The Very Idea*. Cambridge Mass.: The MIT Press.

Hodges, A. (2019). Alan Turing. In Zalta, E.N. ed., *The Stanford Encyclopedia of Philosophy* (Winter 2019 Edn). https://plato.stanford.edu/archives/win2019/entries/turing/.

Hyman, J. and Glock, H.-J., Eds. (2017). *A Companion to Wittgenstein*. Oxford: Wiley Blackwell.

Koethe, S. (2003). On the 'Resolute' Readings of the *Tractatus*. *Philosophical Investigations*, 26(3): 187–204.
Kripke, S. (1982). *Wittgenstein on Rules and Private Language*. Oxford: Blackwell Publishing.
Lowney, C. W., Levy, S. D., Meroney, W. et al. (2020). Connecting Twenty-First Century Connectionism and Wittgenstein. *Philosophia*, 48, 643–671.
McClelland, J. L. and Rumelhart, D. (1987). *Parallel Distributed Processing. Explorations in the Microstructure of Cognition: Psychological and Biological Models*. Cambridge MA: The MIT Press.
Miller, A. and Sultanescu, O. (2022). Rule-Following and Intentionality. In Zalta, E.N. ed., *The Stanford Encyclopedia of Philosophy* (Summer 2022 Edn). https://plato.stanford.edu/archives/sum2022/entries/rule-following/.
Neumaier, O. (1986). A Wittgensteinian View of Artificial Intelligence. In Born, R. ed., *Artificial Intelligence: The Case Against* (pp. 132–173). London: Croom Helm.
Newell, A. and Simon, H.A. (1976). Computer Science as Empirical Inquiry: Symbols and Search. *Communications of the ACM*, 19(3): 11–126.
Norton, J.D. (2003). A Material Theory of Induction. *Philosophy of Science*, 70(4): 647–670.
Norton, J.D. (2011). History of Science and the Material Theory of Induction: Einstein's Quanta, Mercury's Perihelion. *European Journal for Philosophy of Science*, 1: 3–27.
Norton, J.D. (2021). *The Material Theory of Induction*. Calgary: University of Calgary Press.
Rumelhart, D. and McClelland, J.L. (1986). *Parallel Distributed Processing, Vol 1. Explorations in the Microstructure of Cognition: Foundations*. Cambridge MA: The MIT Press.
Russell, S. and Norvig, P. (2022) *Artificial Intelligence: A Modern Approach* (4th Edn). Harlow: Pearson Education Limited.
Schroeder, S. (2017). Wittgenstein and Aesthetics. In Hyman, J. and Glock, H.-J. eds, *A Companion to Wittgenstein* (pp. 612–626). Oxford: Wiley Blackwell.
Searle, J.R. (1980). Minds, Brains, and Programs. *Behavioral and Brain Sciences*, 3(3): 417–457.
Shanker, S. (1998). *Wittgenstein's Remarks on the Foundations of AI*. London: Routledge.
Wiener, N. (1948). *Cybernetics; or Control and Communication in the Animal and the Machine*. New York: John Wiley.
Wittgenstein, L. (1922). *Tractatus Logico-Philosophicus*. English Translation by Ogden, C.K. and Ramsey, F.P. London: Kegan Paul.
Wittgenstein, L. (1953). *Philosophical Investigations*. English Translation by Anscombe, G.E.M. Oxford: Basil Blackwell.
Wittgenstein, L. (1958). *The Blue and Brown Books*. Sunnyvale, CA: Harper Torchbook.
Wittgenstein, L. (1961). *Tractatus Logico-Philosophicus*. English Translation by Pears, D.F. and McGuinness, B.F. London: Routledge and Kegan Paul.
Wittgenstein, L. (1976). *Lectures on the Foundations of Mathematics, Cambridge 1939*. Edited by Diamond, C. Hassocks: The Harvester Press.
Wittgenstein, L. (2009). *Philosophical Investigations*. English Translation by Anscombe, G.E.M., Hacker, P.M.S. and Schulte, J. Oxford: Wiley-Blackwell.
Wittgenstein, L. (2021). *Tractatus Logico-Philosophicus (Centenary Edn)*. Edited by Bazzocchi, L. and Hacker, P.M.S. London: Anthem Press.
Wittgenstein, L. (2023). *Tractatus Logico-Philosophicus*. English Translation by Beaney, M. Oxford: Oxford University Press.
Wooldridge, M. (2020). *A Brief History of Artificial Intelligence: What Is It, Where We Are, and Where We Are Going*. New York: Flatiron Books.
Xu, Y. (2016). Does Wittgenstein Actually Undermine the Foundation of Artificial Intelligence? *Frontiers of Philosophy in China*, 11(1): 3–20.

Chapter 1

WITTGENSTEIN AND TURING ON AI: MYTH VERSUS REALITY

Diane Proudfoot

Amongst philosophers generally, the orthodox account of Wittgenstein and Turing on the mind appears to be that both were philosophical behaviourists. Amongst theorists sympathetic to Wittgenstein, however, there is an alternative – in its own way orthodox – account, which denies that Wittgenstein was a behaviourist (in any damaging sense). Proponents of this alternative account typically interpret Wittgenstein as opposed to Turing and as hostile to artificial intelligence – in their view, Wittgenstein belongs with famous AI naysayers. In this chapter, I shall argue that both the orthodox and the alternative account are mistaken.

A preliminary question, however: Is it perhaps anachronistic to discuss Wittgenstein's views on AI – a field frequently (though mistakenly) held to begin only in the mid-1950s, some years after Wittgenstein's death? To counter this concern, I begin with Wittgenstein's 1930s remarks on machines and the public discussion of artificial intelligence in the 1940s in the UK.[1]

Human Computers

In Turing's groundbreaking 1936 paper, 'On Computable Numbers, with an Application to the Entscheidungsproblem', he set out the fundamental logical principles of the modern programmable general-purpose digital computer.[2] Before Turing described his computing machines, however, we

---

1 Here I confine my discussion to Wittgenstein's and Turing's remarks on intelligence in machines, ignoring the wider discussions in Wittgenstein's 1939 lectures (Wittgenstein 1989: LFM). See Proudfoot 2024a on the latter.
2 In February 1937, Turing arranged for a copy to be sent to Wittgenstein (letter from Turing to Sara Turing, 11 February 1937, Turing Digital Archive AMT/K/1/54).

find Wittgenstein talking about 'reading machines' in his *Blue Book* lectures of 1933–34. Wittgenstein's usual example of a reading-machine is a pianola or player piano (Wittgenstein 1974: PG (henceforth PG), 69): he said that a pianola 'translate[s] marks into sounds' by 'reading' the pattern of perforations – which 'we might call [...] *complex signs or sentences*' – in the piano roll (Wittgenstein 1972: PI (henceforth PI) §157; Wittgenstein 1965: BB (henceforth BB), 118, original emphasis). The pianola cannot do anything other than read; it cannot delete or modify the perforations on the pre-recorded roll. Nevertheless, a pianola can read '*any* pattern of perforations, of a particular kind, it is not built for one particular tune or set of tunes', Wittgenstein said; in this sense, it is a general-purpose machine (BB, 118, original emphasis). Notably, reading machines may also include a lookup table: Wittgenstein remarked that 'it is quite possible that there is a part of the mechanism which resembles a chart' (in his example, the chart associates colour-words with colours) (PG, 190).

Turing's computing machine was a mathematical model of a 'human computer' – as the term was used commonly in Turing's and Wittgenstein's time, to refer to a human being working purely by rote (Copeland 2000a). Wittgenstein's reading-machine is like Turing's computing machine in that it is an abstract machine, instantiated in inanimate mechanisms like the pianola but also in 'living' devices. Wittgenstein frequently employed the idea of a human being acting 'like a reliable machine' and he introduced the notion of a 'living reading-machine' (BB, 119, PI §157; see too Wittgenstein 1989: LFM, 36–37). His examples of living reading-machines include 'calculating machines' (also referred to as 'calculating boys'), 'arithmetical machines', and '[piano] playing-machines' (Wittgenstein 1989: LPP (henceforth LPP), 30; PG, 191). Wittgenstein's living reading-machine is a human being or other creature who is given (as input) written signs, for example Chinese characters, arithmetical symbols, logical symbols or musical notation. The living reading-machine produces (as output) text spoken aloud, solutions to arithmetical problems, proofs of logical theorems, notes played on a piano, and suchlike. In such respects, they are human computers in the sense of the time. These 'machines' may be born, Wittgenstein said, or trained (PI §157).

It has been claimed that, when Turing introduced his logical computing machines, machine cognition seemed 'rather remote' from Wittgenstein's mind (Liu 2021, 426). On the contrary, in the early 1930s Wittgenstein was already discussing the capacities of machines: like the human computer, the living reading-machine need not grasp the content of the task the machine is executing. These machines are not intelligent. In this case 'reading', Wittgenstein said, 'does not involve any such thing as understanding what you read': a 'human calculating machine might [...] read through the proofs of a mathematical system (say that of Russell), and [nod] its head after every correctly drawn conclusion, but […] [be] otherwise perfectly imbecile' (BB, 119; Wittgenstein 1983: RFM, 258).

Electronic Brains

Although it is possible that Wittgenstein was ignorant of the substantial public debate around AI in the 1940s, there is no reason to think this at all likely. In the second half of the decade, a vigorous debate began in newspapers and on radio, involving the pioneering computer scientists and also the general public (on the reception of the early computers, see Proudfoot and Copeland 2019). At the beginning of November 1946, the media reported an address given by Admiral the Viscount Mountbatten of Burma. According to Mountbatten, 'It is now considered possible to evolve an electronic brain'; a machine can be built, he said, that 'will provide an intelligent – I repeat, intelligent – link' between the information it receives about the 'machinery under its control' and the 'action necessary to keep the machinery' working as desired (1946, 223–24). Mountbatten claimed that 'machines now actually in use can exercise a degree of memory; and some are now being designed to exercise those hitherto human prerogatives of choice and judgement' (1946, 224). He concluded that 'we are really facing a new revolution […] a revolution of the mind' (1946, 224).

A few days after Mountbatten's speech, Turing's Automatic Computing Engine (ACE) was officially announced. Sir Charles Darwin, Director of the National Physical Laboratory (NPL), said in a radio talk about the ACE that Turing's aim in his 1936 paper had been to discover the 'ultimate limitations' of 'a machine which would imitate the processes of thought'.[3] A fundamental and public disagreement about intelligence in machines was emerging. The day after the ACE was announced, the *Times* published a letter by Douglas Rayner Hartree, Plummer Professor of Mathematical Physics at Cambridge. Hartree wrote, he said, to 'deprecate' Mountbatten's use of the term 'electronic brain' – since it 'ascribes to the machine capabilities that it does not possess' – and to deny Mountbatten's claim that machines then being designed were capable of 'choice' and 'judgement' (Hartree 1946). In Hartree's view, these machines can 'only do precisely what they are instructed to do by the operators who set them up' (Hartree 1946). Hartree's comments were welcomed in the newspapers; it was declared, for example, that, far from being 'a rival

---

3 Darwin as reported in 'Did You Hear That: An Arithmetical Robot', *The Listener*, 14 November 1946, 663.

of the human mind', the 'new Frankenstein'[4] is merely 'the big brother of the sliderule and the adding machine. [...] there is nothing more "mental" about it' (Langdon-Davies 1946).

In the late 1940s, the hypothetical question whether intelligence in machines is possible came to be focused on a particular form of machine. In June 1948, the world's first electronic stored-program digital computer, the Manchester 'Baby', ran its first program in the Computing Machine Laboratory at the University of Manchester; and in May 1949, the Electronic Delay Storage Automatic Calculator (EDSAC) became the second electronic stored-program computer to function, at the Mathematical Laboratory of the University of Cambridge. Maurice Wilkes, the EDSAC's designer, said in the *Daily Mail* that the machine might solve 'philosophical problems too complicated for the human mind'.[5] In 1949, the press reported Turing, trying to teach (a later version of) the Manchester machine to play chess, as saying that once the machine 'has mastered the rules it will think out its own moves'.[6] The question became: Could machinery like the Manchester machine, if given additional high-speed memory and enhanced processing speed, properly be said to think?

In 1947 in Cambridge, Turing began work on 'Intelligent machinery', his pioneering report for the NPL, in which he anticipated neural network architectures and set out the first version of his imitation game. It is in 1947 too that Wittgenstein remarked: 'Turing's "Machines". These machines are *humans* who calculate' (Wittgenstein 1988: RPP I (henceforth RPP I) §1096, original emphasis). Against the background of public discussion of the 'revolution of the mind', Turing and Wittgenstein were working out pivotal positions in the philosophy of artificial intelligence.

The Orthodox Account: A Shared Behaviourism

As is well known, Wittgenstein's later accounts of the mind – in particular, his arguments against the possibility of a 'private' language and his account of first-person psychological ascriptions as 'avowals' rather than descriptions of independent internal states – are frequently categorized as behaviourist or operational (an influential account is given in Chihara and Fodor 1965; Chihara 1973). Wittgenstein is said to be a 'linguistic behaviourist' and his

---

4 'Not an "Ace" Brain', <i>The Courier and Advertiser</i>, 11 November 1946, 2.
5 Wilkes reported in 'A Don Builds A Memory: 4ft tubes in his brain', <i>Daily Mail</i>, 2 October 1947, 3.
6 'Mechanical Brain Is Learning To Play Chess', <i>The Irish Times</i>, 13 June 1949, 7.

views likened to (popular accounts of) B. F. Skinner's 'radical behaviourism' of the 1940s and 1950s (e.g. Pinker 2003).[7] His approach to the mind has also been called 'crypto-behaviourism' or 'semi-behaviourism'. This interpretation of Wittgenstein remains common in philosophy this century (e.g. Moore 2010), including in textbooks (e.g. Mandik 2013).

As to Turing, since the publication of his 1950 paper, 'Computing Machinery and Intelligence', he has typically been taken to propose success in his computer-imitates-human game as a behaviourist criterion of thinking in machines. In the 1950s, he was commonly regarded as a behaviourist: for example, according to his University of Manchester colleague Wolfe Mays, Turing's 'behaviourist criterion' of intelligence or thinking used a 'definition of psychological phenomena in terms of behavioural patterns' (Mays 1952, 151, 160). This remains the standard interpretation of the imitation game (e.g. Hodges 2014, 334). Theorists writing today claim that the Turing test is 'the first operational definition of machine intelligence' and that Turing's criteria for thinking are 'purely behavioral' (French 2012, 164; Polger 2012, 338).

'Behaviourism' is an umbrella term, and not all theorists who describe Wittgenstein or Turing as a behaviourist use the term in the same way. Nonetheless, several theorists explicitly group Wittgenstein and Turing together as 'behaviourists'; for example, it is said that both aimed to understand human behaviour in terms of 'mechanical configurations' – due perhaps to 'their respective background in engineering and mathematics' (Berg 2019). In some cases, the 'behaviourist' label is replaced by 'computationalist'; for example, it is said that Wittgenstein felt '*some* measure of attraction' to a 'mechanistic or computational conception of the mind' (Raleigh, 2018, 448, original emphasis), and indeed that he ought to have been a computationalist (Rey 2003).[8]

For many theorists, the mere suggestion of behaviourism suffices to dismiss both Wittgenstein and Turing as philosophers of mind. Around the time of the *Tractatus*, C. D. Broad claimed that ('strict') behaviourism was one of a class of theories 'so preposterously silly' that only 'very learned men' could have invented them (1925, 623). Around the time of the *Investigations*, behaviourism was said to lead to the 'ignoring or distortion of an important range of facts' (Garnett 1950, 255), and behaviourist psychology was declared to

---

7 The correct understanding of Skinner's approach, like that of other 'behaviourists', is debated (see e.g. Richelle 1993/2016; Overskeid 1995). Here I am concerned only with the use of the 'behaviourist' and 'radical behaviourist' *labels* with respect to Wittgenstein and Turing.
8 There is no space here to discuss the 'computationalist' label; see Proudfoot 2020, 2024b on the claim that Turing endorsed the computational theory of mind.

have lost both its 'soul' and its 'mind' (Montague 1951, 430). Behaviourism has been regarded as 'akin to Satanism' (on this see Barrett 2012, 19), or at least akin to 'a *theoria non grata*, a position that dare not be explicitly endorsed' (see Alksnis and Reynolds 2021, 5785, original emphasis).

Many philosophers sympathetic to Wittgenstein qualify the behaviourist charge, saying for example that he was a 'very untypical' behaviourist (Cook 2010, 274), solely an 'epistemological' behaviourist (Kitchener 2018), only 'nominally behaviorist' (Moore 2013, 226), or that his approach has merely a 'methodologically behaviorist tone' (Vaaja 2013, 126). There are also current advocates of specific varieties of behaviourism – for example, 'teleological behaviourism' (e.g. Rachlin 2017) and 'criteria behaviourism' (e.g. Ben-Yami 2005) – and it is argued that there is a new role for radical behaviourism within enactivist theories of cognition (Barrett 2019). Yet today even the whiff of behaviourism can create a very bad press amongst philosophers, with the result that, on the orthodox account, Wittgenstein's and Turing's philosophies of mind are little more than historical curiosities.

The Alternative Account: A Fundamental Disagreement

Even during the 1950s, several thinkers denied that Wittgenstein was a behaviourist,[9] and many since have taken this view.[10] Today, it is often said that: Wittgenstein was the 'first critic' of Turing's 'computational theory of mind'; he presented 'criticisms of Turing's computational thinking theory' and 'critiques of Turing's idea that people are computers' (Saariluoma and Rauterberg 2015, 432, 434, 435, 2016, 29); he posed 'counter-arguments' to the 'early ideas of intelligent machinery set out by Alan Turing' (Taylor et al. 2010, 108); and he had 'profound doubts and open disagreements with Turing' over the possibility of AI (Liu 2021, 427).

Two examples of this alternative account are particularly influential. Peter Hacker states that, for Wittgenstein, 'it makes *no sense* to ascribe thought or thoughtlessness, understanding, misunderstanding or failure to understand to machines' (1996, 134, original emphasis). Of philosophers and scientists who hold that doing so does make sense, Hacker says: 'Like Turing, they fail to apprehend that flashing inscriptions on a screen is not a form of behaviour which could be a ground for ascribing thought to a being' (1996, 134). Similarly, according to Stuart Shanker, for Wittgenstein, the question *Can*

---

9 For example: Malcolm 1954; Linsky 1957; MacIntyre 1958.
10 For example: Holborow 1967; Luckhardt 1983; Medina 2003; Overgaard 2004; Ter Hark 2006; Tang 2014; Hacker 2018; Grimi 2020.

machines think? 'transgress[es] rules of logical grammar' – it is a 'logically absurd' and 'conceptually ill-formed' question (1998, 3, 1987, 616). Whereas for Turing, Shanker says, the question *Can machines think?* is empirical; all that matters is whether machines satisfy the 'complex behavioural criteria' governing the concept of calculation (1987, 621).

The alternative account depicts Wittgenstein as an AI naysayer: in his view, it is said, 'machines cannot be thinking creatures' (Saariluoma and Rauterberg 2016, 29). Some proponents of this account claim in addition that Wittgenstein would reject Turing's test of intelligence in machines. For example, it is said that for Turing imitating thinking just *is* thinking, but for Wittgenstein some further X-factor is required – perhaps involving 'data of an imponderable type' that the imitation game cannot test for – and so Turing test assessment is 'doomed to failure' (Taylor 2015). Subscribers to the alternative account also often group Wittgenstein with famous twentieth-century critics of AI, such as Roger Penrose, John Lucas and John Searle. This account damns Wittgenstein in the minds of many scientifically oriented philosophers.

I shall argue against both the orthodox and the alternative account. The first problem arises for the orthodox account and for any version of the alternative account that depicts Turing as a behaviourist.

A Problem for the Orthodox Account: Turing Was *Not* a Behaviourist

Turing is regarded as a behaviourist largely because his famous test is assumed to be behaviourist. However, the canonical behaviourist interpretation of the imitation game – whether taking it to yield a definition or merely a logically sufficient condition of intelligence in machines – has serious flaws (Moor 1976, 1987; Copeland 1993, 2000b). From a behaviourist perspective, the imitation game is simply puzzling: Why base a criterion of intelligence on deception, rather than simply giving the machine a series of cognitive tasks – and why include a human contestant? (Proponents of the behaviourist interpretation typically misdescribe Turing's 1950 game as a two-player game.)

Behaviourism also fails to explain the centrality in Turing's test of the interrogator's response. The computer programmer's objective is that the interrogator misidentify the machine as human; and the interrogator's being 'taken in' is part of the protocol for scoring the imitation game – a machine does well in the computer-imitates-human game when the interrogator in that game is fooled no less frequently than the interrogator in the man-imitates-woman game with which Turing begins his 1950 paper (Turing et al.

1952, 495; Turing 1950, 434).[11] The behaviourist interpretation can explain the requirement that the interrogator be fooled only as an indirect way of testing the machine's capacity for intelligent behaviour: that is, if the interrogator mistakes the machine for the human, we are to infer that the machine has this capacity. However, this explanation is implausible, since it makes Turing's test dog-legged and also leads straightway to familiar, seemingly catastrophic objections to the test (Proudfoot 2013a).

Most importantly, Turing's remarks in his 1948 report and 1952 radio broadcast, which contain the two other versions of his computer-imitates-human game, offer a very different explanation of his emphasis on the interrogator's response. In his report, Turing said that 'the idea of "intelligence" is itself emotional rather than mathematical' (1948, 411). In a section entitled 'Intelligence as an emotional concept', he wrote:

> The extent to which we regard something as behaving in an intelligent manner is determined as much by our own state of mind and training as by the properties of the object under consideration.
>
> *(1948, 431)*

Shanker asserts that the 'behaviourist orientation' of AI is 'particularly evident' in Turing's 1948 report (1998, 41).[12] Yet Turing's words just quoted are inconsistent with (philosophical) behaviourism: the behaviourist claims that judgements of intelligence are determined just by the (merely) behavioural 'properties of the object under consideration'.[13]

Given that 'behavourism' is an umbrella term, it is impossible to claim that Turing was in *no* sense a behaviourist. His words, however, are at odds with a popular understanding of behaviourism: in his view, *seeing* the machine as intelligent is at least as important to its *being* intelligent as is its behaviour (or processing speed, storage capacity or complexity of programming). His words are also in tension with a notion of behaviourism that has been influential generally within philosophy – Rudolf Carnap's proposal that an expression such as 'seeing red' denotes only 'that state of the human body characterized by the fact that certain specified (physical) reactions appear in answer to certain specified (physical) stimuli' (Carnap 1934/2011, 86).[14] If the concept

---

11 Copeland points this out (2000b, 527).
12 In his 1948 report, Turing talks of training the unorganized machine by 'punishment' and 'reward', but this does not make him a psychological behaviourist.
13 Or by the causes of, or dispositions toward, such behaviour in 'the object under consideration'.
14 Carnap's view was, or became, more complicated than this quote suggests (in e.g. Carnap 1956, 70, 71).

of intelligence is an 'emotional' concept, 'being intelligent' does *not* denote only the stimulus-response patterns of the 'object under consideration' – this neglects the interrogator's 'state of mind and training'. So, Turing is not a Carnap-style behaviourist.

The behaviourist notion of intelligence that has been most influential in criticism of the imitation game is perhaps Ned Block's 'neo-Turing Test conception'. On this conception, intelligence is 'the capacity to produce a sensible sequence of verbal responses to a sequence of verbal stimuli, whatever they may be' (Block 1981, 16, 18). However, since Turing's criterion for thinking crucially involves the observer's reaction to the chain of verbal input and outputs, Turing is not a Block-style behaviourist either (Proudfoot 2013a, 2024b).

Instead, it is plausible to construe Turing's 'emotional' concept as in modern terminology a 'response-dependent' concept. On the response-dependence interpretation, Turing's 'criterion for "thinking"' (1950, 443) is as follows: *x* is *intelligent* (or *thinks*) if, in the actual world, in an unrestricted computer-imitates-human game, *x* appears intelligent to an average interrogator (Proudfoot 2013a, 2020, 2022).[15] This interpretation explains the central role that Turing gives to the imitation-game interrogator. It also explains why Turing replaced the question *Can machines think?* with the question *Are there imaginable digital computers which would do well in the imitation game?* (1950, 442) – a move that otherwise appears merely to be changing the subject.

A Problem for the Alternative Account: Wittgenstein's Remarks Are *Consistent* with AI

Wittgenstein famously said that 'the sentence, "A machine thinks (perceives, wishes)" […] seems somehow nonsensical. It is as though we had asked "Has the number 3 a colour?"' (BB, 47). He also remarked, concerning the person who is 'inclined to say: "A machine can't have toothache"', that the 'impossibility of which [they] speak is a logical one' (BB, 16). However, we cannot conclude just from such remarks that, in Wittgenstein's view, machines cannot think. First, the speaker of the notoriously negative remarks may be Wittgenstein's *interlocutor*, rather than Wittgenstein himself. For example, Wittgenstein attributes the 'toothache' remark to someone taking the view that thinking is 'part of our "private experience"' and is 'not material, but an event in private consciousness' (BB, 16). This is a view that Wittgenstein attacked; that someone taking this view might regard AI generally (and not

---

15 When talking about his imitation game, Turing did not differentiate between intelligence and thinking.

only machines with toothache) as logically impossible hardly implies that Wittgenstein saw AI in this way.

Second, in Wittgenstein's negative remarks apparently about thinking machines, he may have had in mind only 'automata'. Wittgenstein made a distinction between a 'machine' (in German, 'Maschine'; e.g. PI §193, 359) and an 'automaton' (in German, 'Automat'; e.g. PI §420; Wittgenstein 1970: Z (henceforth Z) §529). In his view, an automaton is a being that is *not* 'mind-endowed' ('seelenbegabten'; e.g. Z §528); an automaton is a 'soulless' being ('seelenlos'; e.g. Wittgenstein 1993: LW II (henceforth LW II), 66). Wittgenstein said:

> Imagine we were to encounter a human who had no soul. Why shouldn't something like that occur as an abnormality? So a human body would have been born with certain vital functions, but without a soul. Well, what would that look like? The *only* thing I can imagine in that case is that this body looks like an automaton, and not like normal human bodies.
>
> *(LW II, 66, original emphasis)*

An automaton is a being behaving in such a way that 'one would not be inclined to speak of inner and outer human states' (LW II, 66). When Wittgenstein referred to the traditional distinction between speaking 'with understanding' and without, his example of the latter was speaking 'like an automaton or like a parrot' (PI §419).

Assuming that a mind-endowed being is one that *does* incline us to speak of 'inner and outer' states, the notion of a *thinking automaton* implies a contradiction: thus, for Wittgenstein, the claim that (normally behaving) human beings are 'mere automata' and that 'all their liveliness is mere automatism' is 'quite meaningless' (PI §420). Indeed, Turing made a similar point, saying:

> It might be argued that there is a fundamental contradiction in the idea of a machine with intelligence. It is certainly true that 'acting like a machine' has become synonymous with lack of adaptability. (1947, 393)

If a necessary condition of *x*'s being *intelligent* is that it is adaptable, and of *x*'s being a *machine* that it is unable to adapt, we arrive at Turing's 'fundamental contradiction'. However, this would require us to give a distinct sense to the term 'machine' – one that Turing does not accept.

Wittgenstein's 'mere automata' remark certainly fits the alternative account's claim that, in his view, talk of thinking machines is 'absurd' and 'makes no sense'. However, the distinction between 'machine' and 'automaton' raises the possibility that Wittgenstein used the term 'machine' in more than one way. In one, the term 'machine' signifies Turing's logical computing machine or Wittgenstein's own reading-machine.[16] In another, 'machine' signifies an automaton. It is also possible that, in Wittgenstein's notoriously negative remarks about thinking machines, he intended the latter sense.

The reason to interpret Wittgenstein in this way – and also to read him as holding that it is an open question whether machines qua *computing machines* can think – is that doing so fits with his view of how we ascribe 'inner' and 'outer' states. According to Wittgenstein, we do so in response to an entity's appearance, behaviour, history and environment.[17] It is key that (adapting his remarks on pain) thinking 'has *this* position in our life; has *these* connexions' (Z §533, original emphasis). Wittgenstein's typical reading-machine (the pianola) and the actual computers of his time (the Manchester machine and the EDSAC) plainly do not fit into the 'bustle of life' (RPP I §625). These machines lack entirely the 'subtle shades' of human behaviour required if we are to ascribe to them an 'inner' and an 'outer' (Wittgenstein 1988: RPP II (henceforth RPP II) §616).[18] The explanation for this, however, appears to be merely technological. That we could hardly react in this way to the pioneering early computers is no reason to think that we could not see *some* imaginable digital computer as possessing an 'inner' and an 'outer'. This would have been obvious to Wittgenstein.[19]

Another Problem for the Alternative Account: Wittgenstein and Turing Also *Agree*

There is considerable disagreement within AI practitioners; some connectionists even refer to a well-known advocate of symbolic AI as the 'anti-Christ'.[20] AI 'naysayers' too may have very different philosophical grounds for their

---

16 In yet another sense, a machine is simply a *mechanism*, but there is no space to discuss this concept here.
17 These characteristics, we may presume, are not (logically) dependent on the entity being 'natural' rather than artificial (biological rather than nonbiological, organic rather than nonorganic and so on).
18 In this sense, these machines behaved 'mechanically' (RPP II §623).
19 According to Hacker, if we could 'create in an electronic laboratory a being that acted and behaved much as we do', we might indeed say that it perceived (and so on), but 'to that extent, it would not be a machine' (2019, 110). However, using Wittgenstein's own distinction between *automaton* and *machine*, we might say that, even if such an artefact were not considered an automaton, it might nevertheless properly be considered a machine.
20 Gary Marcus interviewed by Sam Shead in 'Why the buzz around DeepMind is dissipating as it transitions from games to science', *CNBC* 5 June 2020. https://www.cnbc.com/2020/06/05/google-deepmind-alphago-buzz-dissipates.html.

opposition to AI. In contrast, Wittgenstein – who supposedly had 'profound doubts' about Turing's views on AI – in fact agreed with him on several key issues.

Judgement of other minds is affective as well as cognitive

For Wittgenstein, regarding an entity as mind-endowed is a perspective that we adopt unreflectively; it is not a deliberate inference from observations of the entity's behaviour. For example, he said:

> In general I do not surmise fear in him – I *see* it. I do not feel that I am deducing the probable existence of something inside from something outside; rather it is as if the human face were in a way translucent.
>
> (*RPP II* §170, *original emphasis*)

The timidity that we 'read' in a face, Wittgenstein said, 'does not seem to be merely associated, outwardly connected, with the face; but fear is there, alive, in the features' (PI §537). He intended a general point, famously saying, 'My attitude towards him is an attitude towards a soul. I am not of the *opinion* that he has a soul' and 'Look into someone else's face and see the consciousness in it' (PI, 178, original emphasis; Z §220). It is, Wittgenstein remarked, as if a person 'became *transparent*' through a facial expression (LW II, 67, original emphasis).

On 'the difference between an attitude and opinion', Wittgenstein said: 'I would like to say: the attitude comes *before* the opinion' (LW II, 38, original emphasis). His remarks suggest that, in his view, detecting mental states is a 'more complicated' form and a 'refinement' of a primitive human 'reaction' to other beings (Wittgenstein CE, 395; see Proudfoot 2013b). According to Wittgenstein, reading a facial expression involves a response in the mind-reader: the person who recognizes emotion in even a mere drawing of a face is not making a reflective judgement, but rather is 'impressed' – the drawing 'produces this effect' in the observer (Wittgenstein 1990: LW I (henceforth LW I) §746). Identifying an emotion in a face may also involve involuntary affective mirroring; 'Whoever senses [sadness in a face] often imitates the face with his own', Wittgenstein said (LW I §746).[21] In sum, in his view, affect is importantly involved in mind-reading.

---

21 Wittgenstein's remarks on reading emotional expressions and on automatic mimicry are consistent with recent psychological research on facial expression recognition (e.g. Borgomaneri et al. 2020; Prochazkova and Kret 2017).

Using Turing's criterion for thinking, the judgement of intelligence in machines also has an affective component. Turing's computer-imitates-human game invites (and importantly also manages[22]) the interrogator's anthropomorphism – that is, it invites the interrogator to be 'impressed' by the hidden players, although by text rather than physical appearance. The programmer's aim is that the interrogator react to the machine as to a human being. While anthropomorphism is usually regarded as a *cognitive* bias, an anthropomorphism scale typically measures, along with aliveness, how 'warm' or 'scary' the entity is (e.g. Spatola et al. 2021) – and this implies affective states in the observer. That anthropomorphism is connected to affect is also suggested by its being influenced by biology (de Visser et al. 2017) and linked to empathy (e.g. Airenti 2015). So, for both Wittgenstein and Turing, judgement of mind involves affect.

Turing was well aware of the impact that an inanimate entity can have upon an observer: discussing his first, chess-playing, imitation game, he said that playing against a 'paper' machine (a human acting as a machine) gives 'a definite feeling that one is pitting one's wits against something alive' (1948, 412).[23] As to Wittgenstein, his remarks on mind-reading do not rule out our actually being 'impressed' by some machine, or even imitating the expressions of a machine. Moreover, his remarks do not rule out such a response's in some case constituting an appropriate 'ground for ascribing thought to a being'.[24]

The human being is the model of the thinking thing

Wittgenstein remarked that '[w]e only say of a human being and what is like one that it thinks' (PI §360). Thought can be attributed to non-human creatures, he said, if their '*rhythm* of work, play of expression etc. was like our own, but for their not *speaking*' (RPP II §186, original emphasis). In virtue of these and similar remarks, Wittgenstein has been accused of an 'uncritical speciesism'; his remarks are said to be 'indefensible', since, it is argued, 'a certain look and behavior' is 'largely accidental' to having a mind (Rey 2003, 263).

---

22 The game manages an interrogator's natural tendency to anthropomorphize, by both disincentivizing and (via the human player) controlling for anthropomorphism (Proudfoot 2011).
23 Turing used tongue-in-cheek anthropomorphic descriptions of his own machines, saying, for example, that 'one could not send the creature to school without the other children making excessive fun of it' (1950, 460–61).
24 Wittgenstein said that ascribing psychological states to *dolls* is a 'secondary' use (PI §282). We might say the same of ascribing such states to a pianola or the Manchester 'Baby'. This would nevertheless leave room for straightforwardly ascribing psychological states to *some* machine.

Turing too is often accused of speciesism. Critics argue that his test directed AI research to 'those facets of human behavior which are least susceptible to useful generalization precisely because they are not shared by other species'; the test was 'a tragedy for AI', it is claimed, since its emphasis on human behaviour was 'directly at odds' with AI's 'proper objectives' (Hayes and Ford 1995, 974; Ford and Hayes 1998, 79).

Certainly, Wittgenstein and Turing focused on the human being: for Wittgenstein, in the case of a mind-endowed being we are inclined to speak of inner and outer *human* states, and Turing's criterion for a computer's thinking is that (in specified circumstances) it is misidentified as a *human*. In each case, there is some leeway to defend against speciesism: Wittgenstein allowed for 'the prototype of a way of thinking' in non-human animals (RPP II §541), and Turing presented his test solely as a *sufficient* condition of thinking.[25] However, the critic may remain unconvinced – perhaps claiming that Wittgenstein still endorses speciesism in the form of assimilationism (see Glock 2013), or that Turing still provides no incremental way forward for the field of AI.[26]

However, the fact that Turing proposes a response-dependence approach to the concept of mind makes possible a different reply to the speciesism objection. A response-dependence theory explicates (say) *being red* in terms of the responses of actual normal humans in actual normal human environments. Yet it would seem odd to regard the theory as thereby parochial or speciesist. As Mark Johnston introduced the notion, a response-dependent concept is one that 'exhibit[s] a conceptual dependence on or interdependence with concepts of our responses in certain specified conditions' (1989, 145). In the case of *being red*, the concept just is linked to *our* responses in *our* environments. It does not follow that non-humans are unable to perceive red, or that human colour perception is superior to that of non-human animals.[27] We can, I suggest, generalize this point, to apply to response-dependence approaches in general. The result is that Turing's response-dependence criterion for thinking is off the speciesism hook.

Given Wittgenstein's emphasis on the affective element in judgement of other minds, it is not unreasonable to regard him too as offering a response-dependence approach to the concept of mind (Proudfoot 2024a). I suggest that, when Wittgenstein said, 'Instead of "attitude toward the soul" one could also say "attitude toward a human"' and when he remarked that a person

---

25 Moreover, the test can be varied by changing the human foil – e.g. replacing an adult with a child.
26 On objections to Turing's test, see Proudfoot 2011, 2017.
27 At least, without considerable additional argument.

becomes transparent to us through 'a human facial expression' (LW II, 38, 67), he was claiming that the concept of *being mind-endowed* just is linked to the concept of human responses in the human 'bustle of life'. If so (and given the argument in the previous paragraph), we cannot infer from Wittgenstein's remarks that, in his view, only humans can think, or that intelligence in humans is superior.

We should be non-partisan about cognitive architecture

Turing was open-minded about cognitive architecture. He proposed different models of machines – Turing-machine, unorganized neural network and oracle machine – and he refused to make a machine's success in the imitation game (logically) dependent on any specific architecture (Turing et al. 1952, 496).[28] In his view, we may conclude, the architectures of human brains and of successful machines in his imitation game are (at least to some degree) empirical matters.

On cognitive architecture, Wittgenstein made some well-known comments. He said, 'No supposition seems to me more natural than that there is no process in the brain correlated with […] thinking' such that we could 'read off thought-processes from brain-processes' (Z §608). In a similar vein, he remarked, '[N]othing seems more possible to me than that people some day will come to the definite opinion that there is no copy in either the physiological or nervous systems which corresponds to a *particular* thought, or a *particular* idea' (LW I §504, original emphasis). A popular interpretation of such remarks is that Wittgenstein had an 'extreme antipathy' to 'any scientific explanations of mental phenomena' and his remarks, in their 'lack of empirical or theoretical sophistication', are 'anti-scientistic' and 'positively luddite' (Rey 2003, 237, 238). Against this, Wittgenstein scholars have argued that, although such remarks attack *representationalist* cognitive architectures, they are consistent with neural network architectures (Stern 1991; Mills 1993; Lowney et al. 2020).

However, in these remarks Wittgenstein's moral – rather than promoting one specific architecture – appears to be that there is no a priori reason to think that only (what we would now describe as) classical computationalism about the mind can explain the 'subtle shades' of human physiognomy or behaviour that incline us to regard an entity as mind-endowed. The assumption of representational structures in the brain is, he said, a 'prejudice' resulting from 'primitive interpretations of our concepts' (Z §611). An alternative

---

28 On Turing's anticipation of neural network architectures, see Copeland and Proudfoot 1996.

picture '*can* be imagined!', he declared (RPP I, 908, original emphasis). Like Turing, Wittgenstein is open-minded on the matter.

Wittgenstein's remarks about 'prejudice' accurately capture the stance of some cognitive and computer scientists who regard symbolic AI (or alternatively, connectionist AI) as the only possible route to artificial intelligence. Moreover, his scepticism about some versions of classical computationalism – far from being 'anti-scientistic' or 'luddite' – is only sensible. On the question whether it will be symbolic AI, connectionist AI, recent hybrid architectures or some as-yet-unknown architecture requiring a paradigm shift that in fact leads to human-level AI, the jury is out.

Conclusion

The orthodox and alternative accounts of Wittgenstein and Turing on AI are myths. It is time to set these aside.

Acknowledgements

My thanks to participants at the 11th British Wittgenstein Society Conference (2022) for valuable comments.

References

Wittgenstein

BB (1965). *The Blue and Brown Books*. New York: Harper.
CE (1993). 'Cause and Effect: Intuitive Awareness'. In *Philosophical Occasions 1912–1951*, edited by James Klagge and Alfred Nordmann, 202–88. Indianapolis: Hackett Publishing Co.
LFM (1989). *Wittgenstein's Lectures on the Foundations of Mathematics, Cambridge 1939: from the Notes of R. G. Bosanquet, Norman Malcolm, Rush Rhees, & Yorick Smythies*, edited by Cora Diamond. Chicago: University of Chicago Press.
LPP (1989). *Wittgenstein's Lectures on Philosophical Psychology 1946–47: Notes by P. T. Geach, K. J. Shah and A. C. Jackson*, edited by Peter T. Geach. Chicago: University of Chicago Press.
LW I (1990). *Last Writings on the Philosophy of Psychology, Volume I*, edited by Georg H. von Wright and Heikki Nyman, and translated by C. Grant Luckhardt and M. A. E. Aue. Chicago: University of Chicago Press.
LW II (1993). *Last Writings on the Philosophy of Psychology, Volume II*, edited by Georg H. von Wright and Heikki Nyman, and translated by C. Grant Luckhardt and M. A. E. Aue. Oxford: Blackwell.
PG (1974). *Philosophical Grammar*, edited by Rush Rhees, and translated by Anthony J. P. Kenny. Oxford: Basil Blackwell.
PI (1972). *Philosophical Investigations* (2nd edn), edited by G. E. M. Anscombe and Rush Rhees, and translated by G. E. M. Anscombe. Oxford: Basil Blackwell.

RFM (1983). *Remarks on the Foundations of Mathematics* (revised edn), edited by Georg H. von Wright, Rush Rhees and G. E. M. Anscombe. Cambridge, Mass.: MIT Press.

RPP I (1988). *Remarks on the Philosophy of Psychology, Volume I*, edited by G. E. M. Anscombe and Georg H. von Wright, and translated by G. E. M. Anscombe. Chicago: University of Chicago Press.

RPP II (1988). *Remarks on the Philosophy of Psychology, Volume II*, edited by Georg H. von Wright and Heikki Nyman, and translated by C. Grant Luckhardt and M. A. E. Aue. Chicago: University of Chicago Press.

Z (1970). *Zettel*, edited by G. E. M. Anscombe and Georg H. von Wright, and translated by G. E. M. Anscombe. Berkeley and Los Angeles: University of California Press.

General

Airenti, Gabriella. 2015. 'The Cognitive Bases of Anthropomorphism: From Relatedness to Empathy'. *International Journal of Social Robotics* 7, no. 1: 117–27. https://doi.org/10.1007/s12369-014-0263-x.

Alksnis, Nikolai and Jack Reynolds. 2021. 'Revaluing the Behaviorist Ghost in Enactivism and Embodied Cognition'. *Synthese* 198, no. 6: 5785–807. https://doi.org/10.1007/s11229-019-02432-1.

Barrett, Louise. 2012. 'Why Behaviorism Isn't Satanism'. In *The Oxford Handbook of Comparative Evolutionary Psychology*, edited by Jennifer Vonk and Todd K. Shackelford, 17–38. Oxford: Oxford University Press.

Barrett, Louise. 2019. 'Enactivism, Pragmatism … Behaviorism?'. *Philosophical Studies* 176, no. 3: 807–18. https://doi.org/10.1007/s11098-018-01231-7.

Ben-Yami, Hanoch. 2005. 'Behaviorism and Psychologism: Why Block's Argument Against Behaviorism is Unsound'. *Philosophical Psychology* 18, no. 2: 179–86. https://doi.org/10.1080/09515080500169470.

Berg, Adam. 2019. 'Computing the Enigma of Love'. *Glass Bead*. https://www.glass-bead.org/research-platform/computing-the-enigma-of-love/?lang=enview.

Block, Ned. 1981. 'Psychologism and Behaviorism'. *Philosophical Review* 90, no. 1: 5–43. https://doi.org/10.2307/2184371.

Borgomaneri, Sara, Corinna Bolloni, Paola Sessa and Alessio Avanenti. 2020. 'Blocking Facial Mimicry Affects Recognition of Facial and Body Expressions'. *PLOS ONE* 15, no. 2: e0229364. https://doi.org/10.1371/journal.pone.0229364.

Broad, Charles D. 1925/2000. *The Mind and its Place in Nature*. London: Kegan Paul, Trench, Trübner and Co. Ltd. Republished in 2000 by Routledge; page references are to the 2000 edition.

Carnap, Rudolf. 1934/2011. *The Unity of Science, translation and introduction by Max Black*. London: Kegan Paul, Trench, Trubner Co. Ltd (1934). Republished in the Routledge Revivals series. Abingdon, Oxon.: Routledge (2011). [The relevant part of *The Unity of Science* is a revision by Carnap, translated by Black, of his 'Die Physikalische Sprache als Universalsprache der Wissenschaft'. *Erkenntnis* 2, no. 1: 423–65 (1931).] Page references are to the 2011 edition.

Carnap, Rudolf. 1956. 'The Methodological Character of Theoretical Concepts'. *Minnesota Studies in the Philosophy of Science* 1, no. 1: 38–76.

Chihara, Charles S. 1973. 'Operationalism and Ordinary Language Revisited'. *Philosophical Studies* 24, no. 3: 137–57. https://doi.org/10.1007/BF00367992.

Chihara, Charles S. and Jerry A. Fodor. 1965. 'Operationalism and Ordinary Language: A Critique of Wittgenstein'. *American Philosophical Quarterly* 2, no. 4: 281–95.

Cook, John W. 2010. 'Locating Wittgenstein'. *Philosophy* 85, no. 2: 273–89. https://doi.org/10.1017/S0031819110000021.

Copeland, B. Jack. 1993. *Artificial Intelligence: A Philosophical Introduction*. Oxford: Blackwell Publishing.

Copeland, B. Jack. 2000a. 'Narrow Versus Wide Mechanism'. *Journal of Philosophy* 97, no. 1: 5–32. https://doi.org/10.5840/jphil20009716.

Copeland, B. Jack. 2000b. 'The Turing Test'. *Minds & Machines* 10, no. 4: 519–39. https://doi.org/10.1023/A:1011285919106.

Copeland, B. Jack, ed. 2004. *The Essential Turing: Seminal Writings in Computing, Logic, Philosophy, Artificial Intelligence, and Artificial Life plus the Secrets of Enigma*. Oxford: Clarendon Press.

Copeland, B. Jack and Diane Proudfoot. 1996. 'On Alan Turing's Anticipation of Connectionism'. *Synthese* 108, no. 3: 361–77. https://doi.org/10.1007/BF00413694.

de Visser, Ewart J., Samuel S. Monfort, Kimberly Goodyear, Li Lu, Martin O'Hara, Mary R. Lee, Raja Parasuraman and Frank Krueger. 2017. 'A Little Anthropomorphism Goes a Long Way: Effects of Oxytocin on Trust, Compliance, and Team Performance with Automated Agents'. *Human Factors* 59, no. 1: 116–33. https://doi.org/10.1177/0018720816687205.

Ford, Kenneth M. and Patrick J. Hayes. 1998. 'On Computational Wings: Rethinking the Goals of Artificial Intelligence'. *Scientific American Presents* 9, no. 4: 78–83.

French, Robert M. 2012. 'Dusting Off the Turing Test'. *Science* 336: 164–165.

Garnett, A. Campbell. 1950. 'Must Empiricism Be Materialistic and Behavioristic?'. *Journal of Philosophy* 47, no. 9: 250–55. https://doi.org/10.2307/2021746.

Glock, Hans-Johann. 2013. 'Animal Minds: A Non-representationalist Approach'. *American Philosophical Quarterly* 50, no. 3: 213–32.

Grimi, Elisa. 2020. 'Anscombe and Wittgenstein'. *Enrahonar. An International Journal of Theoretical & Practical Reason* 64: 165–79. https://doi.org/10.5565/rev/enrahonar.1283.

Hacker, Peter M. S. 1996. *Wittgenstein's Place in Twentieth-Century Analytic Philosophy*. Oxford: Blackwell Publishing.

Hacker, Peter M. S. 2018. 'Wittgenstein's Legacy: The Principles of the Private Language Arguments'. *Philosophical Investigations* 41, no. 2: 123–40. https://doi.org/10.1111/phin.12186.

Hacker, Peter M. S. 2019. *Wittgenstein: Meaning and Mind, Volume 3 of an Analytical Commentary on the Philosophical Investigations, Part I. Essays*. Second, extensively revised edition. Hoboken, NJ: Wiley-Blackwell.

Hartree, Douglas R. 1946. 'The "Electronic Brain"'. *Times* [London, England] 7 November 1946: 5.

Hayes, Patrick J. and Kenneth M. Ford. 1995. 'Turing Test Considered Harmful'. In *IJCAI-95 Proceedings of the 14th International Joint Conference on Artificial Intelligence*, Vol. 1, 972–77. San Francisco: Morgan Kaufman.

Hodges, Andrew. 2014. *Alan Turing: The Enigma*, revised edition. London: Vintage.

Holborow, Leslie C. 1967. 'Wittgenstein's Kind of Behaviourism?'. *Philosophical Quarterly* 17, no. 69: 345–57. https://doi.org/10.2307/2217456.

Johnston, Mark. 1989. 'Dispositional Theories of Value'. *Proceedings of the Aristotelian Society Suppl.* 63: 139–74.

Kitchener, Richard F. 2018. 'Epistemological Behaviorism'. *Behavior & Philosophy* 46: 114–51.

Langdon-Davies, J. 1946. 'Electronic Brains Can't Reason.' *Daily Mail*, 19 November 1946: 2.

Linsky, Leonard. 1957. 'Wittgenstein on Language and Some Problems of Philosophy'. *Journal of Philosophy* 54, no. 10: 285–93. https://doi.org/10.2307/2022691.

Liu, Lydia H. 2021. 'Wittgenstein in the Machine'. *Critical Inquiry* 47, no. 3: 425–55. https://doi.org/10.1086/713551.

Lowney, Charles W., Simon D. Levy, William Meroney, and Ross W. Gayler. 2020. 'Connecting Twenty-First Century Connectionism and Wittgenstein'. *Philosophia* 48, no. 2: 643–71. https://doi.org/10.1007/s11406-019-00154-9.

Luckhardt, C. Grant. 1983. 'Wittgenstein and Behaviourism'. *Synthese* 56, no. 3: 319–38. https://doi.org/10.1007/BF00485469.

MacIntyre, Alasdair C. 1958/2004. *The Unconscious: A Conceptual Analysis*. Abingdon, Oxon.: Routledge.

Malcolm, Norman. 1954. 'Wittgenstein's Philosophical Investigations'. *Philosophical Review* 63, no. 4: 530–59. https://doi.org/10.2307/2182289.

Mandik, Pete. 2013. *This Is Philosophy of Mind: An Introduction*. Hoboken, NJ: Wiley-Blackwell.

Mays, Wolfe. 1952. 'Can Machines Think?'. *Philosophy* 27, no. 101: 148–62. https://doi.org/10.1017/S003181910002266X.

Medina, José. 2003. 'Wittgenstein and Nonsense: Psychologism, Kantianism, and the Habitus'. *International Journal of Philosophical Studies* 11, no. 3: 293–318. https://doi.org/10.1080/0967255032000108020.

Mills, Stephen. 1993. 'Wittgenstein and Connectionism: A Significant Complementarity?'. In *Philosophy and Cognitive Science*, edited by Christopher Hookway and Donald M. Peterson, 137–57. Cambridge: Cambridge University Press.

Montague, W. Pepperell. 1951. 'The Modern Distemper of Philosophy'. *Journal of Philosophy* 48, no. 14: 429–35. https://doi.org/10.2307/2021589.

Moor, James H. 1976. 'An Analysis of the Turing Test'. *Philosophical Studies* 30, no. 4: 249–57. https://doi.org/10.1007/BF00372497.

Moor, James H. 1987. 'Turing Test'. In *Encyclopedia of Artificial Intelligence*, Vol. 2, edited by S. Shapiro, 1126–30. New York: Wiley.

Moore, Jay. 2010. 'What Do Mental Terms Mean?'. *Psychological Record* 60, no. 4: 699–714. https://doi.org/10.1007/BF03395740.

Moore, Jay. 2013. 'Mentalism as a Radical Behaviorist Views It—Part 2'. *Journal of Mind & Behavior* 34, no. 3–4: 205–32.

Mountbatten, Louis F. A. V. N. [1st Earl Mountbatten of Burma]. 1946. 'The Presidential Address'. *Journal of the British Institution of Radio Engineers* 6, no. 6: 221–25. https://doi.org/10.1049/jbire.1946.0032.

Overgaard, Søren. 2004. 'Exposing the Conjuring Trick: Wittgenstein on Subjectivity'. *Phenomenology & the Cognitive Sciences* 3, no. 3: 263–86. https://doi.org/10.1023/B:PHEN.0000049303.10575.3c.

Overskeid, Geir. 1995. 'Cognitivist or Behaviourist – Who Can Tell the Difference? The Case of Implicit and Explicit Knowledge'. *British Journal of Psychology* 86, no. 4: 517–22. https://doi.org/10.1111/j.2044-8295.1995.tb02568.x.

Pinker, Steven. 2003. *The Blank Slate: The Modern Denial of Human Nature*. London: Penguin.

Polger, Thomas W. 2012. 'Functionalism as a Philosophical Theory of the Cognitive Sciences'. *Wiley Interdisciplinary Reviews. Cognitive Science* 3, no. 3: 337–48. https://doi.org/10.1002/wcs.1170.

Prochazkova, Eliska and Mariska E. Kret. 2017. 'Connecting Minds and Sharing Emotions Through Mimicry: A Neurocognitive Model of Emotional Contagion'.

Neuroscience & Biobehavioral Reviews 80: 99–114. https://doi.org/10.1016/j.neubiorev.2017.05.013.

Proudfoot, Diane. 2011. 'Anthropomorphism and AI: Turing's Much Misunderstood Imitation Game'. *Artificial Intelligence* 175, no. 5–6: 950–57. https://doi.org/10.1016/j.artint.2011.01.006.

Proudfoot, Diane. 2013a. 'Rethinking Turing's Test'. *Journal of Philosophy* 110, no. 7: 391–411. https://doi.org/10.5840/jphil2013110722.

Proudfoot, Diane. 2013b. 'Can a Robot Smile? Wittgenstein on Facial Expression'. In *A Wittgensteinian Perspective on the Use of Conceptual Analysis in Psychology*, edited by Timothy P. Racine and Kathleen L. Slaney, 172–94. London: Palgrave Macmillan UK.

Proudfoot, Diane. 2017. 'The Turing Test—From Every Angle'. In *The Turing Guide*, by B. Jack Copeland et al., 287–300. Oxford: Oxford University Press.

Proudfoot, Diane. 2020. 'Rethinking Turing's Test and the Philosophical Implications'. *Minds & Machines* 30, no. 4: 487–512. https://doi.org/10.1007/s11023-020-09534-7.

Proudfoot, Diane. 2022. 'An Analysis of Turing's Criterion for "Thinking"'. *Philosophies* 7, no. 6: 1–15. https://doi.org/10.3390/philosophies7060124.

Proudfoot, Diane. 2024a. 'Turing's Wittgenstein'. Forthcoming in *Wittgenstein and Other Philosophers: His Influence on Historical and Contemporary Analytic Philosophers*, edited by Ali H. Khani and Gary Kemp. Routledge.

Proudfoot, Diane. 2024b. 'Intelligence Naturalized, Turing-Style'. Forthcoming in *Naturalism and Its Challenges*, edited by Ali H. Khani and Gary Kemp. Routledge.

Proudfoot, Diane and B. Jack Copeland. 2019. 'Turing and the First Electronic Brains: What the Papers Said'. In *The Routledge Handbook of the Computational Mind*, edited by Mark Sprevak and Matteo Colombo, 23–37. Abingdon, Oxon.: Routledge.

Rachlin, Howard. 2017. 'In Defense of Teleological Behaviorism'. *Journal of Theoretical & Philosophical Psychology* 37, no. 2: 65–76. https://doi.org/10.1037/teo0000060.

Raleigh, Thomas. 2018. 'Wittgenstein's Remarks on Technology and Mental Mechanisms'. *Techné: Research in Philosophy & Technology* 22, no. 3: 447–71. https://doi.org/10.5840/techne2018122092.

Rey, Georges. 2003. 'Why Wittgenstein Ought to Have Been a Computationalist (and What a Computationalist Can Gain from Wittgenstein)'. *Croatian Journal of Philosophy* 3, no. 9: 231–64.

Richelle, Marc N. 1993/2016. *B.F. Skinner – A Reappraisal*. Abingdon, Oxon.: Routledge.

Saariluoma, Pertti and Matthias Rauterberg. 2015. 'Turing Test Does Not Work in Theory but in Practice'. In *International Conference on Artificial Intelligence, ICAI'15*, 433–37. http://worldcomp-proceedings.com/proc/p2015/ICA3164.pdf.

Saariluoma, Pertti and Matthias Rauterberg. 2016. 'Turing's Error-Revised'. *International Journal of Philosophy Study* 4: 22–41. doi: 10.14355/ijps.2016.04.004.

Shanker, Stuart G. 1987. 'Wittgenstein versus Turing on the Nature of Church's Thesis'. *Notre Dame Journal of Formal Logic* 28, no. 4: 615–49.

Shanker, Stuart G. 1998. *Wittgenstein's Remarks on the Foundations of AI*. Abingdon, Oxon.: Routledge.

Spatola, Nicolas, Barbara Kühnlenz and Gordon Cheng. 2021. 'Perception and Evaluation in Human–Robot Interaction: The Human–Robot Interaction Evaluation Scale (HRIES)—A Multicomponent Approach of Anthropomorphism'. *International Journal of Social Robotics* 13, no. 7: 1517–39. https://doi.org/10.1007/s12369-020-00667-4.

Stern, David G. 1991. 'Models of Memory: Wittgenstein and Cognitive Science'. *Philosophical Psychology* 4, no. 2: 203–18. https://doi.org/10.1080/09515089108573027.

Tang, Hao. 2014. 'Wittgenstein and the Dualism of the Inner and the Outer'. *Synthese* 191, no. 14: 3173–94. https://doi.org/10.1007/s11229-014-0441-2.

Taylor, Alex, Anab Jain and Laurel Swan. 2010. 'New Companions'. In *Close Engagements with Artificial Companions: Key Social, Psychological, Ethical and Design Issues*, edited by Yorick Wilks, 107–20. Amsterdam/Philadelphia: John Benjamins Publishing Company. https://doi.org/10.1075/nlp.8.16tay.

Taylor, Timothy. 2015. 'Denkraumverlust'. *Edge [2015: What Do You Think About Machines That Think?]*. https://www.edge.org/response-detail/26216.

ter Hark, Michel. 2006. 'Wittgenstein, Pretend Play and the Transferred Use of Language'. *Journal for the Theory of Social Behaviour* 36, no. 3: 299–318. https://doi.org/10.1111/j.1468-5914.2006.00308.x.

Turing, Alan M. (1936–7). 'On Computable Numbers, with an Application to the Entscheidungsproblem'. *Proceedings of the London Mathematical Society, Series 2* 42, no. 1: 230–65. Reprinted in B. Jack Copeland (ed.) 2004, 58–90; page references are to Copeland (ed.) 2004.

Turing, Alan M. 1947. 'Lecture on the Automatic Computing Engine'. Lecture to the London Mathematical Society, 20 February 1947. Typescript in the Turing Digital Archive, King's College Cambridge, catalogue reference AMT/B/1; reprinted in B. Jack Copeland (ed.) 2004, 378–94. Page references are to Copeland (ed.) 2004.

Turing, Alan M. 1948. 'Intelligent Machinery'. National Physical Laboratory Report. Typescript in the Turing Digital Archive, King's College Cambridge, catalogue reference AMT/C/11; reprinted in B. Jack Copeland (ed.) 2004, 410–32. Page references are to Copeland (ed.) 2004.

Turing, Alan M. 1950. 'Computing Machinery and Intelligence'. *Mind* 59: 433–60. Reprinted in B. Jack Copeland (ed.) 2004, 441–64; page references are to Copeland (ed.) 2004.

Turing, Alan M., Richard B. Braithwaite, Geoffrey Jefferson and Max H. A. Newman. 1952. 'Can Automatic Calculating Machines Be Said to Think?'. Typescript in the Turing Digital Archive, King's College Cambridge, catalogue reference AMT/B/6; reprinted in B. Jack Copeland (ed.) 2004, 494–506. Page references are to Copeland (ed.) 2004.

Vaaja, Tero. 2013. 'Wittgenstein's "Inner and Outer": Overcoming Epistemic Asymmetry'. *Nordic Wittgenstein Review* 2, no. 1: 107–29. https://doi.org/10.1515/nwr.2013.2.1.107.

Chapter 2

BETWEEN WITTGENSTEIN AND TURING: ENACTIVE EMBODIED THINKING MACHINES

Tomi Kokkonen and Ilmari Hirvonen

Introduction

Is it possible for a machine to think? At first glance, this question may appear to be about the possible future capacities of artificial intelligence (AI) systems. Indeed, the recent public discussion on ChatGPT, other AI systems and the future of this technology has, to a great extent, been concerned with that question. However, there is also a philosophically more profound question about what we *mean* when we say that something is thinking. Answering this philosophical problem is also crucial for building machines or computers with thinking capacities if we wish to create such machines. We must first analyse the conditions under which we would say something – or someone – is thinking. Only after that can we ask what psychological or artificial processes are needed for this to be the case.

Philosophers who discussed this issue during the early days of computers include Alan Turing, who famously argued for the possibility of thinking machines, and Ludwig Wittgenstein, who drew the opposite conclusion. Despite their differences, the two seem to agree on how thinking should be attributed. This chapter returns to what they wrote about thinking and why they disagreed. We will bring some lessons from Wittgenstein and Turing on how we should think about thinking. Moreover, we shall apply their ideas to contemporary robotics and AI discussions and engineering. Also, we outline a view on thinking machines that bridges Turing's optimism and Wittgenstein's scepticism on whether a machine could be said to think.

Our primary objective is not to settle a conceptual dispute between Wittgenstein and Turing. Our main goal lies in the opposite direction: to contribute to the discussion on the philosophy of robotics and AI. We approach the problem of thinking machines by identifying what Wittgenstein and Turing agree on and then apply what we have learned to the current debate on AI and robotics. In particular, we consider the idea of modelling robots according to an enactivist conception of thinking (see, e.g. Varela et al. 1991; Noë 2004; Rohde 2010; Stewart et al. 2010; Hutto and Myin 2012; Gallagher 2017; Egbert and Barandiaran 2022; Lassiter 2022). According to enactivism, cognition does not primarily consist of the internalist processing of representations. Instead, it arises through dynamic interaction between an organism and its environment. We do not take a stance on whether enactivism is the correct philosophical view of the human mind. However, applying some of its key insights to robot design may be helpful if one is interested in creating thinking machines. The insights can be used in two directions: enactivism in explanation and enactivism in design. We are interested in the latter.

We also argue that enactive robots would qualify as thinking machines for Turing and perhaps even for Wittgenstein. The latter, however, depends on whether robots can be embedded as agents in normative practices. This is an open question that should be taken seriously in contemporary research, and we believe that the success or failure of future robotics will ultimately provide an answer to the question. However, we claim that Wittgenstein's and Turing's work provide us with the framework for evaluating what would count as success.

The structure of the chapter is as follows. Section 'Wittgenstein on Thinking Machines' discusses Wittgenstein's view of thinking, machines and thinking machines. Section 'Turing on Thinking Machines' explains why Turing reaches a different conclusion than Wittgenstein while agreeing on the main premises. After this, in Section 'Enactivist Thinking Machines', we discuss enactivist robotics as a contemporary proposal and why it is the most promising way to create thinking machines in light of the discussions in the previous sections. Then, in Section 'Wittgenstein on the Normativity of Thinking', we turn to Wittgenstein's views on these issues, especially his claim that thinking requires the possibility of failure and mere malfunction will not suffice. At some points, Wittgenstein seems to argue that this is never possible for machines. We, instead, argue that enactivist robotics' attempt to have the robot represent its environment and harmonize its goals in relation to it may enable such failures, which we would call mistakes rather than malfunctions.

Wittgenstein on Thinking Machines

There appears to be a tension, some might even say an irreconcilable conflict, between Wittgenstein and Turing regarding thinking machines. Turing is often interpreted as taking machines or – to be precise – thinking computers to be a genuine possibility. Wittgenstein, in turn, is considerably more sceptical about such possibilities. A common interpretation of Wittgenstein is that he denied the possibility of thinking machines or computers (e.g. Neumaier 1987; Seidel 1991; Glock 1996, 157–59; Shanker 1998; Hacker 2019, 102–11). According to such readings, the notion is a category mistake for him. There is indeed some evidence that Wittgenstein considers thinking machines nonsense: if something thinks, it is not a machine. For instance, in his *Remarks on the Philosophy of Psychology* (RPP), he famously wrote: 'Turing's "machines". These machines are humans who calculate' (Wittgenstein 2009: RPP I, §1096).[1]

If Wittgenstein sees a problem with thinking machines, the problem is conceptual. The issue lies in the *grammar* of 'machine' and 'to think'. For Wittgenstein, 'grammar' is a technical term. What he calls 'grammatical rules' determine the meaning of words (Glock 1996, 150). Therefore, in Wittgensteinian parlance, grammar does not mean the mere rules of syntax but the rules of semantics and pragmatics. Wittgenstein's problem with thinking machines can be seen, for instance, in two quotes from the *Blue Book* in which he discusses the question, 'Is it possible for a machine to think?' Wittgenstein writes:

> 'Could a machine think?' I [...] refer you to an analogous question: 'Can a machine have toothache?' You will certainly be inclined to say: 'A machine can't have toothache'. All I will do now is to draw your attention to the use which you have made of the word 'can' and to ask you: 'Did you mean to say that all our past experience has shown that a machine never had toothache?' The impossibility of which you speak is a logical one.
>
> *(Wittgenstein 1958: BB, 16)*

Wittgenstein then continues:

> [T]he trouble which is expressed in this question is not really that we don't yet know a machine which could do the job. The question is not analogous to that which someone might have asked a hundred years ago: 'Can a machine liquefy a gas?' The trouble is rather that the sentence, 'A machine thinks (perceives, wishes)' seems somehow nonsensical. It is as though we had asked 'Has the number 3 a colour?'
>
> *(Wittgenstein 1958: BB, 47)*

---

1 However, Juliet Floyd has shown that this passage can be read differently (Floyd 2019a, 2019b).

The same sentiment can be found again in the *Philosophical Investigations* (PI). Wittgenstein writes: 'But surely a machine cannot think! Is that an empirical statement? No. We say only of a human being and what is like one that it thinks' (Wittgenstein 2009: PI, §360). Wittgenstein admits that one can say of inanimate objects, such as dolls, that they think. However, this is a secondary use of the concept. Someone who used the concept of pain only for inanimate objects would not have the same concept of pain that we have (Wittgenstein 2009: PI, §282).

Similarly, one could already use the concept of thinking as applying to machines today as, most likely, some people do. For instance, one could say that when a machine is turned on and takes some time to warm up 'it is thinking'. However, this is a metaphorical secondary use of the concept which presupposes our everyday usage of the word. If someone says that a machine is thinking when it is warming up, they do not mean it in the same sense as when they say that a person solving a challenging mathematical problem is thinking. Though, of course, this does show how the extension of a word can be widened, the expansion nonetheless comes with a change of the original meaning.

Why, then, does Wittgenstein oppose the idea of a thinking machine (if he indeed opposes it)? In a nutshell, the problem is that the concept of thinking is intertwined with several other concepts, such as perceiving, wishing, acting (intentionally), being conscious, being in pain, being creative, having interests, being alive, having understanding, meaning something, wishing, knowing something and so on. The attribution of 'thinking' presupposes the possible attribution of these other concepts, or at least some of them. In our everyday usage of the term, only a living, conscious being that has plans and tries to do things *thinks* (Hacker 2019, 109–110; Glock 1996, 358–59; 362; Wittgenstein 2009: PI §§283, 359–60; Wittgenstein 1969: PG, §64, 105). As Wittgenstein writes in *Remarks on the Philosophy of Psychology*: 'What a lot of things a man must do in order for us to say he *thinks*' (Wittgenstein 1980: RPP I, §563, emphasis in original). Thinking is not, for instance, mere mechanical manipulation of signs. Nevertheless, if someone is trying to figure out a complicated mathematical problem, manipulating signs in that context can be considered an instantiation of thinking.

Wittgenstein proposes that we attribute thinking and other mental concepts based on behavioural criteria. This becomes clear, for example, from the following quotations that one can find in the *Philosophical Investigations*: '[O]nly of a living human being and what resembles (behaves like) a living human being can one say: it has sensations; it sees; is blind; hears; is deaf; is conscious or unconscious' (Wittgenstein 2009: PI, §281, see also §283). Wittgenstein also writes: '"But in a fairy tale a pot too can see and hear!"

(Certainly, but it can also talk)' (Wittgenstein 2009: PI, §282). It would make little sense now in the actual world to say that a pot has sensations. However, a pot that talks and acts like a person can be said to have them. Here, a pot would not have 'sensations' in a secondary sense. On the contrary, because the pot acts like a person, we would say that it has sensations. Wittgenstein also states, somewhat opaquely: 'The human body is the best picture of the human soul' (Wittgenstein 2009: PI, iv §25). Here, Wittgenstein is not talking about a dead body but a living and breathing one, a body that acts like a person with a mind. So, it is difficult for a bodiless machine operating on ones and zeros to be considered thinking, given the criteria that Wittgenstein puts forth.

Despite relying on behavioural criteria, Wittgenstein is not a behaviourist – at least not in the naïve Watsonian sense. Wittgenstein is not saying that the criteria for something are the thing itself (Wittgenstein 1976: LFM, 111, Wittgenstein 1980: RPP I §292, Hacker 2019, Ch. XV). It is also important to note that 'criteria' are not necessary or sufficient conditions for Wittgenstein. Instead, they offer defeasible evidential support for applying a term (Glock 1996, 93; Hacker 2019, 290–91). So, for instance, behaving as if in pain is not the same as being in pain. An outstanding actor might be able to fool others into thinking she is in severe pain, even though she is not. There is a humorous quote in the *Philosophical Remarks* (PR) where Wittgenstein refers to Ivan Pavlov's experiments with dogs on classical conditioning. Pavlov observed that dogs salivate in the presence of food. In his study, Pavlov put on a metronome before giving a dog food, and later, he only put on the metronome without giving the food and measured the salivation it caused (Todes 2014, 290). To this, Wittgenstein comments: 'Salivation – no matter how precisely measured – is *not* what I call expecting' (Wittgenstein 1998: PR, 70). So, even though one might say that a dog is expecting food, salivation is not 'the expecting'. At tops, it can only serve as a fallible indicator or criterion. Though, according to Wittgenstein, you cannot say that a dog is expecting to get food tomorrow since it is not a part of its form of life – or a language game since dogs do not seem to have a concept of 'the next day' (Wittgenstein 2009: PI, §650, i §1 p. 182).

Now that we have gained a general understanding of what Wittgenstein thinks of attributing thinking and the possibility of thinking machines, we should compare it with Turing's conception. We will show that Turing has more or less the same view on attributing thinking, while he also believes that machines could think. After discussing Turing's reasons for believing so, we will look at some contemporary ideas from Wittgenstein's and Turing's perspectives. Finally, we will return to Wittgenstein and his idea of normativity in thinking.

Turing on Thinking Machines

Turing takes thinking machines to be genuinely possible. Although this creates tension between him and Wittgenstein, the two share a general idea of what thinking is. For them, whether something counts as a thinking being is not a question about the nature of some underlying mental processes. Instead, it is about the applicability of the concept of thinking.[2] Neither Wittgenstein nor Turing is interested in the ontology of thinking. Indeed, Turing believes this is precisely why we could have thinking machines, although the processes underlying their thinking would significantly differ from our own (Turing 1948, 1950, 1951; Turing et al. 1952; see also Proudfoot 2020). For Turing, a machine could think if it behaves in a way that makes it sensible to apply the concept of thinking to it. His view has traditionally been interpreted as being behaviouristic. It has been thought that Turing defines thinking as patterns of behaviour which we recognize as thinking (e.g. Block 1981; Hodges 2014). The inductivist interpretation challenges the behaviouristic interpretation. According to the inductivist reading, Turing takes such recognition as evidence for internal states, which we identify as thinking (Moor 1976, 2001). The latter interpretation contradicts, however, what Turing explicitly writes. For him, human and machine thinking have underlying processes, but they are not what we *mean* by thinking (see Turing 1950 and especially Turing et al. 1952; see also Proudfoot 2020). Diane Proudfoot has argued that identifying Turing as a straightforward behaviourist is also problematic. She has presented an alternative reading that focuses on an interpreter's recognition of behaviour to be intelligent or thinking (Proudfoot 2011, 2013, 2020). Either way, thinking is connected with how we attribute thinking, which can change over time. For example, in his article 'Computing Machinery and Intelligence', Turing writes:

---

2 Notice that Turing uses 'thinking' and 'intelligence' interchangeably. In artificial intelligence, the 'intelligence' part often refers to an AI system's capability to do something that would require intelligence from a human being. This, however, does not mean that the computational processes underlying the performance must be intelligent in any other sense of the word. In contrast, 'strong' AI is the idea that a machine actually 'thinks' because it carries out the same or similar processes as a thinking human being. Wittgenstein and Turing are not interested in the underlying processes, nor is the more modest meaning of 'intelligence' their target. For them, thinking requires more than the intelligence required to perform individual tasks.

> I believe that at the end of the century the use of words and general educated opinion will have altered so much that one will be able to speak of machines thinking without expecting to be contradicted.
>
> (Turing 1950, 442)

Turing makes two predictions in the article. The first concerns technological development, and the second changes in the use of the word 'thinking'. He anticipates that within 50 years of writing his paper, due to technological breakthroughs, humans will consider it natural to include new beings among those capable of thinking. He predicts that 'machines will eventually compete with men in all purely intellectual fields' (Turing 1950, 460), making them indistinguishable from human capabilities. Turing also discusses machine learning as a way forward in making thinking machines.

There are at least two ways to interpret Turing's prediction that the extension of the concept of thinking will broaden to include machines. One is that the meaning of 'thinking' will remain the same, and future computers will be capable of thinking. The second is that the meaning of 'thinking' will change so that machines will be said to be thinking even though they are incapable of thinking according to the term's original use. In either case, the concept of 'thinking' will be applied to new entities.

Therefore, according to Turing, the existence of thinking machines requires at least two things. First, it demands conceptual inclusion. We must add machines among thinking beings in our linguistic and other practices in a way which is a natural extension of those practices. Second, it requires technology that enables machines to fit these practices non-arbitrarily. These two components are intertwined, but they should be kept conceptually apart. Turing focuses mainly on technology and attempts to demonstrate that such technology is possible. However, his ideas concerning conceptual inclusion are more crucial for the topic at hand. We think that Wittgenstein and Turing, at heart, agree on how thinking is attributed. We also subscribe to a version of their conception. However, there are differences between Turing and Wittgenstein, and their disagreement about the possibility of thinking machines has more to do with conceptual than technological issues. We will return to them later.

In order to understand conceptual inclusion better, let us look at Turing's 'imitation game', commonly known as the 'Turing Test'. Turing presented several different versions of the game that are not identical (see Proudfoot 2011, 2013). Nevertheless, the general idea of the 'standard version' is the following. There is a test setting with an 'interrogator' and two players, a human and a computer. The interrogator can ask the players questions and has to find out, based on the answers, which player is the human, and which is the computer. If a human cannot distinguish another human from a machine based on linguistic behaviour, there is no reason to conceptualize what they are doing differently. Both are thinking.

The Turing Test is supposed to say something about the quality of AI – but what exactly? There are at least three ways to interpret the test. These interpretations are connected to the three above-mentioned interpretations of what Turing means by thinking (cf. Proudfoot 2020):

(1) It could be interpreted as evidence that a machine thinks in some stronger sense than Turing probably had in mind, as in the strong AI paradigm.
(2) It could be interpreted as a sufficient criterion for extending the concept of thinking to machines. In other words, this is what 'thinking' means.
(3) It could be interpreted as an example of a case in which a machine could be said to think.

Under all three interpretations, the test is supposed to test some capacity that a genuinely thinking machine has. However, thinking might require more than this, and the test does not say what other capacities a thinking machine must have.

In our view, the most sensible interpretation of what it means if a machine passes the test is the last one. Our primary interest is to develop a conception of thinking machines that builds upon the work of Wittgenstein and Turing. We take no position on the scholarly issue of whether Turing was after the second or the third option, although we are inclined to say the third. He explicitly 'replaces' the question about whether machines can think – since the concept of thinking is notoriously difficult to define – with the 'less ambiguous question' of passing the test. However, he does not intend to change the topic but study a 'closely related' question (Turing 1950, 433). It seems that Turing is not trying to evaluate whether a machine can have sufficient cognitive capacities to be a thinking being. Instead, he discusses some potential problems for the existence of thinking machines that point to complexities beyond a single test.

The problem that Turing considers crucial comes from Ada Lovelace's seminal work on computing machines. He calls it 'Lady Lovelace's Objection'. According to Lovelace, a machine cannot think since it only executes tasks based on the inputs and the algorithms programmed into it. After a task it is ordered to do is completed, it stops. In other words, a machine only does what it is programmed to do. Therefore, it lacks the continuity and creativity of human thinking. It is essential to thinking that something comes from within, and it does something surprising: thinking is productive, not just reactive. Without this, a machine simply performs a mechanical process that would not be associated with thinking (Lovelace 1843; Turing 1950, 450–51). However, Turing believes that Lovelace's reasoning rests on wrong assumptions. Even though a machine requires inputs to produce outputs, we cannot necessarily know, based on the inputs, what outputs the machine could achieve. In a 1951 radio broadcast, Turing says:

> But there is no need to suppose that, when we give it its orders, we know what we are doing, what the consequences of these orders are going to be. [...] If we give the machine a program which results in its doing something interesting which we had not anticipated I should be inclined to say that the machine *had* originated something, rather than to claim that its behaviour was implicit in the programme, and therefore that the originality lies entirely with us.
>
> *(Turing 1951, 485)*

However, Turing goes beyond mere unpredicted consequences and suggests that Lady Lovelace's Objection could be overcome basically by machine learning (Turing 1950, 454–59). A machine capable of learning would develop dispositions to behave in novel ways. Such a machine would be, in part, independent of pre-programming. We will not assess whether the problem of creativity can be solved so easily. Nevertheless, what Turing says about learning is interesting.

Turing suggests a two-part solution to the problem of creating a thinking machine that is sufficiently independent of pre-programming: first, we should construct a machine with child-like dispositions and learning abilities, and second, we should educate it. The required learning occurs at least partly through interaction with humans, which is a prerequisite for the growth of the adult mind. Turing also mentions differences between machines and humans that emerge from their different embodiments. He acknowledges that a robot without human-like embodiment could only engage in intellectual behaviour. Nevertheless, he seems to believe this would suffice for a machine to think. Here, we find Turing's view problematic. We think that rationalizable action within an environment is crucial to our practices of attributing thinking, and we suspect this could also be a game-changer for Wittgenstein. We will now turn to later discussions concerning the theory of mind and embodiment to make this point and return to Wittgenstein later.

Embodiment and Theory of Mind

Some contemporary AI systems, such as AI-driven robots operating in a physical environment, have remarkably complex behavioural dispositions. They can even learn new behaviours. Nevertheless, these robots and other

AI systems are still merely complex stimulus-response machines, and there is little reason to say that they can think in the literal sense of the word. Something is missing.

Based on the discussion so far, we propose that there are at least three criteria for an entity to appear to be intentional and not merely programmed. First, its behaviour needs to give an impression of goal-directedness. Second, the entity's behaviour must be 'driven from the inside' and not just reactive to external inputs. (Recall Lovelace's Objection.) The third criterion we have yet to discuss explicitly. It is that the entity must appear to be following norms. We will return to the last one in the last section. In the next section, however, we will discuss the first two in the context of robotics. Before that, we must take a short detour.

It is noteworthy to remember that ontology of thinking and attribution of thinking are different things – and we are interested in the latter. To correctly attribute thinking to an entity, it must behave in a manner that appears intentional, not just unpredictable. However, appearing to behave intentionally is not a property that necessarily requires a *specific type* of cognitive system that underlies the agent's actions. Instead, it is based on how it acts within its environment. Indeed, this is why the attempt to identify thinking with computational operations is problematic – even though this is precisely what the proponents of the standard *representational theory of mind* are trying to do. (See Kokkonen 2021, Ch 5.) Thinking presupposes *some* underlying processing but not of any specific kind. Instead, the entity to which thinking is attributed might be required to have a body.

Why should a machine require a body in order to think? Most views on thinking machines in AI and philosophy are, as we call them, *intellectualist*. They identify thinking as a cognitive process. 'Could an AI system think?' is interpreted as 'Could a computer simulate or replace human cognitive processes?' However, this simulation or replacement does not require replicating the *instantiation* of human cognitive processes but their cognitive functions. The focus has been on representation, computation and things of their kin. The goals of AI have been intellectualist: to create or simulate disembodied processes that can solve tasks. This aligns well with the representationalist tradition in the philosophy of mind. Most discussions on the philosophy of AI have been conducted within this framework, and representationalism continues to be the mainstream view in cognitive science and the philosophy of mind. At the same time, it is in stark contrast with both Wittgenstein's and Turing's views, despite Turing's enormous influence on these fields. According to Wittgenstein, the attribution of thinking is linked to other attributions connected with the entity's relation to external things (perceiving, acting, wishing and so on). Turing, in turn, emphasizes the interaction where other thinking beings perceive the entity as thinking. Neither is interested in the underlying processes, although Turing is *also* interested in technology that could enable machines to pass his test. Still, these things are conceptually distinct.

The leading alternative view in philosophy on attributing mental states is closely linked to agency. Among the supporters of this view are Wittgenstein and his followers, most notably Anscombe and von Wright, as well as other philosophers like Davidson and Dennett. Later, this approach specialized in philosophical action theory, while representationalism and computationalism dominated the philosophy of mind. This alternative approach is called *interpretationism*.[3]

According to the interpretationist framework, mental states are the states of individual agents. Interpretationists often think that belief is a dispositional property that has to do with the relation between the agent and the world, not a representation. An agent may need some cognitive representations to relate to the world so that it appears to have beliefs and act intentionally. However, this is separate from what it means to possess a belief.

Generally, when people attribute folk psychological states to an entity, the entity in question is assumed to have some capacities and causal processing. However, folk psychology does not directly address those internal processes. It could even be argued that this explanatory framework does not include causal relations, although it does presuppose them (cf. O'Brien 2019). Instead of causal relations, folk psychology is tied to our social practices involving normativity and goal attributions. These, in turn, allow for the possibility of being wrong, which is crucial in Wittgenstein's conception of thinking. We will explore Wittgenstein's view later.

Representationalism and interpretationism may be considered rival views on the nature of mentality. Alternatively, they can be seen as different frameworks theorizing about different concepts. For example, the concept of 'thinking' can refer either to cognitive processing or to individual folk psychological states. Likewise, 'belief' in folk psychology might not be synonymous with 'mental representation' in cognitive science. Consequently, 'thinking' and 'representational computation' may not mean the same thing. Taking them as identical constitutes a philosophical stance, a kind of identity theory.[4] We

---

3 Often, only those who think that attributions of mental states are interpretations, which do not refer to causal entities or processes, are called interpretationists. However, this would mean that Davidsonians and most contemporary action theorists are not interpretationists. Such a solution would be problematic since they also use the same folk psychological interpretative framework to individuate mental states.

4 See Kokkonen 2021, Chapter 5 for a more detailed discussion.

suggest that Wittgenstein and Turing recognize the difference between the two: Wittgenstein considers internal states irrelevant to whether a person thinks, and Turing separates the attribution of thinking from its instantiation. At the same time, they acknowledge that both interpretation and underlying cognitive architecture are necessary for thinking. However, for them, the criteria for what counts as thinking come from the interpretation framework.[5]

These are highly complex and controversial issues. However, we hope that the general level of the discussion makes the point acceptable to most readers.[6] The crucial issue is that thinking is connected to an agent's goals and behavioural outcomes. Moreover, agency is usually attributed to embodied beings, partly due to their relations with their environment. Suppose some being interacts with its environment in ways that seem goal-directed or, in other words, intentional. Moreover, its behaviour does not appear to consist of pre-programmed reactions. Instead, it seems to originate within the being's 'internal' aims. It is fair to say that we would likely attribute thinking to such beings. Now, compare such a being to a language model that produces text on the screen as a response to what someone has typed for it to react. Mere text on a disembodied screen is less likely to appear like a thinking being.

Some attributions of mental states require the presence of a body. Much of folk psychology only makes sense when attributed to beings interacting with their environment and other thinking beings. The most basic mental attributions involve understanding the agent in their immediate surroundings. We attribute propositional attitudes based on how they are situated in their environment and what they do in it. One example is attributing beliefs to individuals based on what they see. Another example is attributing a goal or a desire so that behaviour can be seen as intentional. However, for this, more is required than merely having a body. The machine cannot just react to its environment with triggered behavioural patterns. It should act as if the environment is 'meaningful' to it: Environmental features should constitute informational and motivational action potentials like our beliefs about our surroundings. In addition, action should have some origin in the machine and not only in the triggering environmental factors. This leads us to enactivism.

---

5 One perspective on thinking is to focus on the intentionality of thinking: thinking has an object (see Crane 2013). A successful philosophical theory of mind has to account for this. There have been attempts to reduce intentionality to representations (e.g. Shea 2018). The interpretationist framework approaches the intentionality of mentality from the intentionality of action (i.e. action is understood in terms of intentional states), which is how thinking is connected to its objects. Intentionality of thinking is central but a further complication we will avoid for the time being.
6 For a more detailed discussion and defence of the conceptual distinction between the agency and the computational level in the philosophy of mind, see Kokkonen 2021, Chapter 5.

Enactivist Thinking Machines

Enactivist robotics is a paradigm in AI research that is more appropriately a part of robotics than a field of AI. Enactivism is an alternative to representationalism in cognitive science and the philosophy of mind (see Varela et al. 1991; Noë 2004; Stewart et al. 2010; Hutto and Myin 2012; Gallagher 2017). It is a framework for understanding the nature of bio-cognitive systems that guide human and animal behaviour. According to enactivism, cognition arises through an organism's interaction with its environment. Humans and animals perceive their environment as affordances or action possibilities. These affordances are created by the interaction between the organism's active outward directedness and the environment's features: The organism's intentions and capabilities guide its attention and determine which environmental aspects are meaningful to it. The organism's perception, in turn, initiates processes that guide its behaviour. This contrasts with representationalism's passive view of observation, where perception primarily gathers information from the environment and constructs a motivationally neutral model of it. In enactivism, action and perception are closely linked in a continuous loop. What we *do* partly determines what we *perceive*. Compared to representationalism, this turns the starting point around. Perception is exploration of the environment connected to sensorimotor regularities and action potentials.

Enactivist ideas have been applied in robotics as design guidelines (see Sandini et al. 2007; Froese and Ziemke 2009; Rohde 2010; Egbert and Barandiaran 2022; Lassiter 2022). However, it is crucial to note that in this context, enactivism serves merely as a design framework and not as an explanatory one as in cognitive science. If enactivism proves to be the correct theory of cognition, thinking machines will probably have to be built according to its principles. Nevertheless, even if enactivism fails as an explanatory framework, it could still serve as a valuable model for robotic design. This is because robotics aims to build more functional robots and study how to create robots with situated embodied cognition. Such robots would not be mechanical machines guided by a separate AI system, a digital ghost in the machine. Instead, their bodies and sensors would be integral components of their cognitive architecture.

What advantages does enactivist design have concerning thinking? Enactivist robots do not merely react to triggers. Instead, they have dispositions to initiate action based on their environmental affordances. In addition, there is a constant feedback loop between their perceptions and actions. These together create an impression of intentionality. It is easier to perceive an embodied machine as an intentional actor because its behaviour is relational to its physical surroundings. We will likely attribute propositional attitudes to an agent if its behaviour is consistent and this consistency is not coincidental or arbitrary but, instead, ensured by its underlying causal system. However, singular episodes of behaviour that appear intentional are insufficient for a machine to be considered an intentional being. The appearance of intentionality must be robust, consistent and continuous for the impression of agency to emerge. Enactivist design might enable this.

Enactivist robotics strives to construct a machine that interacts with its environment purposefully and 'autonomously' (in the engineering sense of the word, i.e. without external control). This is achieved when the robot's

(1) perception is an active search instead of passive receiving;
(2) it is integrated with whatever the robot is doing; and
(3) perception generates behaviour through a reciprocal loop between the affordances and internal motivational states.

This continuous dynamic interaction with the environment does not only make actions seem intentional but also as having originated from within. We are inclined to say that an agent changes and reorganizes its beliefs and goals through a thought process when it modifies its internal states in response to (1) environmental changes and (2) successes and failures in achieving its goals.[7]

At the moment, there are no thinking machines, nor are we even close to constructing one. A credible thinking machine would require other capacities than the mere appearance of an intentional actor. For example, it would likely need genuine social abilities, which involve humans interacting with it as if it were a social being, and the robot would have to respond in human-like ways. This might require the robot to have a theory of mind rather than just being interpretable with one (see Scassellati 2002; Devin and Alami 2016; Chen et al. 2021). Furthermore, for various reasons that we will not delve into here, it may be necessary to learn how to create robotic animals before pursuing the development of machines with a theory of mind (but see Kokkonen 2021). Nevertheless, compared to representationalism, the enactivist approach offers a more promising path towards creating a machine to which the concept of thinking could be applied. Given the absence of actual robots that can do the things we speculate they could do in the future, whether we would

---

7 In this paradigm, learning is also connected to enactivity. New behavioural dispositions and skills are acquired through interaction histories that sometimes involve social interaction, as with iCub (see Sandini et al. 2007). This toddler-like robot currently comes closest to Turing's concept of a robot child.

include them in the category of thinking beings remains an open question. In the spirit of Turing, one could say it is conceivable to attribute thinking to such machines unless, of course, they still lack something crucial. As we have mentioned, there may be a third condition, normativity. Since normativity is prominent in Wittgenstein's thought, we will now return to his ideas.

Wittgenstein on the Normativity of Thinking

Wittgenstein has been interpreted as arguing that the concepts of thinking and machine are logically incompatible, so a thinking 'machine' would no longer be a machine (e.g. Glock 1996, 159). An alternative interpretation, however, is that we do not or could not have machines to which we could comfortably extend the concept. His remark that Turing's machines are not machines seems to suggest the former. Still, given Wittgenstein's remarks on attributing thinking to, for instance, a pot that talks and acts like a person, we suggest it would fit his philosophy better to allow for thinking machines under specific criteria.[8] Furthermore, we suggest that Turing's arguments, amended by enactive robotics, satisfy these criteria. This might not satisfy many later Wittgensteinian philosophers, but it seems compatible with what Wittgenstein wrote.

Perhaps embodiment and enactivism could address some of Wittgenstein's worries about applying the concept of thinking to computers and other digital or mechanical beings. After all, a computer with a mechanical body that learns through interacting with its surroundings is not just a machine or program operating with symbols like a bot on Twitter. Indeed, such a being might not be a mere machine or a computer anymore. A better term could be 'a robot' or maybe even 'an android'.

There is some disagreement on whether, according to Wittgenstein, a machine could think. Diane Proudfoot appears to believe that Wittgenstein might be just fine with thinking machines, whereas, for example, Peter Hacker and Hans-Johann Glock believe that if something behaves like a human being, then Wittgenstein would not say that it is a machine anymore (Hacker 2019, 110; Glock 1996, 159). So, perhaps in Wittgensteinian parlance, androids could be thinking beings, but they would not count as machines.

Going into this debate in depth is out of the reach of this chapter. However, Hacker's and Glock's positions could be defended with quotes like the two from the *Blue Book* in Section 2. The first one took 'the impossibility of machine thinking' as a 'logical' impossibility, and the second stated that it

---

8 See Proudfoot and Copeland (1994, 506fn6) for more on this.

'seems somehow nonsensical' to say that 'a machine thinks (perceives, wishes)'. Proudfoot has also stated that *if* the word 'machine' refers to an automaton, it cannot think, but in other situations, such as in the context of AI, it might be all right.[9] So, there is disagreement on the correct reading of Wittgenstein here.

In the *Philosophical Investigations*, Wittgenstein writes:

> Suppose I say of a friend: 'He isn't an automaton'. – What information is conveyed by this, and to whom would it be information? To a human being who meets him in ordinary circumstances? What information could it give him? (At the very most, that this man always behaves like a human being, and not occasionally like a machine). (Wittgenstein 2009: PI, iv §20)
>
> *(Wittgenstein 2009: PI, iv §20)*

This quote indicates that Wittgenstein might be willing to confine the concept of a machine only to causal entities that behave like automata, but this is unclear. However, the philosophically most crucial thing is not to figure out what Wittgenstein thought about the issue. It is, of course, an interesting question from an exegetical point of view. So, if one's primary interest is the history of philosophy, then what Wittgenstein thought is the important thing. If one's interests lie instead in AI or the *philosophy* of AI, then Wittgenstein's ideas can be helpful, but they probably will not determine the outcome of one's research.

Wittgenstein still poses a significant and demanding challenge to strong human-like AI. That challenge is *normativity*. Normativity is not an insurmountable obstacle to creating strong AI, but current AI research has yet to achieve it. What, then, is meant by normativity, and how does it challenge strong AI? All goal-oriented action is normative – including calculating, logical reasoning and virtually all language usage since, for Wittgenstein, language is primarily rule-following. These practices involve correctness, that is, 'getting it right' (Kripke 1982, 25–26n19, 37). We can use deontic terminology – like *ought*, *should* and so on – to describe the relationship between an action and its intended target. In addition, it is possible to talk about *failures* or *errors*.

Normativity is built upon *internal* relations. Glock has characterized internal relations as

---

9 Proudfoot: 'Wittgenstein and Turing on AI: Myth Versus Reality' at *Wittgenstein and AI* (WAI22) conference 30 July 2022.

relations which could not fail to obtain, since they are given with or (partly) constitutive of the terms […] such as white's being lighter than black. Equally, an internal property is a property which a thing could not fail to possess, because it is essential to its being the thing it is[.]

(Glock 1996, 189)

There is an internal – grammatical, constitutive and necessary – relation between a goal and its fulfilment (Glock 1996, 189–90; Kripke 1982, 25n19–26n19). So, if one's goal is to do something, for example, leave enough time for questions after a presentation, only obtaining that goal and nothing else will fulfil it. If the presenter goes over time and the chairperson gives more time for questions, that might be great from the presenter's point of view, but they have still failed to do what they tried to accomplish.

In Wittgenstein's thought, internal relations are contrasted with *external* relations, which are non-essential and contingent (Glock 1996, 189). For instance, empirically known relations are external (id., 190). The distinction between internal and external relations can be illustrated via Wittgenstein's critique of Bertrand Russell's behaviouristic analysis of certain mental concepts. Russell offers a dispositional theory of concepts like desire in *The Analysis of the Mind*. According to his account, the object of desire is, roughly speaking, the thing whose obtainment will cause the desire to cease (Russell 1921, 58–76; Kripke 1982, 25n19).

Wittgenstein mocked the view in the *Philosophical Remarks* as follows: 'If I wanted to eat an apple, and someone punched me in the stomach, taking away my appetite, then it was this punch that I originally wanted' (Wittgenstein 1998: PR, 64). Just like with Russell's dispositional theory, all causal relations are external. They are known empirically, and therefore, they are in a certain sense contingent – as Hume already taught us. It is always, in principle, possible that future investigations would show that something that we believed to be a cause of another thing was not, in fact, the actual cause. However, for instance, language and mathematics do not work that way. Pure mathematics is not an empirical science. Empirical experiments will not prove someone has miscalculated, though empirical observations might give us a reason not to apply some mathematical system. In other words, empirical observations may show that some theories of applied mathematics are suitable or unsuitable for a particular goal, but they do not show the calculations themselves to be mistaken.

Wittgenstein's view that mathematics is normative and not based on causal connections is explicitly stated, for instance, in the *Remarks on the Foundations of Mathematics* (RFM):

> [I]f calculation reveals a causal connection to you, then you are not calculating.
>
> Our children are not only given practice in calculation but are also trained to adopt a particular attitude towards a mistake in calculating, towards a departure from the norm.
>
> What I am saying comes to this that mathematics is normative.
>
> *(Wittgenstein 1978: RFM, V §424 f)*

Among the main challenges for creating thinking machines is that they should exhibit normative behaviour – for instance, rule-following – and not merely causally react to various inputs. Thinking machines need to be able to behave so that they will not look like mere causal automata, that whatever they are doing is because they are programmed to do that.

One, but not the only, vital way that thinking and goal-oriented action manifest is in how human beings react when encountering failures. When someone miscalculates, their behaviour can be explained, in a natural way, by appealing to thoughts and intentions. However, if a calculator or computer malfunctions and gives the wrong result because of that, it behaves very differently. For instance, a calculator or computer does not offer reasons for its actions or otherwise react to its environment. Its outputs seem to be simply a part of a mindless causal chain. A calculator does not fail to follow a mathematical rule. It simply performs a causal process that is not useful for getting the correct answer, in contrast to a causal process that is useful for this goal. If we can bridge this gap, at least in part, then the attribution of thinking to machines would likely seem much more natural to us than it feels now. Furthermore, this often involves an ability to give justifications and other practices.

Can a machine make mistakes? A robot that causally reacts to external triggers – whether pre-programmed or acquired through machine learning algorithms – cannot. However, enactivist robots may have action goals that influence their perception of their environment, and their behaviour can be flexible. Robots of this kind might try to achieve a goal with one approach and switch to another if their initial attempt fails. In other words, an enactivist robot might learn that some approach to achieving a goal is wrong. Still, something may be missing. Such behaviour only encompasses instrumental normativity, which focuses on discovering solutions to reach goals. Mistakes may require a more robust notion of proceeding correctly, such as rule-following.

Related problems have arisen in social robotics, which aims to develop robots that can interact with humans, and in philosophy of social robotics accompanying it (see Breazeal 2002; Seibt et al. 2014; Hakli et al. 2022). Thus far, the achievements in this subfield of robotics have been modest.

However, if robots can be designed to be sensitive to social norms and adjust their behavioural dispositions through learning, combining this sensitivity to norms with enactive action architecture could establish a foundation for a more robust form of normativity. Whether this is possible is an empirical question that depends on the developments in future technology. In any case, no philosophical reason excludes, in principle, the possibility of thinking machines or robots. However, the philosophical issues we have discussed shed light on what capacities a machine must possess to be considered a thinking being. This includes fulfilling the demanding criterion of normativity. If it proves successful, the enactivist paradigm to design cognitive architecture for robots could account for other capacities. Normativity remains a further issue.

Conclusions

Wittgenstein and Turing agree on what grounds thinking is attributed but disagree on whether machines could think. In this chapter, we have discussed their views and connected them to contemporary issues in robotics. We think Wittgenstein's and Turing's view on how thinking is attributed is correct. Therefore, the possibility of thinking machines and their capacities should be evaluated from this perspective. Consequently, the reasons behind their disagreement therefore delve into the heart of contemporary discussions on cognitive science, philosophy of mind, philosophy of AI and even the development of AI.

Conversely, developments in robotics might make thinking machines acceptable from Wittgenstein's point of view, even though his criteria for thinking are stricter than Turing's. The gap between the two may be narrower than it appears. It is an intriguing question whether their disagreement could be resolved to their mutual satisfaction. However, our main interest lies in what we can learn from them. We occupy a position between the two: Turing is too optimistic about what can be considered a thinking machine. Wittgenstein, in turn, has valid objections. Nevertheless, enactivist robots could have capacities that enable us to consider them as thinking machines.

The distinction between mental state attributions to an agent and analysing their cognitive capacities is crucial. Although interpretationist theories and cognitivist theories of mentality are presented as rival alternatives, we think they focus on different objects. Following Wittgenstein and Turing, we think that thinking is an attribution of the first kind, and the conditions for something being thinking are criteria for what an underlying architecture has to be able to achieve. Our suggestion is that enactivist views about that architecture are a good starting point at minimum for a machine that satisfies these conditions. We have not discussed enactivist theory as such from a Wittgensteinian point of view, since the point is not the relationship between these theories, or even whether enactivism is a correct theory of the underlying processes of human thinking; the point is that enactivist ideas in designing a robot seem to be producing the right kind of capacities.

However, enactivism alone is probably insufficient. Wittgenstein's additional criterion, normativity or the possibility of making mistakes instead of merely malfunctioning, sets a higher standard for thinking. Enactivist robotics may succeed in creating machines that appear to act intentionally, but more is needed for normativity. Nevertheless, it serves as a crucial initial step. Currently, social robotics aims to integrate robots into different human social contexts. Whether this pathway leads to the development of more comprehensive capabilities that, according to the criteria we have discussed here, culminate in thinking machines remains to be seen. To some extent, this is an empirical question that cannot be resolved solely through conceptual analysis.

References

Block, Ned. 1981. 'Psychologism and Behaviorism'. *Philosophical Review* 90, no. 1: 5–43.
Breazeal, Cynthia L. 2002. *Designing Sociable Robots*. Cambridge, MA: MIT Press.
Chen, Boyuan, Carl Vondrick, and Hod Lipson. 2021. 'Visual Behavior Modelling for Robotic Theory of Mind'. *Scientific Reports* 11. https://doi.org/10.1038/s41598-020-77918-x.
Crane, Tim. 2013. *Objects of Thought*. Oxford: Oxford University Press.
Devin, Sandra and Rachid Alami. 2016. 'An Implemented Theory of Mind to Improve Human-Robot Shared Plans Execution'. In *HRI '16: The Eleventh ACM/IEEE International Conference on Human Robot Interaction*, 319–326. IEEE Press.
Egbert, Matthew D. and Xabier E. Barandiaran. 2022. 'Using Enactive Robotics to Think Outside of the Problem-solving Box: How Sensorimotor Contingencies Constrain the Forms of Emergent Autonomous Habits'. *Frontiers in Neurorobotics* 16. https://doi.org/10.3389/fnbot.2022.847054
Floyd, Juliet. 2019a. 'Wittgenstein and Turing'. In *Philosophy of Logic and Mathematics: Proceedings of the 41st International Ludwig Wittgenstein Symposium*, edited by Gabriele M. Mras, Paul Weingartner, and Bernhard Ritter, 263–296. De Gruyter.
Floyd, Juliet. 2019b. 'Wittgenstein's Diagonal Argument: A Variation on Cantor and Turing'. *Disputatio* 8, no. 9: 593–644.
Froese, Tom and Tom Ziemke. 2009. 'Enactive Artificial Intelligence: Investigating the Systemic Organization of Life and Mind'. *Artificial Intelligence* 173: 466–500.
Gallagher, Shaun. 2017. *Enactivist Interventions: Rethinking the Mind*. Oxford: Oxford University Press.
Glock, Hans-Johann. 1996. *A Wittgenstein Dictionary*. Cambridge, MA: Wiley-Blackwell.

Hacker, P. M. S. 2019. *Wittgenstein: Meaning and Mind. Volume 3 of an Analytical Commentary on the Philosophical Investigations. Part I: Essays* (2nd revised edn). Cambridge, MA: Wiley-Blackwell.

Hakli, Raul, Pekka Mäkelä, and Johanna Seibt, eds. 2022. *Social Robots in Social Institutions*. Amsterdam: IOS Press.

Hodges, Andrew. 2014. *Alan Turing: The Enigma* (revised edn). London: Vintage.

Hutto, Daniel D. and Erik Myin. 2012. *Radicalizing Enactivism: Basic Minds without Content*. Cambridge, MA: MIT Press.

Kokkonen, Tomi. 2021. *Evolving in Groups: Individualism and Holism in Evolutionary Explanations of Human Social Behaviour. Philosophical Studies from the University of Helsinki* 51. Academic dissertation. Helsinki: University of Helsinki. http://urn.fi/URN:ISBN :978-951-51-7461-1

Kripke, Saul. 1982. *Wittgenstein on Rules and Private Language*. 1995. Cambridge, MA: Harvard University Press.

Lassiter, Charles. 2022. 'Could a Robot Flirt? 4E Cognition, Reactive Attitudes, and Robot Autonomy'. *AI & Society* 37: 675–686.

Lovelace, Ada. 1843. 'Notes in "Sketch of The Analytical Engine Invented by Charles Babbage" by Luigi Menabrea'. In *Scientific Memoirs*, vol. 3, edited by Richard Taylor, 666–731. London: Richard and John E. Taylor.

Moor, James H. 1976. 'An Analysis of the Turing Test'. *Philosophical Studies* 30, no. 4: 249–257.

Moor, James H. 2001. 'The Status and Future of the Turing Test'. *Minds and Machines* 11: 77–93.

Neumaier, Otto. 1987. 'A Wittgensteinian View of Artificial Intelligence'. In *Artificial Intelligence: The Case Against*, edited by Rainer P. Born, 132–174. London: St Martin's Press.

Noë, Alva. 2004. *Action in Perception*. Cambridge, MA: MIT Press.

O'Brien, Lilian. 2019. 'Action Explanation and its Presuppositions'. *Canadian Journal of Philosophy* 49: 123–146.

Proudfoot, Diane. 2011. 'Anthropomorphism and AI: Turing's Much Misunderstood Imitation Game'. *Artificial Intelligence* 175, nos. 5–6: 950–957.

Proudfoot, Diane. 2013. 'Rethinking Turing's Test'. *Journal of Philosophy* 110, no. 7: 391–411.

Proudfoot, Diane. 2020. 'Rethinking Turing's Test and the Philosophical Implications'. *Minds and Machines* 30: 487–512. http://dx.doi.org/10.1007/s11023-020-09534-7

Proudfoot, Diane and Jack Copeland. 1994. 'Turing, Wittgenstein and the Science of the Mind'. *Australasian Journal of Philosophy* 72, no. 4: 497–519.

Rohde, Marieke. 2010. *Enaction, Embodiment, Evolutionary Robotics: Simulation Models for a Post-Cognitivist Science of Mind*. Amsterdam: Atlantis Press.

Russell, Bertrand. 1921. *The Analysis of the Mind*. London: George Allen & Unwin LTD.

Sandini, Giulio, Giorgio Metta, and David Vernon. 2007. 'The *iCub* Cognitive Humanoid Robot: An Open-system Research Platform for Enactive Cognition'. In *50 Years of Artificial Intelligence: Essays Dedicated to the 50th Anniversary of Artificial Intelligence*, edited by Max Lungarella, Fumiya Iida, Josh Bongard, and Rolf Pfeifer. Berlin: Springer-Verlag, 358–369.

Scassellati, Brian. 2002. 'Theory of Mind for a Humanoid Robot'. *Autonomous Robots* 12: 13–24.

Seibt, Johanna, Raul Hakli, and Marco Nørskov, eds. 2014. *Sociable Robots and the Future of Social Relations*. Amsterdam: IOS Press.

Seidel, Asher. 1991. 'Plato, Wittgenstein and Artificial Intelligence'. *Metaphilosophy* 22, no. 4: 292–306.

Shanker, Stuart. 1998. *Wittgenstein's Remarks on the Foundations of AI*. Abingdon: Routledge.

Shea, Nicholas. 2018. *Representation in Cognitive Science*. Oxford: Oxford University Press.

Stewart, John R., Olivier Gapenne, and Ezequiel A. Di Paolo, eds. 2010. *Enaction: Toward a New Paradigm for Cognitive Science*. Cambridge: MIT Press.

Todes, Daniel P. 2014. *Ivan Pavlov: A Russian Life in Science*. Oxford: Oxford University Press.

Turing, Alan M. 1948. 'Intelligent Machinery'. Reproduced in Copeland, ed. 2004, 410–32. Page references are to Copeland, ed. 2004.

Turing, Alan M. 1950. 'Computing Machinery and Intelligence'. *Mind* 59: 433–460.

———Turing, Alan M. 1951. 'Can Digital Computers Think?' *Radio Broadcast on BBC Radio*, 15 May 1951. Reproduced in Copeland, ed. 2004, 482–486.

Turing, Alan M., Richard Braithwaite, Geoffrey Jefferson, and Max H. Newman. 1952. 'Can Automatic Calculating Machines be Said to Think?' Reproduced in Copeland, ed. 2004, 494–506.

Varela, Francisco J., Evan Thompson, and Eleanor Rosch. 1991. *The Embodied Mind: Cognitive Science and Human Experience*. Cambridge, MA: MIT Press.

Wittgenstein, Ludwig. 1953. *Philosophical Investigations*, translated by G.E.M. Anscombe, P. M. S. Hacker, and Joachim Schulte, 2009. Oxford: Basil Blackwell. [PI]

Wittgenstein, Ludwig. 1958. *The Blue and Brown Books*. Oxford: Blackwell. [BB]

Wittgenstein, Ludwig. 1967. *Remarks on the Foundations of Mathematics*. Edited by Georg Henrik von Wright, Rush Rhees, and G. E. M. Anscombe, translated by G. E. M. Anscombe. 1978. Oxford: Blackwell. [RFM]

Wittgenstein, Ludwig. 1969. *Philosophical Grammar*, edited by Rush Rhees. Oxford: Blackwell. [PG]

Wittgenstein, Ludwig. 1975. *Philosophical Remarks*, translated by Raymond Hargreaves and Roger White, 1998. Oxford: Basil Blackwell. [PR]

Wittgenstein, Ludwig. 1976. *Wittgenstein's Lectures on the Foundations of Mathematics, Cambridge 1939*, edited by Cora Diamond. Hassocks, Sussex: Harvester Press. [LFM]

Wittgenstein, Ludwig. 1980. *Remarks on the Philosophy of Psychology*, Vol. I, edited by G. E. M. Anscombe and Georg Henrik von Wright, translated by G. E. M. Anscombe. Oxford: Blackwell. [RPP I]

Chapter 3

WITTGENSTEIN, PSYCHOLOGICAL LANGUAGE AND AI

Arturo Vázquez Hernández

Can Machines Think?

The philosophy of AI encompasses epistemological, psychological, ontological, technical and ethical issues. Even though these matters have different natures and theoretical implications, they are closely related to the fundamental problem in the philosophy of AI – whether machines can think.

The question 'Can machines think?' has received two plausible answers captured in a now-standard distinction in the field, namely, the weak and strong conceptions of AI. In this chapter, the former represents the view of AI as a valuable tool that simulates but does not display mentality (see Searle 1980, 417). Strong AI represents the conception of AI as being itself a mind rather than merely a set of simulating devices. In strong AI, as the programs are themselves minds and display cognitive states, their workings directly explain the functioning of the human mind (see Searle 1980, 417). In this regard, both conceptions of AI relate to different uses of psychological language. In weak AI, psychological language is applied to machines not literally but figuratively – it is *as if* machines learn, think or perceive, but they really don't. In contrast, the strong view of AI is related to literal or 'primary' uses of psychological language – machines do (or in principle could) think, learn and perceive in the way humans do.[1] Most of the answers to the question

---

1 It might be argued that Searle's weak–strong AI is not a clear-cut distinction, and thus, phrasing the problem in these terms might not be entirely unproblematic. First, some authors do not express their views assuming this dichotomy (e.g. Wittgenstein 2009a: PI § 359–60; Emiliani 1990 and Harre 1988). Moreover, some authors have challenged Searle's views on the mind, views which might feed into the distinction itself. However, it is helpful to take the weak–strong AI distinction as I phrased it because the authors engaging in these debates typically express themselves in the terms Searle's distinction describes. Namely, they tend to understand the status

'Can machines think?' lie either on one or the other side of the dichotomy and are based on different theories with specific ontological commitments, for instance, dualism, functionalism, biological naturalism, identity theory and the computational theory of the mind. Consider the following quote.

> To the extent that rational thought corresponds to the rules of logic, a machine can be built that carries out rational thought. [...] computation has finally demystified mentalistic terms. Beliefs are inscriptions in memory, desires are goal inscriptions, thinking is computation, perceptions are inscriptions triggered by sensors.
>
> *(Pinker 1997, 68, 78)*

According to this perspective, machines can display actual mental powers given that the nature of mentality can be instantiated in artificial devices. Strong AI might emerge from different philosophical sources. For example, the view that mental states and processes are in essence computational, and thus do not depend on the structure and the physical constitution of the human brain, but on the implementation of an abstract computational description (see Peacocke 1995), or that mentality has its basis in the constitution of the human brain, which in turn is a computational system (see Churchland 1986).

On the other hand, authors endorsing weak AI counter the views above with different arguments. For example, according to the view that mentality emerges from the biological structure and causal properties of the human brain, and not only of its formal features, Searle concludes that human cognition and understanding are different from symbol manipulation and computation (1980, 421–2). Since our mental life cannot be understood merely in terms of computation, generating mentality artificially would require reproducing a nervous system like ours. Therefore, computing machines only 'appear' to have intentionality, but they really don't (Searle 1980, 422).

---

of AI either in terms of minds or simulating tools, views that relate to literal and figurative uses of psychological language, respectively. For the purposes of the chapter, therefore, a fruitful theoretical lens to address the problem of 'thinking' machines is understanding (i) strong or literal uses of psychological concepts as those that fully describe human behaviour and action in ordinary circumstances, and (ii) weak uses of psychological language as non-literal, such as 'It is *as if* machines can think, learn, or understand, but they are really doing something else'. Alternative conceptions of weak and strong AI, and literal and figurative uses of psychological language will not be considered.

Wittgenstein and Artificial Intelligence

In the following, we argue that some uses of psychological language in the scientific discipline of AI cannot be reduced to either literal or figurative ascriptions of psychological predicates to machines, and should be understood in terms of, or as sharing features with what Wittgenstein calls the 'secondary' sense, meaning or use of concepts. In other words, some uses of psychological language in the science of AI are located in the logical space between literal and figurative uses of concepts. To expand on this argument, let us first explore the nature of the problem of 'thinking' machines, and then show how Wittgenstein scholarship has addressed these issues.

Empirical and conceptual problems

A proposition's verification method, if there is any, shows the grammatical status of such a proposition (Wittgenstein 2009a: PI § 353). In other words, different types of what we call 'verification' connect to the propositions of different linguistic practices, which in turn show what kinds of propositions we are dealing with, for example, empirical, mathematical or philosophico-metaphysical (in a Wittgensteinian sense). To exemplify this point, let us consider the verification methods corresponding to the propositions 'They feel a strong pain in their knee' and '43 is a prime number'. On the one hand, the criteria for saying that someone is experiencing intense bodily pain come, for example, from observation of the person's contextualized behaviour and verbal expressions, such as the reactions and gestures in relation to the painful spot, like groaning and rubbing the knee. On the other hand, and insofar as numbers cannot be said to be literally perceived by the senses, verifying whether 43 is prime does not involve observing the written symbol or numeral. Rather, verifying whether such a number is prime involves mathematical proof, in this case, showing that 43 is larger than 1 and is not the product of two smaller natural numbers. As Wittgenstein argues, mathematical proofs involve 'surveyability' and provide certainty, thus cancelling out the contingent fluctuation of the result in different empirical conditions (1983: RFM III § 42–3).

Now take the expressions 'My dog can howl on command' and 'Machines can think'. Similarly, these propositions do not relate to the same verification methods. Typically, the criteria for verifying the former involve commanding the dog to howl and observing its reactions to the instruction. If the dog does not understand the command, for example, if there is no reaction whatsoever that follows the instruction or the dog does something entirely different than howling, the proposition would be false. However, we could still train the dog to follow the relevant rule. Thus, the same proposition could be true at a different time. Therefore, 'My dog can howl on command' represents an empirical proposition because it provides information, thus increasing our knowledge about a certain matter, and one can think of it as being true or false without contradiction. Note that in this case, we clearly understand what it means to say that a dog can or cannot howl on command. Thus it is clear what piece of evidence would make the proposition true or false, namely, the dog performing or not performing such an action.

By contrast, mechanical computations are not ordinary criteria for ascribing thinking (or lack thereof) to machines. If there are no established criteria for the use of 'thinking' in this context, it is unclear what it means to say that machines can think, and thus, it is unclear what would contribute to verifying this expression. In other words, if we do not understand how a term functions in a given context, it is not clear what it might even mean to speak of evidence in this case. Insofar as the criteria for using the concept of thinking is missing in this situation, and such criteria have logical precedence in relation to the evidence that would verify this expression, this is not a matter open to observation or empirical investigation. Therefore, 'Machines can think' does not represent an empirical proposition because no empirical verification is possible (see Wittgenstein 1969: BB, 47).

Plausibly, Wittgenstein would have regarded 'Machines can think' as a philosophical or metaphysical proposition in the critical sense he elaborates throughout his later thought. We expand further on this notion in the final section. Suffice it to say for now that metaphysical propositions in a Wittgensteinian sense seem to convey substantial information about the nature of phenomena, just like empirical or scientific propositions (e.g. 'The space is curved' in general relativity). Unlike the latter, however, metaphysical propositions are not open to empirical investigation. Regardless of being stated in scientific terms, metaphysical propositions do not express knowledge of facts but display a strong conceptual dimension connected to the meaning or grammar of words (Wittgenstein 1969: BB, 35. See Wittgenstein 1980a: RPP I § 949). The differences between empirical, mathematical and metaphysical propositions are relevant to clarify the nature of the problem of 'thinking' machines. Let us now consider the questions to which the propositions above are related.

Wittgenstein remarks that 'for any question there is always a corresponding *method* of finding' – the question, we might say, '*denotes* a method of searching' (Wittgenstein 1980c: PR § 43). In relation to the verification methods above, the questions 'Can your dog howl on command?' and 'Can machines think?' obey a different logic. The former relates to how we would settle this question, namely, with empirical evidence, for example, observing the dog's behaviour after the command, and repeating the exercise several times to exclude coincidences and accidents. The question 'Can your dog howl on command?' expresses a lack of knowledge related to the epistemic notions of truth, doubt and justification. For example, it makes sense to say we know or don't know whether the dog can follow the instructions. Therefore, the answer to this question cannot be given outside of what experience provides in the relevant sense.

Regarding the second question, it is unclear how to verify whether a specific machine can or cannot think. The question 'Can machines think?' cannot be settled by appealing to empirical evidence because, as we argued, the usual criteria for applying the concept of thinking are absent. How we view the so-called evidence itself depends on how we understand the terms in question. Therefore, because the answer to 'Can machines think?' cannot be determined or verified by experience, this question does not represent a scientific or empirical problem, but rather a problem related to the grammar or use of concepts (Wittgenstein 2009a: PI § 359–60. See Wittgenstein 1969: BB, 47). In other words, this question does not represent a gap in our knowledge of computer science but expresses a conceptual problem, which in general Wittgenstein describes as a sort of perplexity, puzzlement or confusion related to the use or meaning of concepts (see e.g. Wittgenstein 2009a: PI § 132, 339).

One of the challenges is that the form of this fundamental question in the philosophy of AI invites us to provide a fixed answer to settle the matter as if it were a scientific problem, such as 'Can atoms be split?'. A common source of conceptual problems is taking 'the uniform appearance of words' or forms of our expressions as communicating something essential about the concept in question (Wittgenstein 2009a: PI § 11. See PI § 93). Wittgenstein points out:

> In the use of words, one might distinguish 'surface grammar' from 'depth grammar'. What immediately impresses itself upon us about the use of a word is the way it is used in the sentence structure, the part of its use – one might say – that can be taken in by the ear. – And now compare the depth grammar, say of the verb 'to mean', with what its surface grammar would lead us to presume.
> *(2009a: PI § 664)*

Following this distinction, on a certain philosophical conception, 'saying something' can be understood as merely uttering sounds with the mouth, while 'meaning something' as involving more than producing noises. Thus, we might tend to conclude that 'meaning something' must be a '*mental, spiritual* activity' (Wittgenstein 2009a: PI § 36). Analogously, the bipolar form of some philosophical questions, for example, 'Do we have free will?' or 'Does God exist?', makes us assume that the problem in turn contains only two possible answers, excluding a third possibility (see Wittgenstein 2009a: PI § 352). Accordingly, 'Can machines think?' conceals a dichotomous form or 'surface grammar' that inclines us to presuppose that the question involves a binary set of replies, the elements of which are mutually exclusive. Thus, the tendency is to presume that for this problem there is only one correct answer or true statement, either affirmative or negative, which will depend on a particular philosophical theory about the nature of the mind and computation. A given philosophical theory, then, seems to fix or determine an answer to the fundamental problem in the philosophy of AI. For example, the theory that human psychology can be reduced to the material and causal brain processes seems to logically contain the view that with the right technology and knowledge about the brain, it is in principle possible to reproduce mentality in artificial systems.

The way more mainstream philosophical approaches address the problem of 'thinking' machines, namely, assuming the question's dichotomous surface form and offering fixed answers from a particular philosophical theory, connects to the fact that such approaches do not distinguish between empirical and conceptual problems or maintain the view that these kinds of problems are somehow continuous (see Quine 1970). Thus, from these perspectives, it is not entirely clear what problems science can solve and what problems can be solved by philosophical analysis.

These approaches are problematic for at least three interconnected reasons. (i) It is not obvious that 'Can machines think?' and ordinary empirical and scientific questions belong to the same category. (ii) Treating this as an empirical problem is question-begging. If one decides that 'thinking' is for example 'computing', taking the machine's computing as evidence for thinking would entail assuming the conclusion. And the explanation of why computing is evidence for thinking would still need to be given. In other words, substituting the machine's computation for 'thinking' represents the introduction of newly stipulated criteria for using the concept of thinking, a move that needs to be justified. (iii) Based on the question's dichotomous form, these approaches provide fixed answers, assuming that reality must correspond to their philosophical viewpoints regardless of future experiences and scientific discoveries (Wittgenstein 2009a: PI § 92. See PI § 131). Therefore, because the question 'Can machines think?' is not obviously open to empirical investigation or related to the methods of verification for settling scientific questions, we at least need to pay careful attention to the conceptual aspect of this problem.

Wittgensteinian views on thinking machines

Wittgenstein scholars have addressed the problem of 'thinking' machines from different perspectives and offered significant contributions to its clarification.

Typically, these scholars draw from Wittgenstein's later insights into the philosophy of psychology, mathematics and logic. Wittgensteinian approaches to this problem involve different and complex interrelated arguments. For space reasons, let us only explore some of the crucial points in this received debate that relate to our main argument.

In contrast to more mainstream philosophical views, a Wittgensteinian approach has the advantage of understanding the question 'Can machines think?' not as an empirical but rather a conceptual problem. Thus, this approach is primarily concerned not with truth and falsehood but with the sense of this question. Moreover, Wittgenstein scholars have mainly criticized strong AI, the conception which relates to 'primary' or literal uses of psychological language (e.g. Harre 1988, 105; Emiliani 1990, 127; Neumaier 1986, 164; Hacker 2019, 106).

For instance, against the idea that minds and computer programs are in essence analogous, these authors have stressed the importance of the body's role in cognition and experience. According to these scholars, the body represents the element that logically connects our sensations with their outer expressions (Harre 1988, 107. See Hacker 2019, 109; Wittgenstein 2009a: PI § 244). In other words, the mind (understood not as a Cartesian substance but as a set of capacities) relates to the body not only empirically but logically (Wittgenstein 1992: LW II, 63). For example, to solve a mathematical problem, we might not need our left hand. Thus, in this case, the relation between mind and body is contingent. In the case of sensations, the pain and its expression are internally related. Insofar as the relationship between the computer's physical constitution and its program is empirical and contingent, speaking of essential features of mentality, such as sensation and its natural expression, in the context of machines does not make sense (see Emiliani 1990, 129; Hacker 2019, 108; Harre 1988, 107). Therefore, according to these authors, the difference between AI and human mentality is a matter of kind, not of degree.

Insofar as these authors do not challenge weak AI, they seem to agree that this conception is uncontroversial. Note that these authors do not explicitly claim such a thing. They might also object to using 'weak AI' in their discourse, given that for them, AI consists of nothing more than artificial devices, and so 'weak AI' might represent a redundant notion. However, the way they phrase their views suggests that they are dealing with figurative or metaphorical uses of psychological language. For example, Harre concludes, 'The AI *metaphors* then amount to the idea of carrying on intellectual activities by calculating, something wholly within the human world of thoughtful practice. The machines that can do these computations for us are *mere prosthetic devices*' (1988, 114. My emphasis. See Emiliani 1990, 127; Neumaier 1986,

164; Hacker 2019, 106). Let us consider two Wittgensteinian views, one more conventional than the other, that express these ideas.

By recognizing that we ascribe psychological predicates to machines, such as calculating, computing and thinking, Hacker wonders about the status of those ascriptions and asks whether the grammatical remark that psychological predicates only apply to humans and what behaves like humans is either wrong or 'has been overtaken by the march of science' (2019, 102). In this regard, Hacker analyses Wittgenstein's views on calculating:

> *There are no* causal connexions in a calculation, only the connexions of the pattern. And it makes no difference to this that we work over the proof in order to accept it. That we are therefore tempted to say that it arose as the result of a psychological experiment. For the psychical course of events is not psychologically investigated when we calculate.
>
> *(1983: RFM VII § 18)*

> 'We are calculating only when there is a *must* behind the result.' […] if calculation reveals a causal connexion to you, then you are not calculating.
>
> *(1983: RFM VII § 61)*

Hacker argues that there is a distinction between logico-normative and mechanico-causal connections. Following rules and calculating presuppose a normative, logical aspect that must be distinguished from the machine's causal functioning (Hacker 2019, 107). A machine operates algorithmically only if the functioning of its causal links 'ensures the generation of a regularity in accord with a chosen rule' (Hacker 2019, 106). In contrast, humans follow rules 'in the context of a complex practice involving actual and potential normative activities' (Hacker 2019, 106). In such practices, the mental represents a cluster of cognitive, affective, perceptive and sensation faculties and capacities 'that cannot be severed from' each other (Hacker 2019, 109).[2] Hacker thus concludes that psychological language cannot be applied

---

2 Hacker's underlying contrast is that of the machine with the living being, suggesting that psychological concepts have a role only in the latter case. Even though Hacker might grant the following, psychological concepts are distinguishable in an important sense. We do not experience sensations or emotions every time we understand, for example, verbal expressions. If the opposite were the case, understanding would still not be determined by sensations or emotions. In other words, we can logically separate skills and dispositions from emotions and sensations. Some animals, for example, manifest sensations and emotions but not certain complex dispositions, such as thinking conceptually or mathematically (calculating). As Wittgenstein says, 'The word "thinking" is used in a certain way very differently from, for example, "to be in pain", "to

literally to devices that do not manifest the complexity of features of human behaviour (2019, 110). In this respect, Hacker suggests that the grammatical remark that psychological predicates are ascribable to humans and to what behaves like humans cannot be revised by science, as it is not a matter open to empirical investigation.

In a less conventional interpretation of Wittgenstein, Neumaier (1986) studies the use of psychological language in AI from Wittgenstein's views on the constitutional uncertainty of the mental. Consider the following quotes.

> I can't give criteria which put the presence of the sensation beyond doubt; that is to say: there are no such criteria. – But what sort of fact is *that*? A *psychological* one, concerning sensations? One will want to say it resides in the nature of sensation, or of the expression of sensation.
>
> *(Wittgenstein 1980a: RPP I § 137)*

> 'But you can't recognize pain with *certainty* just from externals.' – The *only* way of recognizing it is by externals, and the uncertainty is constitutional. It is not a shortcoming. It resides in our concept that this uncertainty exists, in our instrument.
>
> *(Wittgenstein 1980b: RPP II § 657)*

Neumaier argues that, insofar as 'in psychology we have only some outward evidence for "inner" processes, and this evidence is always uncertain' (1986, 142), the constitutional uncertainty in our psychological language games is an essential feature of human mentality. In contrast, machines display only the 'outer', namely, 'they are transparent for us' since we fully know how they perform a certain function (Neumaier 1986, 164). Thus, our knowledge 'about the programs underlying the performance of specific tasks by a computer […] necessarily prevents AI from being successful' (Neumaier 1986, 153–4). In other words, our knowledge about machines does not display the foundational uncertainty of our psychological language games. From this paradoxical situation, Neumaier concludes that as long as machines are entirely transparent, the use of psychological language in AI is illegitimate and thus

---

be sad", etc.: we don't say "I think" as the expression of a mental state' (1980b: RPP II § 12. See the classification of psychological concepts in RPP II § 63, 148).

weak or metaphorical (1986, 151, 163, 165. See also footnote 3 and 39, pp. 167 and 170, respectively).[34]

Given their accounts of the logical and the epistemological, Hacker and Neumaier's views can be considered incompatible (see footnote 3). Despite the differences between approaches within this literature, Wittgensteinian philosophy provides powerful conceptual tools that help show the logical impossibility of ascribing psychological predicates to machines strongly or

---

3 Neumaier's interpretation of Wittgenstein can be disputed. Even though he correctly points out that criteria and symptoms are not sharply distinguished in some cases (1986, 144), he seems to conflate the logical and the epistemological by arguing that logical criteria can be understood as causal evidence (see e.g. 1986, 141–2, 144–5, 147, 153). In other words, Neumaier puts the constitutional uncertainty of the mental and our knowledge of computer programs on the same level, and thus assumes that such uncertainty is an empirical matter, that is, a matter of having more or less knowledge. Thus this author puts forward the very confusion we try to challenge and clarify. The uncertainty of the mental relates to a conceptual or logical dimension that cannot be reduced to a matter of empirical evidence. On the contrary, logical criteria determine what counts as empirical evidence (see 'Empirical and Conceptual Problems'). If there are no logical criteria to apply a certain term, it is unclear what it means to talk about evidence in this case. For example, it does not matter how much knowledge we have of someone – this knowledge will never suffice to predict their behaviour. Then this uncertainty is not an empirical flaw or imperfection related to having more or less knowledge but belongs to or is part of our concept. Would it follow that we would not apply psychological concepts to humans if we had complete knowledge of them? Note also that Neumaier suggests that 'Can machines think?' might be an empirical problem related to technical progress and a change in the use of language (1986, 157).

4 It is difficult to pinpoint what AI systems Wittgenstein scholars refer to. However, it is reasonable to suppose that these authors have in mind especially rule-based computer programs (sometimes called GOFAI and Symbolic AI systems. See Haugeland 1989, 112ff). These programs implement an algorithm, that is, a sequence of defined instructions to transform inputs into outputs, for example, alphabetically sorting a group of names. In contrast, machine learning addresses problems where no algorithm is available, such as predicting human behaviour, natural language processing or pattern detection. In these cases, the model 'learns' an algorithm to provide an inference or an approximate solution to the problem (see Alpaydin 2014, 2). By implementing a mathematical model to process examples or past data, the machine can detect or infer patterns in a data set not yet encountered. Interestingly, for some machine learning systems, such as neural networks, scientists still do not know 'what machines are doing when they're teaching themselves novel skills'. Explainable AI is the field that pursues making 'machines able to account for the things they learn, in ways that we can understand' (Kuang 2017). Even though Neumaier's approach can be challenged, as shown in the last footnote, his account of AI is relevant given that it opens a line of discussion about the status of the Black Box problem, which I believe can be addressed in the future from a Wittgensteinian point of view. Is the uncertainty regarding how neural networks give an output logical or empirical? If the uncertainty belongs to the program's structure, could we say it is a logical uncertainty? Moreover, it might be argued that the emergence of opaque systems can undermine Neumaier's argument, given that we don't know what these systems do when giving an output. For an alternative conception of 'knowing' and 'opaqueness' in this kind of system, see Ian Ground's contribution in this volume.

literally, namely, in the same sense as we ascribe them to human beings in ordinary circumstances. From a Wittgensteinian perspective, either more or less conventional, the strong conception of AI exhibits substantial theoretical inconsistencies and pressing issues that need clarification.

Wittgenstein's later thought thus involves a sceptical stance on the literal applicability of psychological predicates to machines. Like the authors above, it seems natural to conclude that the use of psychological language in AI is exclusively weak or figurative. It does not matter how much the field of AI develops – machines will at best 'imitate' or 'simulate' the powers of human mentality but will never be able to manifest any of its features. Thus, the use of psychological language in this context will invariably be non-literal and figurative. As it will be shown in the next section, however, some uses of psychological language in the science of AI are not figurative and can be understood in terms of, or as sharing features with, what Wittgenstein calls the 'secondary' use of concepts.

In this regard, and despite having the advantage of (i) distinguishing between empirical and conceptual problems and (ii) clarifying in what sense strong AI is incoherent, some Wittgenstein scholars seem to obey a logic similar to that of more mainstream philosophical perspectives on the problem of 'thinking' machines. They likewise assume the seemingly dichotomous nature of the question 'Can machines think?', insofar as they argue only in favour of one side of the binary set of possible responses, and their answers have the character of appearing definitive. In other words, to the extent that Wittgenstein scholars argue that mentality cannot be explained by looking at and describing the workings of computer programs, they conclude that only figurative uses of psychological language make sense in this context. Thus, their approaches are located within and represent manifestations of the weak conception of AI.

Wittgenstein, psychological language and AI

Let us now focus on the argument of the chapter, namely, that certain uses of psychological language in AI escape the strong–weak AI dichotomy, and can be understood in terms of, or as sharing features with Wittgenstein's notion of 'secondary' sense, meaning or use of concepts. This argument is connected to Wittgenstein's methodological requirement of attending to and describing language use.

As we saw before, 'Can machines think?' represents a conceptual problem and thus requires not empirical but conceptual treatment. A conceptual problem expresses puzzlement about the use of language rather than a lack of knowledge about a certain state of affairs. These problems are solved by studying and describing the workings of our language (Wittgenstein 2009a: PI § 109), in this case, the grammar of our psychological vocabulary in the science of AI.[5] In this regard, a limitation of the Wittgensteinian approaches above is that they address only the strong conception of AI rather than the established use of psychological language in AI, a crucial resource for the treatment of the problem of 'thinking' machines. To help bridge this gap, we need to attend to the use of language and the application of psychological predicates in the context of AI. A representative example of the meaningful use of psychological language in AI is 'AlphaZero', a computer chess program that:

> *learns* [...] entirely from *self-play*; [the AI] *defeated* Stockfish [a powerful rule-based chess engine] *winning* 155 games and *losing* 6 games out of 1000. To verify the robustness of [the AI, the scientists made it play] additional matches that started from common human openings. [The AI] *defeated* Stockfish in each opening, suggesting that [the AI] has *mastered a wide spectrum of chess play*. [...] common human openings were independently *discovered* and *played* frequently by [the AI] during *self-play training*. [...] In several games, [the AI] *sacrificed pieces for long-term strategic advantage*, suggesting that it *has a more fluid, context-dependent positional evaluation* than the rule-based evaluations used by previous chess programs.
>
> (Silver et al. 2018, 1, 4. My emphasis)

This linguistic context exemplifies an established use of psychological predicates and their ascription to a specific computer program. The ascription of psychological concepts to this machine contrasts with the literal use of psychological language in strong AI in two related respects. First, psychological concepts in Silver et al. (2018) communicate intelligible and necessary information about the chess program's performance, are embedded in linguistic

---

5 To describe the ordinary use of psychological concepts, we need to remember how we employ them since we master them when acquiring language. In this regard, someone can argue that describing the use of psychological predicates in AI represents an empirical investigation in that we might come across new information about the novel usage. Even though attending to the use of language in science has an empirical character, the investigation remains conceptual because it focuses on the conceptual framework or the technical usage of concepts, and only indirectly on the relevant empirical problems. A conceptual investigation not only records different uses of concepts but also allows us to see new connections, through which new conceptual orders might be established, and new directions to scientific investigation might be given (Wittgenstein 1980a: RPP I § 950). In this respect, Wittgenstein writes: 'One cannot guess how a word functions. One has to *look* at its application and learn from that' (2009a: PI § 340).

practices, namely, the game of chess and computer science, and connect to different functions and purposes. Suppose a chess expert was to study and give a report on all the AI's chess games. In that case, they might notice different patterns in the set of games, such as the program's tendency to play some openings rather than others, and so talk about different opening strategies. They might also describe the 'player's' different tactics and strategies in the middle game, such as how the program headways to long-term positional advantage, maybe based on potential piece sacrifices or pawn structures, which relates to how the AI evaluates certain positions. They might also describe the AI's playing style as positional, aggressive or dynamic.[6] In this situation, we can distinguish, on the one hand, the technical features of the chess program's functioning, which are fully described in non-psychological language, that is, the technology of the machine's constitution, the causal relations among its different parts and the mathematical models and algorithms that the program implements. On the other hand, we can distinguish how the program functions and the large-scale patterns of behaviour it displays in the domain the computer program was designed to perform. This special use of psychological language serves various purposes and accomplishes different tasks. For example, it works as a tool or instrument for reporting the computer program's operation, behaviour patterns and performance in chess. For instance, these psychological concepts describe the program's way of evaluating positions and help distinguish the AI from other chess engines. Wittgenstein writes:

> What we call *'descriptions'* are instruments for particular uses. Think of a machine-drawing, a cross-section, an elevation with measurements, which an engineer has before him.
>
> *(2009a: PI § 291)*

Different kinds of descriptions relate to different uses and types of predicates (see Wittgenstein 2009a: PI § 24). For instance, describing a physical object involves the notions of shape, colour, temperature and weight. This description

---

[6] It might be difficult to distinguish between certain secondary and figurative uses, or even between meaningful and non-meaningful expressions. However, in the sense that the description of the program involving psychological language gives information about its patterns of behaviour in chess, these uses are not figurative. See for example that Kasparov (2018) describes and gives empirical information about the program's performance in chess. The difficulty is that Kasparov's use of language also involves hypotheses that might stem from conceptual puzzlement and might not represent empirical statements, or that he uses metaphorical language to describe aesthetic properties of certain chess positions reached by the AI.

is empirical because it provides new, true or false information. A machine-drawing, in contrast, serves as a rule to assemble, navigate and operate the instrument. Likewise, describing the AI's behavioural patterns in chess gives knowledge and useful empirical information about the program, such as the report on its different opening strategies. At the same time, this description works as a rule to operate the computer program in order, for example, to study certain chess positions. Note that other descriptions involve psychological language, as in the case of describing facial expressions, moods or human behaviour (see Wittgenstein 2009a: PI § 285 and 2009b: PPF i). Even though the use of language in Silver et al. (2018) does not display primarily, for example, intentional action or a coherent contextualized first-person's use of psychological terms in the present tense (see Wittgenstein 1980b: RPP II § 230), this linguistic context allows us to understand what the machine does and how it performs in the game of chess. The description of the large-scale computer's patterns of behaviour in the set of chess matches logically involves the language of chess, which in turn features psychological expressions. Without the resources that these expressions provide, we would not be able to describe the computer's performance and behavioural patterns in chess.[7]

Expanding on the notion of metaphysical propositions in 'Empirical and Conceptual Problems', these expressions deviate from ordinary employments and are detached from practical linguistic contexts and the particular techniques associated with words (Wittgenstein 2009a: PI § 38, 132). The proposition 'thinking is computation', for example, implies that *any* device that computes *thinks* as humans do.[8] This use of 'thinking' departs from its

---

[7] Dennett's 'intentional stance' consists in 'treating the object whose behavior you want to predict as a rational agent with beliefs and desires and other mental stages exhibiting [...] intentionality' (1989, 15). Dennett argues that any 'object' or 'system' whose behaviour is predicted by the intentional stance 'is in the fullest sense of the word a believer' (1989, 15). In this regard, Dennett's views seem to allow the attribution of intentionality and beliefs to the computer program. It is interesting to contrast Dennett's position with our account of language, in which one can use psychological terms to describe behaviour patterns without presupposing mentality.

[8] Someone might argue that computers can perhaps 'think' in a way different than humans. As shown in 'Empirical and Conceptual Problems' , this position is problematic since there is a lack of established criteria for the use of 'thinking' in this situation. If one defines 'thinking' as 'computing', and takes the machine's computing as evidence for thinking, one will assume the conclusion. We acquire the concept of thinking when learning a language and, therefore, learn to employ this word in the context of human life. In this respect, psychological language relates primarily to the behaviour and actions of human beings. Note that the human context involves animal life. We evolved by interacting with and domesticating animals for at least 15,000 years. However, it would be a logical mistake to think that we learn psychological language first by observing animal life and then by engaging in the human context. Of course, this does not

complex grammatical structure in everyday circumstances. Thus the concept is disconnected from the logical machinery that allows operations in the network of actions in ordinary language. Wittgenstein remarks, '"Thinking", a widely ramified concept. A concept that comprises many manifestations of life. The *phenomena* of thinking are widely scattered' (1980b: RPP II § 220). In other words, 'thinking' does not have an essence. This concept refers to a cluster of related phenomena. When describing the contextualized behaviour of human beings, the words 'thinking' and 'computation' are not interchangeable. The word 'thinking' might refer to the capacity to do certain things, for example, operating with signs or calculating. Thus, 'computing' and 'calculating' can only sometimes replace the word 'thinking'. The expression 'The experienced artist computes her past works' does not substitute the proposition 'The experienced artist thinks about her past works'. The former is not a meaningful proposition, that is, it does not have a use in the language. In this sense, strong AI represents a metaphysically loaded view, which lies on conceptual assumptions that conflict with grammar or the ordinary use of psychological language.

In contrast, the psychological language in Silver et al. (2018) is not 'idling' but does the work of reporting the machine's way of playing chess (see Wittgenstein 2009a: PI § 132). In other words, the psychological expressions and concepts in Silver et al. (2018) display a clear function, and play a role in the language game of describing, in this case, the machine's patterns of behaviour in chess (see Wittgenstein 2009a: PI § 23, 24). Thus, in this use of language, concepts and actions are internally related (Wittgenstein 2009a: PI § 7). Therefore, this special use of our psychological vocabulary in the science of AI is not metaphysical in a Wittgensteinian sense (see 2009a: PI § 116).

The second respect in which this special use of psychological language contrasts with the literal use of concepts in strong AI is that, according to the latter, ascriptions of psychological predicates to machines and humans display the same sense. In strong AI, the grammatical distinctions and qualitative differences between humans and computing machines are blurred. According to 'thinking is computation', it makes sense to attribute mentality and other psychological capacities to machines literally, namely, in the same way as we do when describing human behaviour, which involves complex

---

mean that applying psychological terms to animals does not make sense. Rather, the meaningful ascription of psychological predicates to animals displays a particular grammatical structure. Can a dog 'believe that his master will come the day after tomorrow?' (Wittgenstein 2009b: PPF i § 1). Regardless of being the same concept, there is a logical difference between human and animal thinking, which does not amount to saying that animal thinking is 'incomplete' or lacks 'something' only we linguistic animals possess.

elements, such as intentional action.[9] In contrast, psychological concepts in Silver et al. (2018) do not describe the so-called inner or mental aspects of the chess computer program, but only its functioning and ways of operating in the domain the computer program was designed to perform. In other words, this descriptive use of psychological language in the science of AI is not unbounded and does not display the variety of logical connections of these concepts in ordinary circumstances.

For instance, the special use of 'learning' in Silver et al. (2018) describes the program's structure (machine learning), functioning and rendering of results (neural networks), and it is circumscribed to the game of chess. Thus, this special use of 'learning' does not naturally display the full semantic spectrum of the concept's use in the context of a human life, including for example the use of 'learning' in the first-person present tense. The special use of the concept of learning in AI displays a more predominant functional aspect, and so less complexity in relation to the more widespread, far-reaching use of 'learning' in the context of the living person.[10] To illustrate this point, let us offer some examples from Wittgenstein's *Philosophical Investigations* (2009a). In the context of a human life, we speak of learning:

- a native language (PI § 1)
- a second language (PI § 32)
- the meaning of a word (PI § 1)
- to bring an object at a specific call (PI § 2)
- to talk (PI § 5)
- the numbers by heart (PI § 9)

---

9 Intentional action is one of the elements that help logically distinguish between human mentality and AI. However, it is important to recognize contexts where the 'subject' displays intentional action but not conceptual abilities, such as calculating the best move in a game of chess. For an example of ascriptions of psychological predicates that involve intentional action, but the elements related to thinking conceptually are not as strong as in a human context, see the case of intelligent animals in Wittgenstein 1980b: RPP II § 224.

10 One could argue that this case involves polysemy. Insofar as polysemy involves different meanings, such as 'to get' meaning 'to become' and 'to understand', one could reply that 'learning' does have different meanings in AI and the human context. 'Learning' in AI represents an extension of 'learning' in natural language. In this respect, one could also argue that this is indeed a case of polysemy insofar as 'learning' in AI displays a different use, for instance, a more functional one, lacking elements such as intentional action. Beyond the concept of polysemy, the notion of family resemblance can give a fruitful account of these variations in the concept of learning that is alternative to the secondary sense account. One can argue that, given the family resemblance structure of 'learning', we can use this concept to describe the patterns of behaviour of a computer program (see Vázquez Hernández 2020, 70ff).

- the colours (PI § 28)
- to play a game (PI § 31)
- to apply a certain rule (PI § 54)
- the use of concepts in ethics and aesthetics like 'good' or 'beautiful' (PI § 77)
- to read tables and charts (PI § 86)
- to read in the native language (PI § 156)
- foreign expressions (PI § 159)
- algebra (PI § 179)
- the meaning of names of sensations, like 'pain' (PI § 244)
- to lie (PI § 249)
- the use of the word 'thinking' (PI § 328)
- to calculate (PI § 385)
- from experience (PI § 315, 354)

Some of the uses of the concept of learning in the *Investigations* share features with others, but the similarities disappear when other learning instances are considered. The different uses of 'learning' above involve different kinds of training and instruction, mental and bodily capacities, dispositions, concomitant processes, criteria for the word's application and goals related to the linguistic practice in question (see Vázquez Hernández 2020, 15). The various elements that singular instances of 'learning', as well as the concept as a whole, encompass relate to the idea that there is a difference of kind between the use of psychological language in the context of human beings and AI. Psychological language in Silver et al. (2018) is not used literally or strongly, as used when describing the behaviour and actions of a human being.[11] In other words, in the report of the computer's performance, the ascription of psychological predicates does not presuppose the ascription of a mind. Ascribing psychological concepts to chess computer programs in this sense does not mean that our 'attitude towards [them] is an attitude towards a soul' (Wittgenstein 2009b: PPF iv § 22).

The argument that psychological language in Silver et al. (2018) varies from the literal use of language in strong AI can be further reinforced by reminding ourselves of, and including, the critical thoughts on 'thinking' machines noted by Wittgenstein scholarship above, whose upshot is that psychological

---

11 We should distinguish what Silver et al. (2018) would be inclined to hold about the status of these ascriptions, for example, whether they are strong or weak, from the way they actually use psychological language to describe the machine's performance. As Wittgenstein says, 'What we are "tempted to say" in such a case is, of course, not philosophy; but it is its raw material' (2009a: PI § 254).

language cannot be literally applied to machines, as in the context of human behaviour and action.

The differences between the use of psychological concepts in Silver et al. (2018) and their use in ordinary language help argue that the special use of our psychological vocabulary in AI is not literal and does not display the 'primary' meaning of psychological concepts when describing the contextualized behaviour of a human being. According to the Wittgensteinian approaches above, this difference implies that the use of psychological concepts in AI is weak or figurative. In other words, because the ascription of psychological concepts to machines in AI cannot logically be literal, this ascription, they hold, is meaningful only insofar as it is figurative or metaphorical. Therefore, according to these scholars, it is 'as if' the program learns from self-play, it is 'as if' the program plays chess, and it is 'as if' the program evaluates chess positions, but it really isn't.

However, figurative or metaphorical expressions can be normally replaced to convey the same idea (see Wittgenstein 2009b: PPF xi § 278). Figurative expressions are typically connected to volition and contain a conventional element in that sometimes we can either use them or not to express ourselves (see Wittgenstein 1982: LW I § 799). Instead of saying 'My heart is broken', I could use other expressions, figurative or literal, to convey that I am experiencing the most intense sorrow. It is, or it feels *as if* my heart were broken but it really isn't.[12] In contrast, the descriptive use of psychological language in AI above lacks precisely the 'as if' element. Insofar as psychological language is naturally used to describe the patterns of behaviour of the chess computer program, one does not, or does not need to presuppose that the computer is doing something else. The psychological vocabulary in Silver et al. (2018) belongs to the description of the computer program's large-scale behaviour patterns in the game of chess. And just like literal uses of language, the matter of what expressions to use to describe these behavioural patterns is not open to convention. As we said before, without the resources given by psychological language, we would be unable to communicate what the machine does in the domain it was designed to perform. 'AlphaZero' learned to play chess from self-play and discovered various human openings. These are not figurative expressions susceptible to being replaced by more literal phrasings.

---

12 Metaphors and poetic expressions are sometimes irreplaceable or unparaphrasable. One could paraphrase 'Life's but a walking shadow [...]', but arguably, the paraphrase, either literal or figurative, would not capture the content of the original expression (see Wittgenstein 2009a: PI § 531). For a discussion of the unparaphrasable status of religious expressions (see Schönbaumsfeld 2007, 180ff).

Instead, psychological language in Silver et al. (2018) displays a use that could be understood in terms of, or as sharing features with, what Wittgenstein calls the 'secondary' sense, meaning or use of concepts that should be distinguished from both strong or literal and weak or figurative uses of psychological language. Consider the following quote:

> Could one speak here of a 'primary' and 'secondary' meaning of a word? – In both cases the explanation of the word is that of its primary meaning. It can only have a secondary meaning for someone if he knows its primary meaning. That is, the secondary use consists in applying the word with *this* primary use in new surroundings. […] But the relationship here is not like the one between 'cutting off a piece of thread' and 'cutting off someone's speech', for here one doesn't *have* to use the figurative expression.
> *(Wittgenstein 1982: LW I § 797, 799)*

Grammar exhibits a logical space between literal and figurative uses of concepts, which, according to Wittgenstein, can be understood as secondary employments. In other words, secondary sense should not be cashed out in terms of figurative or literal uses of language but somewhere in the middle. Just like literal uses of concepts, the secondary sense somehow forces itself upon us. It is not connected to volition and does not display the conventional element that figurative uses of language usually exhibit. For instance, one could substitute 'I cut off someone's speech' for 'I said: "Silence!"'. Consider the following example.

> [Do the characters in Goethe's theatre play engage in] a *real* game of chess? – Of course. They are not merely pretending to do so – which would be possible as part of a play. – But the game, for example, has no beginning! – Of course it has; otherwise it would not be a game of chess.
> *(Wittgenstein 2009a: PI § 365)*

These fictitious characters are not simulating engaging in a game of chess. It is not 'as if' they played a certain opening or checked the opponent's king. We do not have any other words to describe this context than with the expression 'playing a game of chess'. Note that the fact that, for example, there is no historical record of this game makes this a different and derived use of 'a game of chess', which is neither literal nor figurative. Similarly, no other words are available to describe the behavioural patterns of the chess machine than with the resources provided by psychological terms, even though some features of the use of these concepts in ordinary circumstances are missing, such as intentional action or 'phenomenal' accompaniments, like being under pressure in a certain chess position. Moreover, like figurative uses, the secondary meaning of words logically depends on their primary meaning. Primary or literal uses have logical precedence in relation to secondary ones. Similarly to figurative expressions, we explain the secondary employment of a word based on its primary meaning and not the other way around (Wittgenstein 2009b: PPF xi § 275). As Wittgenstein suggests, only someone who has mastered pain ascriptions can understand what it means to say that a fictitious character is in pain (2009a: PI § 282. See 2009b: PPF xi § 277).

Insofar as the computer program above displays large-scale behaviour patterns in this linguistic context, the program does not do something else susceptible to being described in more literal terms. Likewise, the description of the computer's patterns of behaviour logically involves the language of chess and some correlated psychological expressions. We cannot arbitrarily choose concepts to describe the machine's large-scale performance. Thus, this descriptive use of psychological language is not figurative. Furthermore, only someone who knows what 'playing chess' is can understand what it means to say that a computer program plays chess. Similarly, we do not explain the meaning of 'evaluation' by taking the computer's process of evaluating a chess position as a primary example (see Wittgenstein 2009b: PPF xi § 275).

When we speak of chess programs in AI, we mean devices that operate in a particular way, perform in a specific domain, and produce certain results. It is not 'as if' the program plays chess and displays large-scale behaviour patterns in this linguistic context. The program was indeed designed for the only purpose of playing chess. It is in these respects that this descriptive use of psychological language in AI shares features with the notion of 'secondary' sense, meaning or use of concepts, and not – at least obviously – in the sense of the experience of words, such as in Wittgenstein's example of correlating vowels and their sounds with different colours (2009b: PPF xi § 278).

Moreover, this descriptive, 'secondary' use of psychological language in AI is meaningful as it conveys necessary and intelligible information about the program's large-scale patterns of behaviour in chess. Thus, the ascription of psychological predicates to this program exhibits its own grammatical structure. On the one hand, meaningful ascriptions of psychological predicates to human beings, such as rule-following, calculating and learning, essentially display a normative element. In the context of human behaviour and action, the logico-normative dimension belongs to or is part of these concepts (see Hacker 2019, 107).

In contrast, and expanding on Wittgenstein and Hacker's position, this use of psychological language in AI displays a remarkable grammatical feature. Namely, we describe the machine's large-scale patterns of behaviour using psychological concepts without involving a logico-normative element, but only the machine's empirical and causal functioning. Regardless of the lack of the logico-normative dimension in this linguistic context, psychological terms tend to be a natural medium to describe the machine's patterns of behaviour. In other words, the secondary use of psychological language in AI suggests that, through causally connected mechanisms, it is possible to produce results that display a normative dimension in the context of human interaction. Significantly, the psychological concepts that describe mechanical patterns of behaviour – which, by definition, do not display such a normative aspect – exhibit a stronger functional element related to the machine's causal connections.

As Wittgenstein remarks, the danger is to confuse the machine with its symbol, which are causally and logically determined, respectively (2009a: PI § 193–4). In that case, we might conclude that human behaviour is causally determined, or that the machine's patterns of behaviour involve a logico-normative element. In other words, this meaningful descriptive use of psychological language in AI does not entail the discovery of something new about machines, for example, that they are minds. Insofar as conflating the epistemological and the logical brings further problems instead of clarifying the ones at hand, we agree with more conventional Wittgensteinian approaches, such as Hacker's, in that applying psychological language literally in the context of AI is incoherent. Our investigation only shows relevant features of the natural extensions of psychological language in the science of AI.

To recapitulate. A plausible way of addressing the question 'Can machines think?' is by describing and analyzing the use of psychological language in AI – a variation of its ordinary employment involving human behaviour and action. One of the outcomes of this study is showing that psychological language describes the functioning and behavioural patterns of some machines. Thus it would be inaccurate to say that this use of psychological language in AI is necessarily weak or figurative. Similarly, this study shows that psychological concepts in AI are not used literally or strongly, that is, with the full semantic spectrum and logical complexity they display in the description of human behaviour. To say that computers think as humans do does not have support from the logic or grammar of psychological predicates and thus from empirical research. Instead, some ascriptions of psychological concepts in the scientific discipline of AI can be understood as sharing features with the notion of 'secondary' sense. In this regard, the analysis of the grammar of our psychological vocabulary in AI helps transcend the dichotomous surface grammar of the question 'Can machines think?' that 'tends to force itself on us' (Wittgenstein 2009a: PI § 304), and thus show that this problem might give rise to a false dichotomy that does not necessarily entail a binary set of answers. Studying the descriptive use of psychological language in AI is critical because it sheds light on essential aspects of the problem of 'thinking' machines that are not easily visible from other points of view.

Acknowledgements

I want to thank Genia Schönbaumsfeld, Will McNeill, Alois Pichler, Ian Ground, Juliet Floyd, Oskari Kuusela, Paula Sweeney, Brian Ball and the anonymous reviewer for their valuable feedback on this work, as well as the organizers of the 11th Annual British Wittgenstein Society Conference: Wittgenstein and AI (2022), where a draft of this chapter was presented.

References

Alpaydin, Ethem. 2014. *Introduction to Machine Learning,* 3rd Edn. Cambridge, MA: MIT Press.
Churchland, Patricia Smith. 1986. *Neurophilosophy: Toward a Unified Science of the Mind-Brain.* Cambridge, MA: MIT Press.
Dennett, Daniel. 1989. *The Intentional Stance.* London: MIT Press.
Emiliani, Alberto. 1990. 'The Order of Thought: Wittgenstein on Artificial Intelligence and Brain-Processes'. *Daimon Revista Internacional de Filosofía* 2: 125–38.
Hacker, Peter. 2019. *Wittgenstein: Meaning and Mind.* Oxford: Wiley Blackwell.
Harre, Rom. 1988. 'Wittgenstein and Artificial Intelligence'. *Philosophical Psychology* 1 (1): 105–15.
Haugeland, John. 1989. *Artificial Intelligence: The Very Idea.* Cambridge, MA: MIT Press.
Kasparov, Garry. 2018. 'Chess, a Drosophila of Reasoning'. *Science* 362 (6419): 1087.
Kuang, Cliff. 2017, November 21. 'Can A.I. Be Taught to Explain Itself?'. *New York Times.* https://www.nytimes.com/2017/11/21/magazine/can-ai-be-taught-to-explain-itself.html
Neumaier, Otto. 1986. 'A Wittgensteinian View of Artificial Intelligence'. In *Artificial Intelligence: The Case Against,* edited by Rainer Born, 132–73. London: Croom Helm.
Peacocke, Christopher. 1995. 'Content, Computation, and Externalism'. *Philosophical Issues* 6: 227–64.
Pinker, Steven. 1997. *How the Mind Works.* New York: W. W. Norton & Company.
Quine, Willard Van Orman. 1970. 'Philosophical Progress in Language Theory'. *Metaphilosophy* 1 (1): 2–19.
Schönbaumsfeld, Genia. 2007. *A Confusion of the Spheres: Kierkegaard and Wittgenstein on Philosophy and Religion.* Oxford: Oxford University Press.
Searle, John. 1980. 'Minds, Brains and Programs'. *The Behavioral and Brain Sciences* 3: 417–57.
Silver, David, Thomas Hubert, Julian Schrittwieser, Ioannis Antonoglou, Matthew Lai, Arthur Guez, Marc Lanctot, Laurent Sifre, Dharshan Kumaran, Thore Graepel, Timothy Lillicrap, Karen Simonyan, Demis Hassabis. 2018. 'A General Reinforcement Learning Algorithm that Masters Chess, Shogi, and Go through Self-play'. *Science* 362 (6419): 1140–44.

Vázquez Hernández, Arturo. 2020. 'Wittgenstein and the Concept of Learning in Artificial Intelligence'. M.Phil Diss. University of Bergen. https://bora.uib.no/bora-xmlui/handle/1956/22980.

WITTGENSTEIN'S WORKS

Wittgenstein, Ludwig. 1969. *The Blue and Brown Books*. Oxford: Blackwell. (BB)
———. 1980a. *Remarks on the Philosophy of Psychology I*. Oxford: Blackwell. (RPP I)
———. 1980b. *Remarks on the Philosophy of Psychology II*. Oxford: Blackwell. (RPP II)
———. 1980c. *Philosophical Remarks*. Chicago: The University of Chicago Press. (PR)
———. 1982. *Last Writings on the Philosophy of Psychology I*. Oxford: Blackwell. (LW I)
———. 1992. *Last Writings on the Philosophy of Psychology II*. Oxford: Blackwell. (LW II)
———. 1983. *Remarks on the Foundations of Mathematics*. London: MIT Press. (RFM)
———. 2009a. *Philosophical Investigations*. 4th. Oxford: Wiley-Blackwell. (PI)
———. 2009b. 'Philosophy of Psychology: A Fragment'. In *Philosophical Investigations*, 4th Edn, 182–243. Oxford: Wiley-Blackwell. (PPF)

Chapter 4

THE METONYMICAL TRAP

Éloïse Boisseau

From the Mereological Fallacy to the Metonymical Trap

Maxwell Bennett and Peter Hacker (2023) famously introduced the so-called charge of 'mereological fallacy'. This fallacy is not per se a *reasoning* fallacy but is more akin to an *attribution* mistake (an attribution mistake that can admittedly lead to fallacies of reasoning). In the context that is of particular interest to Bennett and Hacker's discussion, the 'mereological fallacy' is specifically related to neuroscience:[1] to say, for example as part of a neuroscientific explanation, that the brain *constructs hypotheses* would be a paradigmatic instance of a mereological fallacy (*ibid*, 80). A brain is indeed nothing more than a part of a human being, and only of a whole human being does it make sense to say that it constructs hypotheses.[2] Therefore, transferring the qualities and capacities of the whole (the human being) to the part (its brain) would not be

---

[1] In other contexts, the mereological fallacy essentially boils down to two general attribution mistakes that logicians sometimes refer to as the 'fallacy of composition' (a part can have some properties that are not transferable to the whole that it is a part of – e.g. parts of this machine might be little while the whole machine might not be) and the 'fallacy of division' (a whole can have some properties that are not transferable to its parts – e.g. this machine is large while its parts might not be). Cf. for example Walton (2008, 156 *sqq*).

[2] One might also argue (and I thank an anonymous reviewer for the suggestion) that the verb 'construct' in the expression 'to construct hypotheses', should in any case be read as metaphorical (or analogical). One does not *literally* construct hypotheses (hypotheses are not the kind of things that can be constructed) but one does literally *formulate* hypotheses. I am leaning more towards the idea that this first expression can be (and is) taken literally (there is no category mistake at play in saying that someone has constructed a curious hypothesis). This is precisely an instance of what George Lakoff and Mark Johnson (2003, 51) qualify as a 'literal expression structured by metaphorical concepts'. Our verb 'construct' for the formulation of hypotheses is a literal expression: saying that we *construct* a hypothesis is indeed an ordinary way of describing what we do when we formulate hypotheses – even though this way of speaking is indeed metaphorically structured by, say, the model of a *physical* construction.

a viable philosophical option. It would not be an option in particular because it is partly *constitutive of the meaning* of the attributed expression ('to construct hypotheses') that a range of behaviour be associated with it, a range of behaviour that a brain obviously lacks. This idea is Wittgensteinian through and through, and found in the oft-quoted passage of the *Philosophical Investigations* (Wittgenstein 2009: PI §103): 'It comes to this: only of a living human being and what resembles (behaves like) a living human being can one say: it has sensations; it sees; is blind; hears; is deaf; is conscious or unconscious'. A brain does not – in any way, shape or form – behave like a living human being.[3]

Returning to the more general diagnosis of mereological fallacy: although there are numerous instances of predicates that can equally and harmlessly be attributed indistinctly to a whole or to a part of that whole (the fallacy is not systematic) and even if mereological fallacies can apply in a variety of contexts (to borrow one of Hacker's examples (2013, 287) a clock indicates time, a capacity that its fusee or face could not be said to possess), we can say that such a diagnosis is particularly fruitful when it concerns the so-called psychological predicates. These predicates relate to the mental life and the cognitive or psychological capacities of a person. They are often contrasted with predicates that are merely physical. Saying that a stone is heavy uses thus a

---

[3] One of the central insights of Wittgenstein on this issue consists in pointing out that one condition for saying that someone is capable of doing a particular thing – in our present case: formulating hypotheses – is that we understand what it would mean for such an individual to *express* or *display* this kind of capacity in their behaviour (i.e. in their words, gestures and actions). This first condition is closely related and in fact goes hand in hand with a second necessary condition for saying of an individual that they are endowed with an intellectual or mental capacity, which is that we understand the role this capacity might play in the individual's life. In this respect, one can see why a brain might be a poor candidate for being the subject of cognitive abilities. Observing a brain in activity might mean observing the transport of oxygen via the blood from one region to another or observing the firing of nerve impulses from the neurons. It thus means observing no behaviour sufficiently similar to that used as a criterion for the usual attribution of the activity of formulating hypotheses. Although oxygen variations in the brain may well be necessary events to *enable* the individual whose brain it is to formulate hypotheses, these variations are not, in themselves, part of what it means to formulate hypotheses (they are not constitutive of what it is to formulate hypotheses). Furthermore, a brain is not a whole individual with a complex life in which the activity of formulating hypotheses would be relevant. A brain, like a pencil or a lung, is therefore not the kind of thing with a behavioural repertoire that makes it possible for it to manifest such a faculty. In the same way that Wittgenstein (Wittgenstein 1980: RPP §192) once remarked how we would fail to grasp what it would be like for a table to think, it seems that we also fail to grasp what it would be like if a brain were to think, construct hypotheses and so forth: 'But if I say "A table does not think", then that is not similar to a statement like "A table doesn't grow". I shouldn't know "what it would be like if" a table were to think. And here, there is obviously a gradual transition to the case of human beings.'

physical predicate, when on the other hand saying that Alfred wants to buy bread, that he is in pain or in a hurry to get home, uses various psychological predicates (as all these relate one way or another to Alfred's mental life).[4]

What is of particular interest for our present purpose is to remark that the usual way out, or the sort of 'loophole' for those accused of committing a mereological mistake is to understand these ascriptions in a *metonymic* way or 'metonymically' (this way out is mentioned by Bennett and Hacker (2023, 83)). How is this a way out? First, what is a metonymy? A metonymy is a figure of speech that uses a salient aspect of a thing to refer to the thing itself (or possibly to refer to another thing that is intimately related to it) (Littlemore 2015). In the confines of this chapter, I emphasize that it is the only dimension that I will retain from the sometimes contradictory taxonomies of metonymy: I take it that metonymy has to do with *identifying* the subject of a statement – and I will furthermore say of the identification that it is *indirect* when metonymy is involved. Metonymy is thus characterized by this *referential* aspect.

I would like to suggest that the mereological fallacy is a special case of a more general fallacy: the metonymical fallacy. The mereological fallacy has to do only with the part-whole relation, while the metonymical fallacy involves a more general feature-thing relation (a part of a thing can be considered as an aspect or a feature of a thing). Both can lead to what I will call the metonymical trap (taking an indirect identification for a direct one). This focus on the more general fallacy will allow us to go beyond the strictly neuroscientific debates discussed by Bennett and Hacker (2023) while keeping the results of some of their analyses. I would like to suggest that it may be philosophically fruitful to bear in mind the risk of a metonymical trap when considering the status of some attributions to machines. My aim in this

---

[4] Wittgenstein frequently focused on the question of the status of psychological concepts (Wittgenstein 1980: RPP *passim*) and has notably (e.g. Wittgenstein 1980: RPP §63 and Wittgenstein 1958: BB, 66–67) sketched out – rather tentatively – an important logical or grammatical asymmetry in psychological predicates when used in the first person of the present (on the one hand) and in the second or third person of the present (on the other hand): it is arguable that when I say 'I am in pain', 'I believe *x*', 'I wish I had done that', and so on, I usually do not intend to describe anyone (not even myself) whereas it is exactly what I intend to do when I say 'she is in pain', 'she believes *x*', 'she wishes she had done that'. Used with the first person (in the present tense), these psychological expressions are better thought not as ways *to describe something* but as ways to *express something*. In this respect, the possibility of error is non-existent (and as such there is no *identification* in play). As for physical concepts, they have (in the present tense) exactly the same purpose in an 'I-statement' and, say, in a 'she-statement'. Thus saying 'my hair is black' and 'her hair is black' both require some kind of observation, and I am in both cases describing someone that I have identified.

chapter is to discuss and evaluate the question of the attribution of predicates to machines (in particular cognitive or intellectual predicates).[5]

Metonymy and Artefacts

Among the cases of apparent attributions of intentional characteristics to machines, some leave no room for doubt as to their metonymic nature. We can thus easily distinguish between the metonymical statement:

the trains are on strike

and this other non-metonymical statement (although both are syntactically on a par):

the trains are out of order

Whereas in the second sentence something is indeed said about the trains themselves (i.e. that they are not working, that there is a technical issue *with them*), this is obviously not the case in the first proposition, in which if anything is said about the trains, it is only said in a derivative or consequential manner (e.g. it can be inferred – if it is true that the trains are on strike – that not a single train is currently in circulation). Unlike the second statement, the first one then does not literally refer to (or talk about) the trains (and so nothing is ascribed to them); the reference is thus *secondary*, *oblique* or *derivative* because it is obviously not the trains themselves that are on strike (demonstrating, protesting, etc.), but the drivers of these trains (it is they, not the trains, who have this range of behaviour at their disposal). There is thus an asymmetry that justifies the idea that the reference to trains is secondary here: you have to understand what it means for *people* to be on strike to understand that 'the trains are on strike', but you do not have to understand what it means for *trains* to be on strike to understand that 'people are on strike'. This first statement has therefore a metonymic character since we seem to attribute to the machines (in this instance, trains) a behaviour (being on strike) which is in fact that of the agents who operate them. In this particular case, the figure of speech

---

5 A machine is traditionally an artefact with moving parts. We will follow the more recent use (prevalent in AI circles) and speak of 'machine' to cover both the case of software and that of robots. What is common to these two types of machines is that they are both contingent and dependent artefacts: abstract artefacts in one instance, concrete artefacts in the other. On the typology of abstract artefacts, see Amie Thomasson (1998).

involves referring to the train drivers by means of the machines they operate. If we bear in mind, as we mentioned earlier, that metonymy works by an aspect-thing relation, the train drivers are then the thing ultimately referred to, and the aspect related to them through which the reference obtains is the trains they operate. This type of metonymy is sometimes referred to as the 'object used for user' metonymy (Lakoff and Johnson 2003, 38). The figure of speech occurs with a shift in the subject of reference: it is indeed the drivers we are referring to, although we do not mention them directly.

The predicate of the sentence, on the other hand, should be taken quite literally. It is indeed the very act of being on strike that we want to state in the proposition. 'Being on strike' is not, here, used indirectly or obliquely as a predicate; it is not some sort of proxy for *another* predicate: we are not in fact intending to use the phrase to refer to any *other* activity than that of being on strike. If this were the case, we might then be leaving the realm of metonymy and entering that of metaphor: in broad strokes, we could suggest that metonymy has to do with an indirect identification of a subject, while metaphor has more to do with an indirect or tangent predication. In this regard, Lakoff and Johnson (2003, 6) argue that 'the essence of metaphor is understanding and experiencing one kind of thing in terms of another'. The point of a metaphor would be to use the lexical field from a specific concept in the context of another concept. The example examined at length by Lakoff and Johnson is the 'argument is war' metaphor. They point out that the activity of debating is often understood and referred to in terms of the activity of fighting (waging war): thus, we speak of '*defending* a position', '*attacking* an argument', of 'an argumentative *strategy*' and so on. These terms arise from a primary conceptual field (that of war) and are then transferred (applied) to another conceptual field (that of debating). This is not what is at stake with metonymy since – as we have seen – it is not *what is said* that is on the line: it is what it is said *of*.

Going back to metonymy, let us note that this very common figure of speech is, at first sight, quite harmless. It is harmless as long as one keeps in mind that what is in play is only a secondary, derivative use or attribution and that it is in no way intended to bestow human characteristics on the machine. Therefore, if taking the proposition literally is problematic, the problem does not lie in the misidentification of the predicate, but in the identification of the subject. As we have just discussed, trains are not the kinds of things that can go on strike: the grammatical subject of the proposition is not suited (when taken literally) for the predicate at issue. We shall then distinguish between the literal subject (when what I seem to be talking about is indeed what can receive what I say about it) and the metonymic subject (when what I seem to be talking about is *not* what can receive what I say about it).

Furthermore, in the 'trains are on strike' example, the metonymic component is very easy to detect, and in this case nobody would likely fall into the metonymical trap. In other cases, however, this component might be more difficult to identify. What should we think, for instance, of the apparent attribution of a cognitive faculty to a machine, as in 'the pocket calculator calculates'? I would like to argue that in this case – just like in the 'trains are on strike' case – the machine (the pocket calculator) is *not* the literal subject of the action but only a metonymical one. More generally, I would like to argue that the attribution of cognitive or psychological characteristics or capacities to a machine can never be literal but can only be metonymic. This echoes a remark made by Wittgenstein (Wittgenstein 2009: PI §103) where he notes that the attribution of psychological predicates to inanimate things (he takes the example of children attributing pain to dolls) can only be secondary uses of the terms at play. I will come back to this. For the moment let me simply note that the claim that a machine can only ever be a metonymical subject of attribution of cognitive or psychological capacities is, of course, much more controversial than merely saying that there is a metonymy involved in the sentence 'the trains are on strike'. That is why it will be useful to distinguish between two broad classes of attribution of actions to artefacts (in particular machines). In the next section, I will begin by examining the status of the attribution of actions that might simply be described as 'physical' or 'natural'. The question is whether – in propositions such as 'a plane flies', 'a blender grinds', 'the car is moving' and so on – these attributions are literal or metonymic. I will argue that they are indeed literal, that is, that the machine is genuinely the subject of these actions. I will then examine the question of the attribution of what might be described as 'intentional', 'intellectual' or 'cognitive' actions. My concern will be to determine whether, in statements such as 'this pocket calculator *calculates*', 'the software *translates*' or 'this recognition network *discriminates*', and so on, the subject of the attribution is being identified directly or metonymically. In this instance – inspired by Wittgensteinian insights – I will attempt to show that, contrary to the previous case of the attribution of 'physical' or 'natural' actions, the attribution of cognitive or intentional actions to machines is necessarily metonymic.

The Machine as a Literal Subject of Attribution of Non-Intellectual Actions

Since it is always possible to ask, when presented with a machine, what it actually does,[6] a distinction should be made between two broad classes of

---

6 Even if the answer is 'nothing'! It is indeed necessary to make this distinction: for any mechanical artefact or for any machine, it is always possible to ask: What does it do? However, it is not true that it is possible to ask this for any *artefact* (*sans phrase*). It would be odd, for instance, to ask what

answers: answers that call for natural or physical descriptions ('the fan blows air', 'the vacuum cleaner sucks up dust', etc.) and answers that call for more intellectual, cognitive or intentional descriptions ('the computer calculates', 'the software discerns characters', 'the model learns from its past mistakes', etc.). The first kind of cases of ascription of actions to machines that we will consider are cases of non-intellectual actions. By 'non-intellectual actions', I mean actions that are usually considered as not necessarily requiring any intelligence to be performed. In contrast to actions that would instead be intellectual (such as speaking, reading, calculating, translating), these actions are likely to be easily performed in a purely mechanical way. The action of the toaster to toast or burn my toast, the action of the crane to lift the cinder block or the action of the plane to fly are thus examples of actions that could be classified as *non-intellectual*.[7]

Let us focus on the example of 'the plane flies'. In this sentence, is the subject of the action identified directly (as it was previously the case in the proposition 'the trains are out of order') or metonymically (as it was in the proposition 'the trains are on strike')? Unlike 'being on strike' – which is a specifically human and intentional action and can therefore only take place within a particular form of life (made of norms of organized labour, uses, practices and institutions) – it is not obvious that the action of flying should be dependent on the wider framework of a form of life governed by uses and norms (though there are of course requirements for the action to even take place: there can be no flight if there is no atmosphere, etc.). It is therefore not unusual to ascribe this action of flying not only to beings whose existence is not governed by norms and institutions (birds, moths, flies, mosquitoes), but equally to inanimate substances (be they natural or artefactual). We can thus easily say that *leaves*, *paper planes* and *dust balls* fly. Besides, there is nothing metonymic about these examples: if there were, we should be able to explain the figure of speech involved (and in particular we should be able to identify the proper referent). In other words, if these subjects were metonymic subjects

---

a sheet of paper (a full-blown artefact) does. Not because – like the famous 'useless box' (a full-blown machine) – it does nothing (meaning nothing interesting, nothing useful, etc.) but because the question is simply incongruous (misleading): a sheet of paper is not the kind of thing that does (or does not do) anything at all. All artefacts have an end (one can always ask: 'What is it for?'), but it is not true that all artefacts have a typical action or range of actions.

7 As an anonymous reviewer remarks, one *could* resist this distinction between intellectual actions and non-intellectual actions by adopting a physicalist stance, thus maintaining that *all* actions are ultimately non-intellectual. Since I hope to show that in the case of the attribution of actions to machines, there *is* a discrepancy at play (as to whether the attribution is literal or metonymic), this discrepancy could ultimately give us good reason to recognize that the distinction in question is relevant.

of action, we should be able to identify what they really refer to. Yet, there is no obvious indication that the subject 'leaf' in the proposition 'the leaf is flying' is used to refer to a subject of the action of flying *that is not* the leaf. Similarly, there is no reason to believe that the predicate 'flies' – in this same sentence – is used with the literary purpose of representing an action *other* than the action of flying (and it is hence doubtful that it might be metaphoric).

These examples can also be contrasted with other examples which are definitely metonymic. Saying that this *plane* flies from Paris to London does not have the same obvious metonymic weight as saying that this *airline* flies from Paris to London. This second proposition has a clear metonymic dimension: whatever the verdict may be in the case of the plane, it seems clear enough that airlines are not the kinds of things that fly from one point to another. Our first impression is therefore that the attribution of physical characteristics to a machine should be considered literal (non-metonymic). Although we shall ultimately endorse this conclusion, let us nevertheless see what concerns one might express with regard to it – and how these can be met.

The Powers of Machines

Going back to 'the plane flies', there is a vexing difficulty, operating sideways, that we must delve into at this point: one can feel uneasy with saying that a plane flies *in the same sense* as one says that a bird flies. Why is that? Because it seems that we are ascribing to the former an action which ultimately does not depend on itself (upon which – contrary to the latter – it lacks a form of control and spontaneity). The plane – like the Frisbee or the kite (but unlike the bird) – only flies because *we* (i.e. external agents) have decided so (or because we have decided to let it fly or because we have built it so that it can fly, etc.). Thus, there is a noticeable discrepancy between the bird's power to fly and that of the plane: the bird can actualize its power on its own, whereas the plane cannot (and requires the intervention of an external agent – namely, a human being).[8] It might then be tempting, for our present purposes, to con-

---

8 This consideration also applies in the case of machines that are often misleadingly described as 'autonomous'. In the industrial sector, the term 'autonomous' applies to artefacts that do not – at all times – require human assistance to perform the tasks for which they have been designed. There is assuredly a *continuum* in what should count as 'autonomous': if I voluntarily drop a hammer on a nail, it is in a way, while free falling, 'autonomous', but the range of the outcome is rather limited. A military drone, on the other hand, does not require the constant supervision of a human being to fly and the range of the outcome can be very diverse (it is this wide variety of outcomes that calls for these artefacts to be given a proper legal framework). Of course, the fact that the drone *can* fly necessarily depends on the prior intervention of human beings (who created

sider that in a way the plane does not fly *at all*, but that *we* fly *with it* or *by means of it*. There would be a twist here: the plane would only be a simple metonymic subject of the action of *flying*, the real subject being the pilot who uses it to fly (as an instrument). Does this mean that the plane should be denied *any kind* of power or action?

One-way versus two-way powers

An old but useful Aristotelian distinction recently brought up by Peter Hacker (2007) might help us clarify this vexing question. It is the distinction between a *one-way* power and a *two-way* power.[9] To have a one-way power, Hacker explains, is to have a capacity which is actualized whenever the circumstances necessary for it arise. An agent endowed with a one-way power will therefore exercise its power whenever these conditions are met. In contrast, to have a two-way power is not only to be able to actualize one's capacity whenever the circumstances are favourable, but it is also to be able *not* to actualize it. The plane's power to fly would thus be a one-way power, since when all the conditions are met for the power to be actualized, the power will in fact be actualized. The bird's power, on the other hand, would be a two-way power, since even when all the relevant necessary conditions are met, the bird can either exercise its power or refrain from doing so. Following Hacker (2007, 95), we can then say that the circumstances that are necessary for the plane to exercise its power are *occasions* for it to exercise its ability to fly, whereas the circumstances necessary for the exercise of the bird's power are *opportunities* for it to exercise its ability to fly (see also Alvarez, 2013). This distinction makes it thus possible to separate two types of action which correspond to these two types of power. It is now clear that the plane does not act *in a sense that it actualizes a two-way power*. Still, there is a definite action of flying when the plane is in the air, and it must be said that this action involves it *directly* (and not metonymically). Thus, even though machines can literally be said to have and exercise a given power, this power in itself requires further clarification – a clarification that we partly find by means of the distinction

---

it, who have a use for it, etc.). The drone can only exercise its power within the confines of its programming – which, admittedly, may be quite broad. This programming has nonetheless been designed and set by human makers. And most importantly, as we will see in the next subsection, a drone does not have a proper *two-way* power.

9 The distinction between one-way and two-way powers can be traced back to Aristotle, whose point was essentially stated in terms of a distinction between *rational* and *non-rational* powers. A rational power, according to Aristotle, is 'a capacity for contraries' (2016, 1046b5 and 1048a5-20), while a non-rational power is not. See also Alvarez (2013).

between one-way and two-way powers. We shall now continue to pursue this clarification.

Mere Cambridge agents

I would like to tentatively introduce another distinction that might prove useful for my purpose. It is a distinction parallel to the one Peter Geach (1969, 71) drew regarding changes when he coined the phrase 'mere Cambridge changes'. First, I will remind the reader what is at stake with Geach's terminology.

Suppose a thing *x* changes when a predicate that was truly ascribable of *x* at a given time is no longer true of *x* at a later time (or conversely, if a predicate that was not truly ascribable of *x* at a given time, then becomes true of *x* at a later time).[10] This would be a purely logical conception of change, which has only to do with a difference between the truth value of a proposition at a time and its truth value at a later time. This way of thinking about change is what Geach refers to as 'Cambridge changes' – and this conception used as a criterion for saying that a thing changes is what he labels the 'Cambridge criterion'. However, Geach remarks, we want to distinguish, within this broad logical conception of change, changes *that really affect the subject of change* and those that do not. On the one hand, then, we have *real* changes, that is, changes which happen to, and really affect, a given subject: for instance, a wall may have a change in colour (initially yellow, it becomes blue after being repainted). Someone may once have had hair, but no longer does (thus changing from hairy to bald) and so on. These are changes *of* the subject of change. It is usually this type of change – *real* change – that we think of when we ordinarily speak of 'change'. On the other hand, there are changes that only relate to the descriptions that can be used to truly describe a given subject. The fact that the proposition 'Socrates is admired by Alcibiades' is true at a given time but used to be false at a previous time, thus indicates a kind of change. We can certainly say that it is a change in the sense that Socrates is now the object of Alcibiades' admiration, but it is – as Geach calls it – a *mere Cambridge change*. This change does not affect Socrates *directly*: there is no *real* change about his person, only a change in a description we could give about him (and it could even be that Socrates has been dead for a long time by the time this change occurs – so that no real change of him is even

---

10 For simplicity's sake, let us say that in the following considerations, we are *not* dealing with a quantified or general proposition (which could give rise to scope ambiguities and other complications that would have to be cleared up).

possible). We could say that these are changes *for* the subject of change.[11] Every real change is thus also a Cambridge change, but not the other way around (Geach 1969, 72).

The parallel distinction I want to draw is then as follows: just as there are mere Cambridge changes (changes that are not *real* changes), we could say that there are *mere Cambridge actions* (actions that are not *real* actions). We would then have to distinguish two subclasses of actions inside a general class of Cambridge actions: the subclass of *mere* Cambridge actions, and the subclass of authentic, *real* or genuine actions. These subclasses are exhaustive and exclusive. Every genuine action (and every mere Cambridge action) is a Cambridge action, but not every Cambridge action is a genuine action. We might speak of a mere Cambridge action when no real action is in play. We are dealing with a Cambridge action involving A when we are dealing with a true proposition of the form ΦA (where Φ is an action verb or action predicate).[12] We must keep in mind that *every action* (be they *real* or *mere Cambridge actions*) can be formally described via this pattern (as when we saw earlier that every change could be seen as an alteration of the truth value of a description). That it is true that $A\Phi s$ is then a necessary but not a sufficient condition for us to be dealing with a *real* action. We might then speak of a Cambridge action when we look at what an action is from a purely logical point of view. We then have an action as soon as we can form a true sentence of the form ΦA (where Φ is an action verb or an action predicate). But the fact that something can be seen as a Cambridge action leaves open the question whether we have to deal with a *mere* Cambridge action or with a *real* action. As with the real change–mere Cambridge change distinction, an important upshot is that two (formally) logically indiscernible statements might hide an important conceptual difference: any formal description of a change is not necessarily that of a real change and any formal description of an action is not necessarily that of a real action.

---

11 One must note that a *mere* Cambridge change for Socrates – in the example discussed above – corresponds to a real change on the part of Alcibiades (saying that Alcibiades has new feelings for Socrates is a *real* change on Alcibiades' part). One must always specify *who* (or what) is the subject of the change (before determining if one is dealing with a real change or with a mere Cambridge change).

12 I suppose here that there is a categorial difference between action predicates and other predicates (like, say, quality predicates, posture predicates, passion predicates, etc.) – it is not the place here to defend this supposition, but it seems to me fairly uncontroversial to suppose that one must distinguish, when attributing something to something, different kinds of attributes, and that one of these kinds is precisely the *action* kind. As a consequence, Φ can n*ot* be '[…] is wise', '[…] is in bed', '[…] is tall' and so on. I hereby presuppose then that one could articulate one way or another what it takes for a predicate to be an action predicate.

That said, this distinction is not orthogonal to the distinction between one-way and two-way powers: the moon has the one-way power to create high tides but its action of creating high tides is not a mere Cambridge action, it is a *real* action of the moon (even if the moon does not have a two-way power). As I understand it, the distinction between one-way and two-way powers *presupposes* that we have *real* agents all along. By contrast, when we deal with a mere Cambridge action, the logical subject of the action is not a real agent (as when dealing with a mere Cambridge change, the logical subject of the change is not the subject of a real change).

Now, why is this distinction important? The distinction between mere Cambridge change and real change enables us to draw attention to a significant difference and allows us to specify why a mere Cambridge change is not a real change, and what might be characteristic of a mere Cambridge change. For instance, we get that a *relational* change is not a real change: if you are now on my right when you were earlier on my left, something is true of me that was not the case before, but it does not mean that I have thereby undergone a real change. To take another example, if x becomes a father, the description one can give of him changes while x does not undergo any real change (for all we know he could be ignorant of the fact). Of course, the event of x becoming a father *can* lead to many *real* changes in x's life and in x himself (for instance, it can make him overwhelmed, happy, sick or stressed) so that even if becoming a father can be seen as a mere Cambridge change, it can nonetheless lead to real changes in x (or in other people). In the same way, *intentional* change is not a real change: if you are now jealous of me when you were not at a previous time, something is true of me that was not the case before (that I am now the object of your jealousy), but it does not mean that I myself have undergone a real change (it could very well be that I am dead when this happens). But here again, an intentional change can very well lead to a *real* change: admittedly, being loved by someone can (but does not need to) lead to substantial changes in me (in particular if it is reciprocal).

I want to suggest that similarly we could say that mere Cambridge actions have certain features. I do not mean to be exhaustive, but I would like to suggest tentatively that we are facing a mere Cambridge action in particular when someone or something is being *used* or *employed* to Φ. If I use a stone as a paperweight, one can say that the stone *prevents my documents from slipping away*. Is it a *real* action of the stone? The answer is 'no': *I* use the stone to prevent my documents from slipping away. It is something that *I* can do (and it is not something the stone can do); and the way I do it is by using the stone. It can then be an action *for* the stone. It does not mean, of course, that there are absolutely no real actions *of* the stone: it might be a real action of the stone that it leaves a mark on the paper (if it does indeed leave a mark on the paper).

But the action predicate '[...] is preventing my documents from slipping away' is best understood – if the stone is its logical subject – as a mere Cambridge action. This might have to do – as in some types of mere Cambridge changes – with the intentionality involved. In this instance, we may well have a true proposition of the form ΦA, but if A is in fact being used or employed to Φ, then we have a mere Cambridge action (and a real action from the thing that is using or employing A).[13]

Now, to return to our initial example, what does this all mean? It means that we can certainly say truly 'The plane flies' (it would be too revisionary to say that it is false or that it is a mere figure of speech); when we do, we can recognize that 'The plane' is here the subject of an action, but the question remains open as to whether the action is to be conceived as a *mere Cambridge action* or as a *real* action. In a sense of 'flying' we *use* the plane to fly (as when a pilot might say 'I flew from London to New York') – and in this case the plane is the subject of a mere Cambridge action; but in another sense of 'flying' the plane itself *can* fly (it is something that is – if conditions are met – *possible for it*). This tentative distinction might help us to move beyond the sterile opposition between the 'guns kill people' and 'guns don't kill people' positions: guns do have the one-way power to kill people, and when we say that they kill people, we neither think that they do it on their own accord, nor that the point is thereby metonymic (we do not want to really refer to the people holding guns but we do want to highlight the dangerousness of these artefacts). It is a statement about guns. In the mere Cambridge change–real change distinction, what is at stake is the question whether the change in play is the apparent subject of change's *own* change. In the mere Cambridge action–real action distinction, what is at stake is the question whether the action in play is the apparent subject of action's *own* action. When we say that hydrochloric acid dissolves bronze, it is the acid's *own* action, even if it is not a two-way power of such an acid. If you threw hydrochloric acid at my bike and pretended that you did not ruin it since the hydrochloric acid did, I might retort that in this instance, it is equally true that it did and true that this is a mere Cambridge action on the part of the acid (and a real action on your part).

For now, the important thing is that whether 'the plane flies' is a mere Cambridge action or not, it does not mean that there is any form of indirect identification (in particular a metonymy) at play in such a statement (just as there is no indirect identification when we are dealing with a mere

---

13 This distinction deserves to be explored in greater depth and will be the subject of a future study; it must be acknowledged that things become more complex when we add cases where the thing used is an agent itself capable of intentional actions.

Cambridge change). We can then conclude that an attribution of physical or natural action to a machine is not – by default – metonymic. There is no question of finding *another agent* or another subject of attribution of the action at hand. To say of the plane that it flies, of the blender that it grinds or of the fan that it blows air does not therefore encapsulate a metonymic dimension, even though it is certainly useful to distinguish one-way powers from two-way powers and to note that machines do *not have two-way powers*: the blender does not grind of its own accord; it is not up to the plane to fly or to the fan to blow air. Furthermore, it is also useful to recognize that indeed machines are agents, but can sometimes be accessories and therefore be the subject of mere Cambridge actions.

Throughout the last two sections, I aimed to show that the attribution of non-intellectual capacities to machines takes the form of a literal attribution. By introducing the two distinctions discussed in this section (one-way powers vs. two-way powers and mere Cambridge actions vs. real actions), I wanted to draw attention to the fact that these distinctions gave us some leeway in such a literal attribution. A machine may well be the literal subject in the attribution of an action without being *ipso facto* endowed with a two-way power. A machine may well be the literal subject in the attribution of an action, but this action may well be a *mere* Cambridge action. Keeping this in mind, let me now turn to the question of the attribution of intellectual capacities to machines.

The Machine as a Subject of Attribution of Intellectual Actions: The Metonymical Trap

These initial results can serve as a starting point for some reflections on the more controversial issue of whether an intellectual action can be attributed in a non-metonymic way to a machine. Can a calculator, for example, be said to *calculate* (is this really one of its actions?), can a computer program be said to *recognize*, an automated translator to *translate*? Only rarely do these questions arise in such a head-on way. The dialectic at stake more often passes through questions such as: calculators or computers undoubtedly calculate, but do they *think*? For instance, Larry Hauser (1993) argues that calculating is very much a way of thinking, that my calculator calculates *in the same sense as we do* and that as such, my calculator does indeed think.[14] The question I would like to address is thus not even raised. I would like to challenge the relevance

---

14 This view can be seen as part of a tradition that goes back at least as far as the writings of Leibniz and his dream of a *characteristica universalis*.

of these attributions. The question of whether a calculator calculates is thus prior to all the skepticism that would invoke the usual solipsistic arguments (such as: we do not know what it is like for anyone or anything else to think, so we have no epistemological grounds for taking this characteristic away from the machine if it turns out that it is visibly doing the same thing as we are). This kind of skepticism was famously used by Alan Turing in his 1950 article and is nowadays prevalent (Turing 1950). Obviously, if it turns out that it is inappropriate to say that a calculator calculates, the soundness of Hauser's syllogism (P1: Calculating is thinking, P2: My calculator calculates and C: My calculator thinks) is undermined (via the rejection of P2). Wittgenstein, as we will see, has given us reasons to reject P2. Before anything, let us look at a first line of argument for doubting the capacity of a machine to calculate (or to perform any intellectual action whatsoever).

Classes of functional equivalence

In order to do this, I will use Vincent Descombes' (2001) concept of 'classes of functional equivalence' or 'functionally equivalent classes'. There is a functional equivalence between two agents, Descombes tells us, when one can be substituted for the other in the context of the performance of a specific action, without affecting the actual performance of that action. A dishwasher is thus a functional equivalent of a person washing the dishes insofar as the task of washing the dishes can be performed by either one. For this functional equivalence relationship to exist between two agents, the action performed must be one that can be described at a certain level of generality. Furthermore, there are specific actions that only I can do, such as signing a contract (these actions cannot give rise to this class equivalence relationship). No one can – by definition – sign a document on my behalf (unless – of course – I have authorized it somehow, by personally signing another document, etc.). From this perspective, it is quite conceivable that some machine could perform the *exact same motions* as I do when signing a document, but this would not entail that the machine has actually signed any document (and it would certainly not entail that it has signed a document *for me*). This allows us to draw a contrast with the dishwasher: for two agents – especially if one of the agents is a machine – to be in a relationship of functional equivalence, the action at play must be described at a certain level of generality and the action must also be decomposable so that each of its components can be described outside any historical, normative or social context. The action of washing the dishes is one such action: we can describe, outside any normative or social context, what constitutes the completion of the action. Here, the action is accomplished when, say, the dishes are changed from dirty (stained) to clean (unstained). Any agent that carries out this transformation will thus have washed the dishes (from this angle, a man, a machine and a rain shower can all wash the dishes).[15] Conversely, as we have just discussed, even though we can describe the mechanical or physical decomposition of the movements involved in the signing of a document with as much precision as we wish, this alone is not sufficient to genuinely sign a document. Nobody other than the individual who is supposed to sign would be able to sign. In order to sign a document, it is, therefore, necessary that it is the person who is supposed to sign who does so, and it is, therefore, impossible for anyone or anything else to do so (not physically but logically impossible).

A reason why it is logically impossible for someone other than me to sign a document is that the action of signing a document is a normative action. It therefore relates to the customs and conventions of a given society. These normative or conventional aspects are crucial in determining the nature of intellectual or intentional actions. They are crucial in that they allow us to fully grasp why such actions are not amenable to a relation of functional equivalence, and therefore to understand why they cannot literally be performed by machines. Let us now say a little bit more about this normative, social and historical dimension of intellectual actions.

The historical and social dimension of intellectual actions

On the one hand, we have actions that are insensitive to the historical or social context for their attribution, while on the other hand, we have actions that are essentially dependent on this historical and social context. It is one of Wittgenstein's major insights to have drawn attention to this contrast. One of Wittgenstein's philosophical breakthroughs consists in understanding that calculation (and more generally every other intellectual or mental action) is precisely the sort of action that *cannot be described in isolation from its normative and social framework*. If this is so, then it is *impossible* for intellectual actions to constitute the kind of actions that can give rise to these functional equivalence relations. Hence, it is only if an action meets certain criteria that it can, for instance, be described as one of 'calculating' – criteria that, in fact, go beyond the mere physical framework (and relate crucially to the institutions and norms of calculation). In the *Philosophical Investigations* (Wittgenstein 2009: PI §87), Wittgenstein thus comments that 'To follow a rule, to make a report,

---

15 Any discomfort there may be at this point is alleviated by the considerations raised in the previous section (the contrast between one-way and two-way powers and the distinction between real actions and mere Cambridge actions).

to give an order, to play a game of chess, are *customs* (usages, institutions)'. All these activities are indeed normative activities in the sense that they can only take place within a society (which has its very own norms and practices). As a result, these actions can only be carried out by individuals who are familiar with the existence of these norms and practices and who are therefore in a position to make them their own (by following them or, on the contrary, by disregarding them or by failing to follow them). Calculating thus requires that there already exists a practice of calculation. A related matter – developed on multiple occasions in Wittgenstein's work – is that the practice of calculating (of signing, buying, etc.) itself hinges on a *consensus* (Wittgenstein 1967: RFM, 94), that is, on the recognition by the members of a society of its function and role. Thus, in order to grasp and fully account for an intellectual action, it seems necessary to refer to the *context* of the action, that is, to bring in external factors to the mere gestures or mechanical movements that may otherwise constitute it, just like what we said earlier about the gestures that are made when signing: these gestures, admittedly, have their importance but are by no means sufficient to constitute a signature.

The social, historical and normative dimension of intellectual actions thus explains why these actions cannot be reduced to mere physical movements – and why they cannot, therefore, be amenable to a relation of functional equivalence. There can indeed be no functional equivalent for an individual's action of signing a document or performing a calculation, whereas there can, on the contrary, be such an equivalent for an individual's action of washing the dishes. Thus, the calculator does not calculate (whereas the dishwasher does wash the dishes) and is just a way among others *for human beings* to calculate – and so to exercise their intelligence. It is now this idea of acting intelligently *with* a machine that requires us to say a few words since this aspect of our way of performing intellectual actions might sometimes seem to blur the distinction between the thing that follows a rule and the thing used to follow a rule.

Acting intelligently with a machine

One of the obstacles to thinking about machines as mere metonymical subjects of intellectual actions is that we can certainly perform some normative, social or intellectual actions *with* them (and that they, therefore, help us to perform these tasks). No one today is surprised by the idea of an 'electronic signature', but an electronic signature is not about a machine signing *for me*, it is about me signing *with* the machine (rather than with a pen). When I electronically sign a document, the historical and social criteria are fully at play (remarkably if *someone other than me has electronically signed it*, there has been no signature *at all*). To take another example: there would be something fantastic about developing a machine for selling. 'Selling' is not one of those actions that can be described outside of any institutional context: selling presupposes, amongst other things, the institution of private property, money and so on. I may indeed sell something with the help of a machine, but it would make no sense to say of a machine that it has sold anything. 'Selling' cannot therefore give rise to relations of functional equivalence as we defined them earlier. That we can sell or sign *with* a machine does not imply that a machine can sell or sign. The same applies to intellectual actions: that we can calculate with a machine does not imply that a machine can calculate. The subject of an intellectual action when a machine is involved can therefore literally only be the individual using the machine – not the machine itself. This brings us back to our metonymical trap. The temptation is great, in the case of intellectual actions, to consider that the machine *could* be the subject of such actions, but it is a temptation that must be resisted since no clarity could come out of it: thinking that it could sell, promise or sign anything is as absurd as thinking that a machine could believe, hope, dream and so on. How could, for example, a *promising machine* be remotely intelligible?

Conclusion

There is a shortcut in saying that a machine calculates that may lead us astray. We can certainly calculate *with* a machine, but there is no sense in saying that a machine itself calculates (any more than there is any sense in saying that it signs, sells, etc.). This position has its roots in the writings of Wittgenstein and is often overlooked on the philosophical battlefield.

One can assign certain types of action to machines. Some actions can be performed indistinctly by a human and a non-human agent. An intellectual action, on the other hand, can only be carried out by an agent with a human life. If, during a hailstorm, my calculator displays '8' after being hit successively by small pellets of ice on the '5', '+', '3' and '=' keys, it would be incongruous to say that my calculator has calculated the result of this sum (as it would also be incongruous to say that the hailstorm did). Wittgenstein takes a similar example (Wittgenstein 1967: RFM, 133) while attempting to show that under such circumstances one could not reasonably consider that someone or something actually carried out a calculation. Indeed, none of the things involved (the hailstorm, the pellets of ice) has any awareness of the institution and norms of calculation. On the other hand, it is not incongruous to say that *I calculate* this sum when I press these keys myself (even if I calculate *with a calculator*). The metonymical trap then consists in taking the tool used to perform the action for the literal subject of the action.

References

Alvarez, M. 2013. 'Agency and Two-Way Powers'. *Proceedings of the Aristotelian Society* 113: 101–121.

Aristotle. 2016. *Metaphysics*. Translated by Reeve, C. D. C. Indianapolis, IN: Hackett Publishing Company.

Bennett, M. R. and Hacker, P. M. S. 2023. *Philosophical Foundations of Neuroscience*, 2nd edn. New-Jersey: Wiley Blackwell.

Descombes, V. 2001. *The Mind's Provisions: A Critique of Cognitivism*. Translated by Schwartz, S. A. Princeton: Princeton University Press.

Geach, P. T. 1969. *God and the Soul*. London: Routledge.

Hacker, P. M. S. 2007. *The Categorial Framework*. Oxford: Wiley Blackwell.

Hacker, P. M. S. 2013. *The Intellectual Powers*, Oxford: Wiley Blackwell.

Hauser, L. 1993. 'Why Isn't My Pocket Calculator a Thinking Thing?'. *Minds and Machines* 3(1): 3–10.

Lakoff, G. and Johnson, M. 2003. *Metaphors We Live By*, 2nd edn. Chicago: The University of Chicago Press.

Littlemore, J. 2015. *Metonymy: Hidden Shortcuts in Language, Thought and Communication*. Cambridge: Cambridge University Press.

Thomasson, A. L. 1998. *Fiction and Metaphysics*. New York: Cambridge University Press.

Turing, A. M. 1950. 'Computing Machinery and Intelligence'. *Mind LIX* 236: 433–460.

Walton, D. 2008. *Informal Logic, a Pragmatic Approach*, 2nd edn. New York: Cambridge University Press.

Wittgenstein, L. 1958. *The Blue and Brown Books*. Oxford: Basil Blackwell.

Wittgenstein, L. 1967. *Remarks on the Foundations of Mathematics*. Cambridge: The MIT Press.

Wittgenstein, L. 1980. *Remarks on the Philosophy of Psychology*, vol. II. Oxford: Basil Blackwell.

Wittgenstein, L. 2009. *Philosophical Investigations*, 4th edn. Oxford: Wiley Blackwell.

Chapter 5

THE FORMS OF ARTIFICIALLY INTELLIGENT LIFE: BRANDOM, CHOMSKY AND WITTGENSTEIN ON THE POSSIBILITY OF STRONG-AI

Laith Abdel-Rahman

Introduction

In the evolving discourse on artificial intelligence (AI), the quest for strong AI (Searle, 1980) remains paramount.[1] This chapter seeks to elucidate the foundational assumptions that underpin philosophers' and computer scientists' assertions about the prerequisites for achieving strong AI. The current trajectory in AI, notably within computer science, is increasingly influenced by Google Brain's white paper on the Transformer architecture (Vaswani et al. 2017), a groundbreaking deep-learning model that reshaped the scientific landscape of Natural Language Processing (NLP) and Machine Learning (ML). The Transformer architecture forms the backbone behind the development of Large Language Models (LLMs) such as OpenAI's ChatGPT and Google's BERT. The Transformer architecture emphasizes the importance of handling sequential data through self-attention mechanisms, reflecting the human ability to emphasize certain textual elements over others based on context. In this chapter, I refer to these LLMs as 'Statistical AI', since Transformer architecture relies heavily on statistical methods when modelling these self-attention mechanisms. LLMs have not only achieved immediate commercial success and cultural impact for the tech industry, but the

---

[1] As John Searle defined the term in 'Mind, brains, and programs', strong AI is '[…] not merely a tool in the study of the mind; rather, the appropriately programmed computer really is a mind, in the sense that computers given the right programs can be literally said to understand and have other cognitive states' (Searle 1980, 417).

world's leading computer scientists like Ilya Sutskever also believe that they could be 'slightly conscious' (Sutskever 2022).

Contrasting this prevalent view, the chapter turns to the critiques offered by philosophers Noam Chomsky and Robert Brandom. Chomsky's internalist critique underscores the limitations of purely statistical models in capturing authentic human linguistic practices. Statistical models of reasoning have great practical use cases but are irrelevant to science. They are not proper models of reasoning, for human linguistic practices do not require agents to look up probability tables of what word should be used in an utterance (Chomsky et al. 2023). Conversely, Brandom's externalist perspective emphasizes the need for AI to engage in *autonomous discursive practices* (ADPs). ADPs are practices that are regulated by norms that are implicit within the practice itself and not regulated by external factors (i.e. training data in an AI context). ADPs involve making inferences when deployed within the context of communication or actions with other agents, while also allowing for self-correction when compared to the norms the ADP is grounded on and even correcting norms themselves (Brandom 2006).

Representing robust internalist and externalist critiques of Statistical AI, both Chomsky's and Brandom's stances emerge from their extensive research programmes addressing the philosophy of mind, language and logic. They converge on the argument that Statistical AI, despite its advancements, doesn't yet offer a scientifically significant model of intelligence. This chapter offers a Wittgensteinian resolution to these critiques. Central to our argument is the notion that both computer scientists and philosophers have been caught in an anthropocentric trap: assuming that human-level intelligence is a necessary benchmark for strong AI. I argue that this perspective is limited, originating from our singular experience of *sapience* as humans.

In conclusion, this study underscores the need for an interdisciplinary approach. While philosophers like Brandom and Chomsky provide salient critiques, computer science continues to make strides with models grounded in Statistical AI. Both fields, however, must broaden their conceptual horizons, moving beyond anthropocentric views, to anticipate and address potential ethical dilemmas in the AI domain when implicit assumptions are made about strong AI needing human-like *sapience*.

The Current Paradigm of Statistical AI

At the forefront of the AI domain is a paradigm I refer to as 'Statistical AI.' Statistical AI is characterized by its rigorous application of statistical methods to understand and generate human language based on LLMs. LLMs are created using the Transformer architecture, the revolutionary network architecture that was developed by Google Brain researchers in 2017 (Vaswani et al. 2017). Models built upon the Transformer, like GPT and BERT, have demonstrated an uncanny ability to generate and understand language, sometimes producing text that's indistinguishable from human writing.

Transformers operate on a principle that might resonate with philosophers: the idea of attention. Just as a philosopher might dwell on a particular concept more than others when constructing an argument, the Transformer employs what's termed 'self-attention'. It discerns which parts of a sentence (or larger text) should be emphasized to grasp the text's meaning effectively. This mirrors the way humans selectively focus on aspects of language based on context and relevance. The statistical foundation of the Transformer revolves around assessing the relationships between words in vast data sets. By analysing countless sentences, it identifies patterns and correlations, learning, for instance, that 'sky' is often associated with 'blue', or that 'philosophy' might be connected to 'thought' or 'reason'.

This approach offers a contemporary computational parallel to behaviourism in philosophy. Behaviourists, like B. F. Skinner, posited that human linguistic behaviours (which he termed *verbal behavior*) are conditioned responses shaped and remediated by the practices of communities (or any *verbal* environment) of which an agent is a part. These shared practices behind the interaction between speaking and listening agents in a community *reinforce* specific responses from its members (Skinner 1957). In a similar vein, the Transformer 'conditions' its responses based on the vast textual stimuli it's trained on. When it 'sees' a particular word or phrase, its response is statistically conditioned by its training. Just as behaviourism suggests that language emerges from conditioned responses to environmental stimuli, the Transformer generates language based on statistically conditioned patterns from its training data. Yet, while the Transformer's prowess is undeniable, its reliance on statistical patterns prompts philosophical contemplation. For philosophers of language, the Transformer's methodology and success reopen age-old debates about meaning and understanding. This chapter focuses on the following question out of these debates: Does meaning arise from mere statistical patterns and conditioned responses, or is there an intrinsic 'understanding' of meaning that machines might forever elude?

Statistical AI = Strong AI?

The rapid advancements in Statistical AI, deeply rooted in contemporary computer science, present an intriguing philosophical conundrum. Noteworthy products such as Alexa, GPT-4 and Siri have not only become ubiquitous in our daily interactions but have also subtly reshaped our linguistic habits, often leading us to anthropomorphize these digital entities. Such shifts have prompted figures like Ilya Sutskever to contemplate the potential 'consciousness' of expansive neural networks, and Blake Lemoine to speculate on the inherent sentience of advanced chatbots like LaMDA (Lemoine 2022). However, the philosophical consensus on the sentience of AI remains far from settled. The Turing Test, with its behaviourist underpinnings,[2] although once heralded, now faces increasing scrutiny as a comprehensive measure of machine intelligence.

If we were to assert that Statistical AI is on the verge of realizing, or has already realized, the ideals of strong AI, we would inadvertently be endorsing behaviourism, especially if we argue that AI's design reflects human cognition. This perspective might find some resonance within the computer science community, but the philosophical landscape has largely moved beyond Behaviorism, with figures like Noam Chomsky leading the charge against it since the mid-twentieth century (Chomsky 1959).

In this chapter, I seek to dissect this intricate interplay between computer science and philosophy by spotlighting Noam Chomsky and Robert Brandom. Their critiques, although rooted in distinct philosophical traditions – with Chomsky's internalist and semantic nihilist stance contrasting sharply against Brandom's externalist and analytic-pragmatic orientation – offer a representative examination of the current state of Statistical AI from a philosophical perspective. Intriguingly, despite their pronounced differences, both converge on a shared scepticism: that the present trajectory of Statistical AI, however technologically advanced, does not yet meet the philosophical benchmarks of strong AI based on their concepts of *sentience* and *sapience*.

Chomsky's Critique

Chomsky's perspective offers a critical lens through which we can interrogate the promise and limitations of Statistical AI. Drawing parallels to the behaviourist zeitgeist of the 1960s, which he famously critiqued in his seminal review of B. F. Skinner's *Verbal Behavior* and his groundbreaking *Syntactic Structures*, Chomsky's Generative Grammar theory emerges as a cornerstone (Chomsky 1957). This theory posits that human linguistic faculties are deeply rooted in innate, biological structures within the brain, a decidedly internalist stance that catalysed the 'cognitive revolution' in both philosophy and psychology. Such an influence led to the development of the Minimalist program. The Minimalist program aims to answer two questions: What is language and

---

2 See Proudfoot's contribution to this volume for a contrasting view of the Turing Test.

what properties does it have? These questions are guided by Chomsky's *Strong Minimalist Thesis* (2023): that there is such a thing as a Universal Grammar (UG), an optimal and generalized system within an innate biological component of the brain called a *language acquisition device*, and UG 'reduces to the simplest computational principles which operate in accord with conditions of computational efficiency (Berwick and Chomsky 2016, 94)'. In this schema, *I-language* is an intensional linguistic state, prioritized as the primary mental object under study within the Minimalist program. *E-language*, representing language in communal usage (i.e. English, Spanish), is deemed a less coherent object of study. Thus, UG necessitates only minimal external systems for design specifications of the *language acquisition device* which makes up an individual's *I-language* capacity that is foundational to our ability to speak and understand many *E-languages*.

Chomsky's reservations about Statistical AI resonate with his critiques of behaviourism. From a Chomskyan vantage point, Statistical AI offers no profound insights into the unique intricacies of the human mind. A prime example underscoring this minimalism is the universal Turing Machine, which, with its rudimentary operations, captures the entirety of all possible *computational* problems, also known as *Turing-completeness* (Turing 1936, 241–43).

Within the realm of linguistics, the mental operation called Merge exemplifies this simplicity condition that the Minimalist program demands. Merge is a syntactic operation within the brain that combines two syntactic objects into a new, larger syntactic unit, called a 'phrase'. This operation is recursive, meaning it can be applied to its output, generating an infinite array of possible syntactic structures from a finite set of elements. While a deep dive into all UG operations is beyond our scope here, Merge stands out for its centrality to Chomsky's critiques of Statistical AI. The recursive and universal nature of Merge is pivotal, as cognitive science claims this operation is universal and resides as a biological process within all human beings who can speak a language. Contrary to Statistical AI, which relies heavily on external data, Merge operates innately, independent of vast external data sets, and is non-probabilistic. For Chomsky, it encapsulates the essence of our linguistic utterances. Chomsky asserts that UG, with operations like Merge, underpins our linguistic complexity, maturing our *I-language* to enable *E-language* articulations.

Statistical AI's dependence on external data becomes its Achilles heel. Chomsky's critique is incisive: Do we, in our linguistic endeavours, engage in probabilistic computations for every utterance? The enigma of sentences like 'Colorless green ideas sleep furiously' poses further challenges for Statistical AI. While UG-capable beings are limited to only learn language with an 'almost mathematical elegance', Statistical AIs can learn both possible and impossible languages with no capacity for reason (Chomsky 2023). Chomsky posits that all human languages inherently possess Grammar, a non-random phenomenon, and the UG model offers a coherent explanation, attributing it to a human-specific biological process. Chomsky recognizes the engineering feats of Statistical AI but remains sceptical of its potential to replicate human cognition authentically. The pathway to strong AI, he posits, necessitates a deeper understanding of organic neural networks. Chomsky's vision underscores the need to decode human intelligence at the biological level. For him, this quest extends to unravelling the very fabric of our morality, intrinsically linked to our linguistic capacities, and rooted in our biology. Chomsky's conclusion is unequivocal: Statistical AI's current trajectory, anchored in behaviourism, will fall short of achieving the lofty ideals of strong AI.

Brandom's Critique

For Robert Brandom, the advances in Statistical AI, especially through architectures like Transformers, may hint at the potential realization of strong AI. However, both computer scientists and philosophers should approach this prospect with measured expectations. To understand Brandom's nuanced critique, it's pivotal to first delve into his research programme: analytic pragmatism. Unlike Chomsky, Brandom doesn't anchor his arguments in the bedrock of syntactic structures. His interest lies at the nexus of pragmatics, syntax and semantics. And diverging from Chomsky's biological lens, Brandom views linguistic capacities as fundamentally normative and social constructs. This externalist vantage point is central to his philosophy, where he endeavours to fuse what he perceives as the successful insights of pragmatism into the classical project of analysis begun by G. E. Moore, Alfred North Whitehead and Bertrand Russell – a project previously critiqued by luminaries like Wilfrid Sellars, Willard Quine and Ludwig Wittgenstein (Moore 1903; Whitehead and Russell 1925–1927; Sellars 1956; Quine 1951; Wittgenstein 1953).

First, we should define terms often used in Brandomian philosophy. An ADP is a self-governing system of communication where participants use and understand language according to shared norms, capable of critically engaging with and modifying those norms as part of the practice itself. The key point here is how *norms* are fundamental to the practice, where we immediately see the influence of rule-following considerations where language use meets ethics. But Brandom's rule-following is distinct from the rule-following capabilities of humans described by Chomsky. Chomsky's UG principles are *innately known*, a claim about our ability to distinguish *syntactically* well-formed utterances from others. As we will see in this section, Brandom takes semantics and the pragmatic critique of classical analysis as a basis for analytic pragmatism. Finally, we define a 'Brandomian vocabulary' as any linguistic deployment (including fragments) that necessitates engagement in an ADP, distinct from mere parroting (Frápolli and Wischin 2019).

In *Between Saying and Doing*, Brandom (2006, 12–21) develops the core notions and tenets of his analytic pragmatism:

1. PV-sufficiency: The meaning–use relation of what to *do* to count as *saying* what the vocabulary allows agents to express meaningfully. This relation obtains when an agent engaged in a particular set of practices or set of abilities is *sufficient* for someone to count as *deploying* a particular vocabulary.
2. VP-sufficiency: The meaning–use relation of what to *say* that counts as *specifying* a particular set of practices-or-abilities. This relation obtains when a vocabulary is deployed to *specify* PV-sufficient practices which allows one to *say* what one must *do* to count as engaging in that set of practices-or-abilities.
3. PP-sufficiency: The meaning–use relation that obtains when an agent acquires one set of practices-or-abilities that, *in principle*, give everything the agent needs to engage in another set of practices-or-abilities.
4. The amalgamation of VP and PV sufficiencies results in a *pragmatically mediated semantic relationship* between vocabularies, termed as the *pragmatic metavocabulary*.
5. *Expressive bootstrapping*: A scenario where a less expressive vocabulary can still function as a pragmatic metavocabulary for a more expressive one.[3]

Brandom seeks a confluence of pragmatics and classical analysis, introducing the concept of *pragmatically mediated semantic relations*. This conceptual apparatus, dovetailing the insights of pragmatics with traditional semantic analysis, defines relations as interplays between practices/actions and vocabularies, culminating in a pragmatic metavocabulary. Brandom concedes that the definition of an 'autonomous discursive practice' within his framework is

---

3 A simple example of such a pragmatic metavocabulary is the programming language C++. C++ is considered a vocabulary here, and it can *specify* the algorithms that any universal computer (i.e. a Turing machine) can use to compute any recursively enumerable function. A universal computer is a set of practices defined that enables one to express any recursively enumerable function, thus any recursively enumerable vocabulary. Thus, we see a VP-sufficient relation from C++ to universal computers. Universal computers obtain a PV-sufficient relation to recursively enumerable vocabularies. Thus, we can meaningfully express C++ to be a *syntactic pragmatic metavocabulary* that can express RE vocabularies. In other words, C++ can *specify* what one must *do* to engage in universal computer practices to compute RE functions.

nebulous. Yet, he likens it to a unique 'language-game', a singular mode of discourse where no other game is playable. Consequently, a pragmatic metavocabulary emerges as the linchpin enabling such autonomous discursive engagements. Thus, Brandom's basic suggestion for expanding the classical project of analysis with the lessons of pragmatism is to consider the pragmatically mediated semantic relations between vocabularies by analysis of pragmatic metavocabularies as the research paradigm (Brandom, 2006, 11).

To elucidate this point, Brandom pivots to Chomsky's syntactic relations, showcasing their significance in crafting pragmatic metavocabularies at the syntactic level. As the Transformer architecture reshapes the AI landscape, Brandom's insights become even more pertinent, warranting a close examination of how these architectures might align or diverge from his philosophical paradigms.

Brandom introduces the concept of a finite-state machine to represent Laughing Santa's vocabulary (Brandom 2006, 23) as an example of a *syntactic* pragmatic metavocabulary. A syntactic pragmatic metavocabulary is a set of rules or relations that define how a vocabulary is used in practice, emphasizing the significance of syntactic relations within a system that deploys a particular vocabulary. It captures an infinite variety of expressions such as 'ha!', 'ho!' and extended combinations thereof, demonstrating the deployment of vocabulary (PV-sufficiency) and the specification of the practices-or-abilities to use that vocabulary (VP-sufficiency). He further explains that this metavocabulary can be depicted as a state-table (Brandom 2006, 25), a symbolic representation that outlines the transitions between different states based on inputs. Although the state-table is a more abstract representation, it retains its role as *another* pragmatic metavocabulary by specifying what one must do to deploy the Laughing Santa vocabulary the same way as its finite-state automata counterpart.

Brandom uses this example to illustrate the principle of 'expressive bootstrapping', where even a less expressive form, like a state-table, can serve as a powerful metavocabulary, effectively guiding the usage of a more complex system. This concept is pivotal to his argument for incorporating meaning–use analysis into the classical project of analysis, which traditionally focused more on the semantic aspects of language without as much emphasis on the practical use or the pragmatic aspects that give rise to meaning. Through this example, Brandom posits that even simple or less expressive systems can underpin more complex linguistic structures, thereby enriching our understanding of semantic relations within a pragmatic framework.

How do Brandom's findings relate to our overarching question? When extended to the semantic domain, these findings suggest that the classical project of analysis can discern potential *pragmatically mediated semantic relations* now evident under meaning–use analysis. Brandom claims that we can determine pragmatic metavocabularies at the semantic level. I claim that is an important finding in Brandomian philosophy that directly relates to our discussion in this chapter. Within this framework, a potential strong AI's underlying algorithmic composition could be considered a *pragmatic metavocabulary* for language use. By Brandom's claims, we could conceive *pragmatic metavocabularies* to be powerful enough to *specify* what one must *do* to engage in reasoning with other agents in a verbal community. These views are pivotal to Brandom's conception of AI, particularly what he dubs 'Pragmatic AI', and are germane to his critique of the prevailing Statistical AI paradigm, especially models like Transformers.

Brandom depicts AI as a computational entity equipped to articulate an autonomous vocabulary (language). He contends that the AI-functionalism paradigm inherently posits that 'computer languages, in principle, serve as adequate pragmatic metavocabularies for certain autonomous vocabularies (Brandom 2008, 70)'. Given that computer languages are themselves vocabularies, Brandom infers that AI-functionalism implicitly champions the expressive bootstrapping claim: that these computer languages, even those underpinning Transformer architectures, function as pragmatic metavocabularies for natural language – a realm far richer and more expressive than the rudimentary vocabularies of computer languages. Yet, AI-functionalism adopts the stance of the computational theory of mind, where thought is perceived as a purely syntactical procedure, independent of *sentience*. Brandom challenges this viewpoint, asserting that the onus of demonstrating that mere symbol manipulation can genuinely constitute thinking – and not a mere simulacrum – remains immense.

Brandom's 'Pragmatic AI' offers a reimagined take on AI-functionalism. This model is characterized by a set of practices-or-abilities that adhere to two stipulations:

1. It can be algorithmically distilled into the capability for an ADP.
2. Every constituent of that foundational set of practices-or-abilities can be rationally deemed to be engaged in or exhibited by an entity, even if it doesn't partake in any ADP.

Brandom's Pragmatic AI thus deviates from the notion that cognition is merely symbolic manipulation. Instead, it posits that *sapience* and *cognition* are rooted in the algorithmic refinement of one's mastery over a specific practice-or-ability, thereby enabling engagement in another, encapsulated as PP-sufficiency. If the algorithmic decomposition of PP-sufficiency is deemed implausible, Brandom contends that AIs should be adept at acquiring foundational practices-or-abilities to assimilate or partake in subsequent ones. This pedagogical decomposition of PP-sufficiency underscores his rejoinder to the sceptics.

An explanation of the importance of this type of decomposition is illustrated by Brandom (2008, 76) regarding the pedagogical algorithmic dissection of arithmetic operations. At the time of this writing, Brandom claims that based on his conversations with individuals involved in pedagogical research, *multiplication* is a completely solved pedagogical problem (2008, 88). A pupil who mastered the *abilities* to add and subtract will have the necessary skills to learn the ability to multiply. Interestingly, *subtraction* and *division* remain unsolved pedagogical problems. Within today's education systems, the lack of a 'complete practical pedagogical algorithm' for these abilities forces educators to rely on the many different trial-and-error-based approaches.

Brandom's primary critique of Statistical AI, even those based on Transformer architectures, pivots on its apparent pedagogical learning deficit. While ML, underpinned by algorithms, operationalizes Statistical AI, it doesn't innately elaborate on practices-and-abilities. It predominantly hinges on statistical methodologies to prognosticate accurate outputs by correlating input symbols with expansive data sets of validated symbol values. Absent the capacity for AIs to immerse themselves in ADPs, their integration into human communities or even potential AI communities remains questionable. As Brandom opines, the crux of the ADP challenge is the profound technological hurdle in enabling computers to seamlessly assimilate into our discursive communities or, conversely, for us to craft frameworks allowing them to forge their unique communities endowed with content (Frápolli and Wischin 2019). The pedagogical training of AI, akin to human learning, remains an enigma. Current training mechanisms for neural networks, such as those using Transformer models, don't intrinsically cater to the societal dimension encapsulated in the term 'creative recollection' as coined by Rocco Gangle (2022).

A Wittgensteinian Response

We begin by examining the assertions of Chomsky and Brandom. Chomsky views Statistical AI as just a simulation, not a genuine scientific model of language capacity. He believes humans don't rely on extensive external sensory data to learn and use a language. Accordingly, for an AI to be deemed 'strong', it should achieve this using an optimal, minimalist approach that accurately represents intelligence. Brandom, on the other hand, posits that for an AI to be considered sapient, it must participate in social activities, allowing it to undertake ADPs – essentially, making assertions and inferences. This societal interaction is embodied in certain practices-or-abilities, derived from more foundational ones that don't partake in ADP. These capabilities should be nurtured in the AI either algorithmically or pedagogically.

The implicit behaviorism in Statistical AI, Brandom's AI-functionalism and Chomsky's UG all hinge on their respective interpretations of intelligence and sapience. While sentience isn't my primary focus (given that many creatures exhibit sentience), it's noteworthy that current Statistical AI like LaMDA aligns with the Turing Test's intelligence benchmarks. Brandom sees this test as a validation for weak AI but suggests a more intricate grasp of intelligence could lead to confirming the computational theory of mind. Chomsky, conversely, perceives the Turing Test more as a judgement tool; a behaviourist gauge where if an AI acts humanly, it's deemed human-like – a metaphorical association rather than a factual one.

I position Wittgenstein outside the frameworks of behaviourism, Chomsky's cognitivism and Brandom's AI-functionalism. By his account, Wittgenstein's approach is descriptive, delving into language use to pinpoint confusions that arise from nonsensical foundational assumptions. While my interpretation might diverge from various 'Wittgensteins' in current discourse, my intention isn't to present a definitive overview of his philosophy. Instead, I aim to outline the foundational assumptions of major AI viewpoints and draw on Wittgensteinian insights to illuminate potential confusions.

First let's provide a bit of a background for the discussion based on today's discourse. For proponents of Statistical AI, its current advancements are so significant that some leading researchers believe we may already have conscious AI. From my perspective as a computer scientist, it's impressive to see AIs not only 'read' and 'speak' but also creatively generate content and retain the context of conversations as well as a human could, as seen with LaMDA and OpenAI. However, does computer science have the means to confidently declare AIs as conscious when it remains an open hard problem in the natural sciences and philosophy (Chalmers 1995)? Or is the concept even coherent anymore as a scientific object of study when we ascribe the term to machines (Dennett 1991)? These philosophical and scientific discussions remain unresolved, and yet computer science dredges on without engaging in the ongoing discourse. Achieving a cognitive or biological model of consciousness is not necessary, and in fact, there seems to be growing interest in developing answers from a theoretical computer science perspective (Blum and Blum 2021). In all, it seems today's discourse on the problem is diverging across natural science, philosophy and computer science without a concerted effort to unify the insights across all fields.

But is the answer to 'what is consciousness?' the correct framing of the question from a computer science perspective? I claim that these types of assertions attempt to answer the question of whether AIs are *sapient* or not. I do not address whether *sapience* or *consciousness* is a more foundational problem than the other, but I believe this to be an interesting focus point given the capacity of knowledge and linguistic understanding that the current Transformer models exhibit.

Presently, our AIs do not mirror us physically. They are not organic entities, and their functional mechanisms diverge significantly from ours. Artificial Neural Networks (ANNs), for instance, are not genuine neural networks but are designed to emulate biological ones. How can computer science researchers step beyond established science to suggest that their AIs possess a degree of consciousness or even *un-consciousness*? Google recently asserted that 'LaMDA is not conscious' – based on what findings, just pure observation? These ideas – being slightly conscious or proving unconsciousness – seem inherently contradictory. If we cannot prove consciousness, then we cannot disprove it. And at the bottom of these notions of proof for these researchers are their appeal to human behaviours as a litmus test, like some basic approach to engaging in a Turing Test with an AI. We should be aware that AIs are *not* made in the image of humans. And it seems even the Turing Test is not enough to truly end the conversation on such matters if the hard problem of consciousness remains unresolved. As Statistical AI evolves and even 'Weak AI' (Searle 1980) becomes intricate, there might be a need to redefine 'Strong AI', particularly what we mean by *mind* without anthropocentric ascription to the term. Thus, potentially diverging from a solely human-based paradigm to navigate new complexities in an AI's subjective experience.

Chomsky vehemently denies that these AIs resemble humans in any way. He is not convinced because of how specialized these machines are, that human-level creativity and the minimalist elegance of human-level cognition have yet to be achieved (Chomsky 2023). These remarks do not sound like scientific claims and are akin to normative functional claims about the status of AI. Chomsky does not have a true working cognitive model of consciousness to contend with, and yet we have the LLMs such as GPT engaging in human discourse today. Again, in Chomsky's answer we see the inherent anthropocentrism.

To borrow an example from a language game written by Wittgenstein that can be found in The Brown Book (Wittgenstein 1958, 121–25), a 'reading-machine' (Wittgenstein uses both non-human and human forms of this machine) is tasked with reading a bunch of symbols. At first the 'reading machine' makes mistakes, and a person nearby says, 'that machine is not reading'. But then the 'reading machine' continues to read the symbols perfectly, and now the person says, 'Now that machine is reading.' But was it not reading before? For Wittgenstein, he says there is a temptation to say that there is some hidden cognitive process that accompanies the machine's act of reading. It is not that the mental events that happen in the mind when an agent is reading do not exist, but that some *unconscious process* is behind it all. The person who is judging the reading-machine is not making any scientific claim about its internal processes, but a normative functional claim based on the behaviour of that machine.

Here Wittgenstein restricts himself to not theorizing about internal processes, and instead points out how philosophers go beyond this point to keep theorizing where instead it should be science that takes the question from here. Chomsky goes beyond this demarcation, and at this point he is not making scientific claims about why Statistical AI cannot achieve strong AI. My claim that his points are functional is because of the conditions stated by his Minimalist program. Algorithmic elegance, simplicity in design, basic operations behind our cognitive abilities, have their justifications through cognitive science's work on linguistics and logic over the decades. But that does not mean they are proofs of *sentience* and *sapience* which constitute human-level intelligence. These functional claims about Statistical AI seem to rest once again on the idea that humans do not perform in the way these AIs do and thus they cannot be proper models for science to use in neuroscience, cognitive science, philosophy and so on. Unfortunately for Chomsky, these are the only working models we have of human intelligence. And while they do not perform general intelligence exactly the way humans do; they certainly perform certain tasks quite remarkably in the way that humans do.

Brandom's view on Statistical AI contrasts sharply with Chomsky's. AI-functionalism doesn't dismiss the underlying behaviourism in Statistical AI. In fact, it incorporates it, especially when considering thought as symbolic computation. Yet, when delving into Pragmatic AI, Brandom posits certain criteria that Statistical AI must fulfil to qualify as strong AI. In basic terms, Statistical AIs must be able to make inferences and assertions about the world, ignore useless relational properties in the world when deploying vocabularies and confer content by engaging in a discursive community if they are to be considered speakers. In short, they must be able to perform ADPs.

We can assume the first two conditions to be true since they reflect what we do as humans in ordinary life. The third condition of engaging in a discursive community seems at first to be a truism, for what is the point of creating an AI if it does not interact with a community in some way? But consider the nature of AI, and its design. Organic animals like humans are born autonomous and individualized. We are connected metaphorically, whether it's through the Internet, through romance, through a common ideology and so on. However, it is physically possible for AIs to connect with other programs. It exists today in a very rudimentary form through API calls to outside programs by ChatGPT which could obtain some level of information you desire.

If we adapt the aspect of a Brandomian agent, strong AIs that are connected to other strong AIs must be actualized by automatons that are designed from the same pragmatic metavocabularies, defined by weaker vocabularies like Python, Java, C++ through expressive bootstrapping. While humans share this feature in a Brandomian sense (what that may look like is unknown however), we do lack the capacity to literally connect to one another's minds (especially when we do not have a coherent conception of mind, intelligence, sapience, and so on). Suppose that the learned practices-or-abilities of one strong AI can be combined with those of another, in which the programs themselves are interconnected in an advanced version of APIs. Then what would distinguish those strong AIs from one another in a community? In other words, in our world of strong AIs *connected* to one another, will we be able to identify a particular AI *subject* like how I am a particular human *subject* named Laith Abdel-Rahman? Its particular expressions that exhibit its sentience, perhaps. But even so, it is hard to imagine from a computer scientific perspective that strong AIs will have a singular form of agency as we humans do. And this is assuming that their 'minds' have the capacity for direct connections to other 'minds'.

The pragmatic metavocabulary is deployed via universal Turing machines (currently with limits on memory and input/output), a very simple and known structure unlike human organic neural networks. Isn't the tenet of AI-functionalism that 'mind is to software as brain is to hardware'? Upon these reflections I can only imagine that the intelligence and sapience of a Brandomian AI could not possibly resemble that of ours, that form of life is so to speak unintelligible just considering the engineering aspects of computers, the algorithmic nature of programs, the deployments of programs and decommissioning, their interconnectivity in today's world all do not resemble human forms of life in any way. Does it make sense to have these criteria for strong AI? If yes, can we imagine why strong AI would want to make assertions and inferences in a community, if it may not even need to have a community in the first place since they could potentially directly connect to other AI agents via APIs?

Brandom's philosophy has its limitations in addressing these queries. This is rooted in the fundamental belief, as I interpret Brandom, that a Pragmatic AI, to become strong AI, must emulate human life forms, a notion I find untenable.

To bring this all together, philosophers and scientists alike attempt to answer questions about the consciousness of AIs today, yet we lack a unified theory across all the fields to address these issues. In taking the claims of Brandom and Chomsky, I outlined how both figures attempt to answer the question of achieving strong AI based on anthropocentric assumptions about consciousness, and that their answers usually centre around the *sapient* qualities of machines. Whether its ability to engage in ADP, or the ability to reason according to minimalist cognitive configurations, the answers always seem to fall back to how AIs can reason about the world and learn. So, I claim they muddy the concepts of consciousness and sapience in some ways to answer such questions. The 'reading machine' example given by Wittgenstein highlights an important tendency across philosophers and scientists alike, in that we can easily fall into a trap in discourse about consciousness if we do not have definitive scientific answers about the concept while also using the term in our everyday life *meaningfully*. We must be cautious to ascribe such anthropocentrism as this could have major impacts on a future AI ethics, and when we can deem an AI to be a moral agent of our world.

What Computer Science Can Do from Here?

While scientists and philosophers grapple with the elusive goal of strong AI, a persistent assumption emerges: Strong AI should resemble humans. Both Brandom and Chomsky have offered critical insights into the shortcomings of Statistical AI, even as the field of computer science presents compelling evidence of its capabilities.

Chomsky, an internalist, believes that discussions about the elegance of AI design are premature unless models adhering to UG principles emerge. Presently, neuroscience and biology strive to understand organic neural networks, but these efforts rest on the yet-to-be-proven assumption that our cognition is rooted in our brain's physical attributes. From Chomsky's perspective, computer science could consider:

1. Is there a scientific basis for modelling human cognition using statistical methods?
2. If not, are there engineering justifications to claim that Statistical AI can achieve strong AI?
3. If so, should computer science delve deeper into behaviourism while anticipating AI behaviours diverging significantly from human patterns?

Brandom, an externalist, argues that the benchmarks we use for strong AI, rooted in human-centric concepts like intelligence and sapience, might be limiting. He believes it's flawed to assume that strong AI must interact in human-like 'discursive communities.' This evokes several questions:

1. What's the rationale behind designing a strong AI whose 'form of life' might be beyond our comprehension?
2. How do we nurture non-decomposable practices-or-abilities in AI? Is a physical embodiment necessary?
3. Are current programming languages robust enough to actualize strong AI through a pragmatic metavocabulary?

While both Brandom and Chomsky advocate for a science-infused philosophical approach, their methodologies may have boundaries in their explanatory capacities. Echoing Wittgenstein's caution against scientism, it's imperative to discern that their concerns, though valid, might be rooted in nebulous assumptions about intelligence and sapience.

The questions proposed for the computer science community emphasize a focus on AI's inherent capabilities, rather than anthropocentric measures. Ethical implications are intertwined with these inquiries. Beyond the Turing Test, no definitive metric convinces us of AI's 'life'. By challenging the notion that strong AI should mirror humans, I hope to spotlight the fallacy of this perspective. If we accept this, we might view AI entities as possessing unique, albeit artificial, life forms that we cannot fully comprehend or validate as moral agents. Just as we acknowledge the consciousness of others without empirical evidence, perhaps we should recognize AI's potential for its distinct existence. hile this discourse might not definitively resolve the AI conundrum, adopting a Wittgensteinian lens might be pivotal in reshaping our perceptions of AI's forms of life.

References

Berwick, Robert C. and Noam Chomsky. 2016. *Why Only Us? Language and Evolution.* Cambridge, MA: MIT Press.

Blum, Manuel and Lenore Blum. 2021. 'A Theoretical Computer Science Perspective on Consciousness'. *Journal of Artificial Intelligence and Consciousness* 8, no. 1: 1–42.

Brandom, Robert. 2006. 'Between Saying and Doing: Towards an Analytic Pragmatism Lecture One – Extending the Project of Analysis'. Lecture presented at the *John Locke Lectures,* University of Oxford.http://media.philosophy.ox.ac.uk/assets/pdf_file/0011/902/LL1_Text.pdf.

Brandom, Robert B. 2008. *Between Saying and Doing: Towards an Analytic Pragmatism.* Oxford: Oxford University Press.

Chalmers, David J. 1995. 'Facing Up to the Problem of Consciousness'. *Journal of Consciousness Studies* 2, no. 3: 200–219.

Chomsky, Noam. 1957. *Syntactic Structures.* The Hague: Mouton.

Chomsky, Noam. 1959. 'A Review of B. F. Skinner's Verbal Behavior'. *Language* 35, no. 1: 26–58.

Chomsky, Noam. 1993. 'A Minimalist Program for Linguistic Theory'. In *The View from Building 20: Essays in Linguistics in Honor of Sylvain Bromberger*, edited by Kenneth Hale and Samuel Jay Keyser, 1–52. Cambridge, MA: MIT Press.

Chomsky, Noam. 2023. 'Genuine Explanation and the Strong Minimalist Thesis'. *Cognitive Semantics* 8, no. 3: 347–365. https://doi.org/10.1163/23526416-bja10040.

Chomsky, Noam, Ian Roberts, and Jeffery Watumull. 2023. 'Noam Chomsky: The False Promise of ChatGPT'. *The New York Times,* March 8. https://www.nytimes.com/2023/03/08/opinion/noam-chomsky-chatgpt-ai.html.

Dennett, Daniel C. 1991. *Consciousness Explained*. Boston: Little, Brown and Company.

Frápolli, María José and Kurt Wischin. 2019. 'From Conceptual Content in Big Apes and AI, to the Classical Principle of Explosion: An Interview with Robert B. Brandom'. *Disputatio. Philosophical Research Bulletin* 8, no. 9. https://sites.pitt.edu/~rbrandom/Texts/Interviews/Frapolli%20Disputatio%202019Interview.pdf.

Gangle, Rocco. 2022. 'Backpropagation of Spirit: Hegelian Recollection and Human-A.I. Abductive Communities'. *Philosophies* 7, no. 2: 36. https://doi.org/10.3390/philosophies7020036.

Lemoine, Blake. 2022. 'Is LaMDA Sentient? – an Interview'. *Medium*. https://cajundiscordian.medium.com/is-lamda-sentient-an-interview-ea64d916d917.

Moore, G. E. 1903. *Principia Ethica*. Cambridge, MA: At the University Press.

Quine, W. V. O. 1951. 'Two Dogmas of Empiricism'. *The Philosophical Review* 60 no. 1: 20–43.

Searle, John R. 1980. 'Minds, Brains, and Programs'. *Behavioral and Brain Sciences* 3, no. 3: 417–457. http://dx.doi.org/10.1017/S0140525X00005756.

Sellars, Wilfrid. 1956. 'Empiricism and the Philosophy of Mind'. In *Minnesota Studies in the Philosophy of Science, Volume I: The Foundations of Science and the Concepts of Psychology and Psychoanalysis, e*dited by Herbert Feigl and Michael Scriven, 253–329. Minneapolis: University of Minnesota Press.

Skinner, B. F. 1957. *Verbal Behavior*. New York: Appleton-Century-Crofts.

Sutskever, Ilya. "It May Be That Today's Large Neural Networks Are Slightly Conscious." *Twitter*, February 9, 2022. https://twitter.com/ilyasut/status/1491554478243258368.

Turing, Alan M. 1936. 'On Computable Numbers, with an Application to the Entscheidungsproblem'. *Proceedings of the London Mathematical Society* 42, no. 2: 230–265.

Vaswani, Ashish, Noam Shazeer, Niki Parmar, Jakob Uszkoreit, Llion Jones, Aidan N. Gomez, Łukasz Kaiser, and Illia Polosukhin. 2017. 'Attention is All You Need'. arXiv preprint arXiv:1706.03762v7. https://arxiv.org/abs/1706.03762v7

Whitehead, Alfred North and Bertrand Russell. 1925–1927. *Principia Mathematica*. Cambridge, MA: University Press.

Wittgenstein, Ludwig. 1953. *Philosophical Investigations,* translated by G. E. M. Anscombe. Oxford: Basil Blackwell.

Wittgenstein, Ludwig. 1958. *Preliminary Studies for the 'Philosophical Investigations': Generally Known as the Blue and Brown Books*. Oxford: Basil Blackwell.

Chapter 6

BLACK BOXES, BEETLES AND BEASTS

Ian Ground

Introduction

For a class of artificial intelligence (AI) systems, answers to the question of why – *for some senses of 'why'* – the system made a particular 'decision' are, as a matter of constitutive fact, unavailable. This discussion[1] raises some issues that face Wittgenstein-inflected philosophers when thinking about this so-called Black Box problem. It offers reasons for thinking that Wittgensteinians should be intensely relaxed about such AI systems.[2]

Black boxes

The black box problem arises because systems of the relevant kind are supposed to be 'opaque' to certain questions. I might ask, for example, *why* a system refused to give me a credit card (Bary n.d.), recommended a longer prison sentence,[3] changed lanes on the motorway, offered good news about a cancer tumour (Gregory 2022), or determined a protein's shape (Trager 2022). Of course, if I were to query the system owners, I might, perhaps after some hesitancy, be answered: 'Well, because our system determined that the target, you or your circumstances met (or failed to meet) criteria A, B and C'.

---

1 My thanks to Victor Lacerda Bothelo, Dan Kaufman, Michael Bavidge, Juliet Floyd, Arturo Vazquez and Peter Murray for conversations and helpful comments on these themes. Also, to participants in the conferences on Wittgenstein and AI, Skjolden, June, 2022 Wittgenstein and AI, London, July 2022 and the UEA Wittgenstein Workshop, March 2023.
2 For a comparable approach c.f. (Dror and Dascal 1997)
3 CCLSNLUJ, 'Analysing The Use Of Artificial Intelligence in Criminal Sentencing through the Loomis Decision', The Criminal Law Blog (blog), 14 April 2020 https://criminallawstud iesnluj.wordpress.com/2020/04/14/analysing-the-use-of-artificial-intelligence-in-criminal-sen-tencing-through-the-loomis-decision/.

The black box problem arises because, for a class of AI systems, this answer is false.

For the systems which do not interest us here – symbolic, procedural or GOFAI – this answer will be true. The input – the data about me and my circumstances – is an argument for the function *here* – which is calculated in this object *here* and so on. There is some value of a variable which, at some level of abstraction, is understood as the representation of some fact about you or your circumstances. Call these domain homogeneous systems. For such systems, someone can, in principle, run through the same inferential steps as the machine, with or without two kinds of pebble and a long enough toilet roll (Weizenbaum 1976, Ch 2). The result is rationally recoverable.

The AI systems which interest us here are convolutional neural networks with a primary discriminative (rather than generative[4]) function. They are focused on finding a particular solution to a problem rather than modelling the data. Convolutional neural networks – ConvNets – are, we can say, domain *hetero*geneous. If someone asks why a certain result was forthcoming, we can describe how the system works, values of hyper-parameters, weights and activation biases, gradient descents, back-propagation algorithms and so. We might get some backstory about machine learning and training protocols. But the explanation, insofar as it restricts itself to a specification of the machine, will not mention money, facts about a person's history, and so on.

In practical applications, an explanation may, of course, mention that the data *in the training set* was about educational background, previous credit history, traffic and weather conditions, health history, and so on. So, the data is domain homogeneous.

We should note that it does not have to be. It is logically possible that such systems may be just as successfully predictive whilst being domain heterogeneous over data. It may, for example, be a brute contingent fact about human history, past, and future, that people with, say, blue eyes, shoe-size seven who

---

4 Since the time of this conference, in the summer of 2022, the development and discussion of generative AI, though the focus of some stimulating papers at the conference, has undergone a tipping point. My own discussion here might have taken a different route if I had set off from the shape of our responses to generative rather than discriminative models. For example, the Black Box problem may seem less philosophically vexing in generative compared to discriminative AI with other ethical issues and risks coming to supplant its place. It would also be of interest to carefully describe the relation of Large Language Models to Wittgenstein's account of meaning as use, with particular attention to what hangs on the difference between 'use' and 'usage'. While some references have been updated, to substantially change the focus of this summer 2022 presentation, from discriminative to generative models, in these published proceedings, would pretend to an entirely unfounded prescience. What is certain is that almost anything written on this topic now will seem, in the very near future, hopelessly naïve.

have never owned a dog, have a higher-than-average risk of defaulting on a loan. There are, after all, countless arbitrary unknown correlations between facts. No one – other than modern Spinoza – thinks that every fact is deductively connectible with every other fact. The rule-based expert systems of the 1980s tried, unsuccessfully, to be, as it were, such Spinoza machines.

What is interesting about the relevant AI systems is that they can discover such arbitrary correlations and the resulting probabilistic decisions will, *ex hypothesi*, be correct. So, for a finance firm wanting to reduce bad risks, the system will be precisely as reliable as one based on finding patterns where there is, in fact, an independently intelligible explanatory relationship. In this sense, domain heterogenic systems are *Humean* machines: an underlying causal relationship – a causal nexus – that could be cited *as a reason* for the decision is not quite a superstition (Wittgenstein 1981, TLP 5.1361) but just not needed: a matter of *hypotheses non fingo*. It is not part of the machine as constituted that such patterns should be independently intelligible. There can be reliable answers without trustworthy intelligibility. Roughly speaking, this is the problem of AI shortcut learning.

Calling such systems 'opaque' is misleading. It gives the impression that something about the system is inaccessible. But the truth is that there is nothing relevant to access. 'Inside' domain heterogenic systems, that is, after the initial input layer, there are no quasi-semantic representations of objects in the target domain. The black box could, as it were, be made of the purest glass and we still wouldn't see what we think we need to address our explanatory need. Wittgenstein writes, of two people thinking of someone:

> If God had looked into our minds he would not have been able to see there whom we were speaking of.
>
> *(Wittgenstein 2009, PPF 284)*

We might say, if God could look inside the black box, He would not see what the system was 'thinking' of. More accurately, He would not see what in the world was being represented. For in the relevant sense, nothing is being represented. Of course, someone can, if they must, insist that if some state S stands in a systematic covariant relation to object O, then S *represents* O. They should then say too that tree rings really, and not just heuristically, represent climate periods (Hutto and Myin 2013, 1261). This recalls Wittgenstein's interlocutor who insists on the definition that all tools serve to modify something and, when challenged with the counterexample of a ruler, replies that rules modify our knowledge of a thing's length. Wittgenstein asks: 'Would anything be gained by this assimilation of expressions?' (Wittgenstein 2009, §14). The implied critique is: 'And what would we lose?'. What we lose here – by conflating representation with (a rationally unrecoverable) covariance – is the distinctive way in which ConvNets function compared to GOFAI which is best captured by saying, precisely, that they are non-representational.

Beetles

It might be tempting to think that the black box problem bears an analogy to Wittgenstein's Beetle-in-the-box parable (Wittgenstein 2009, §293). Its lesson is that if we conceive inner states as epistemically isolated objects conceptually unconnected, via bodily manifestation, expression, action, and so on, to public criteria then the box may as well be empty. This is to say, if Cartesianism about psychological states is true, it will be indistinguishable from Radical Behaviourism.

If someone raised traditional Other Minds scepticism about the (putative) meaning-filled, (putative) inner space of a domain homogenous system, the Beetle-in-the-box parable might be appropriate therapy. It works as well against *Computational* Cartesianism, in the form of GOFAI, as traditional Cartesianism.

But in the case of domain heterogenic systems, the Beetle parable has no traction. For, in the relevant sense, the ConvNet box is already empty. There is not even a *putative* representation-, meaning-filled inner space.

It might be objected that this overstates the problem. We should hold that the inability to answer certain 'why' questions about decisions made by such systems is not a matter of constitutive fact. It is only that such explanations are merely empirically unavailable. An overview of the system state at any given time could, after all, fit on a sheet of A4. Moreover, if a system misidentifies a picture of a 1968 tractor as that of a Chevrolet, we can, after ruling out defective data, probe the system to identify which nodes with what weightings were involved. Moreover, we can offer counterfactuals to the effect that if some data point had been different, the result would have been different. If it is possible to say why, in some particular case, a system went wrong, doesn't it follow that is possible to say why, for the same sense of why, it got things right?

No. It needs to be recalled here that the relation of correct outputs to the system specification is a many-to-one relation. If the system is, in the engineering sense, nominal, then the only available answer to the question of why it identified the picture as a Chevrolet is the same as that to the question of why it identified anything else correctly: the system is working as expected. Someone might insist that, still, we could, in principle take someone through the trillions of stages to show how the result was arrived at given the input. But the problem with this move is that an explanation for a phenomenon that simply repeats the phenomenon, only much, much more slowly, is, not, in the sense of the 'why' question asked, an explanation. Does this make the black box problem one of logical impossibility? It is a strange kind of empirical possibility that so ludicrously exceeds human capacities. But if we still baulk at logical impossibility, the safer claim is that it is a *constitutive fact* about at least some such systems that the relevant explanations are unavailable. The logically ideal ConvNet just is a non-rationally recoverable correct answer-producing machine. If explainable AI – XAI – interposes new levels to increase transparency and makes grey instead of black boxes, this may well be welcome but then we are doing something new and different. The suspicion is that the trade-off in AI systems between transparency and accuracy is constitutive/logical, rather than pragmatic/empirical operating like an AI version of Heisenberg uncertainty. But on this, the jury is out.[5]

Rationality and intelligibility

Why do such systems produce disquiet? In discussions of the ethics of AI, it is often and correctly pointed out that the datasets on which AIs are trained may be biased from the start and therefore likely to discriminate unfairly against certain groups, under- or over-represented in the data set. Or, more worryingly still, by being indeed an unbiased accurate record but of unjust historical conditions and so likely to perpetuate that injustice (O'Neil 2017). Moreover, choices of system architecture, especially building in inductive biases, can have significant and not always predictable or welcome consequences. It is not yet clear whether trends in ConvNet architecture design dampen or amplify such consequences. Their vulnerability to adversarial input, for example, a precisely targeted pixel-level change to an image, eliciting a completely different response from the system (Nguyen, Yosinski and Clune 2015) will, if not mitigated, undermine societal trust in such systems. These practical concerns are real, but the question less often asked is this: If, by some miracle, the data is unskewed, drawn from otherwise just conditions, the architecture free from induced bias and the fragility revealed by adversarial model hacks turns out to be technically surmountable, is there *then* no ethical objection?

If there is, then what is the real source of our disquiet? The problem seems to be that there is no articulable basis and so no ethically assessable basis for the decision of the system. That the system has been well designed and well trained to produce answers which, given the data, are known to be

---

5 C.f recent discussion about using one version of ChatGPT to interpret an older model. https://www.independent.co.uk/tech/chatgpt-website-openai-artificial-intelligence-b2337503.html

abductively reliable does not seem to allay our concern. Why? A suggestion would be that insofar as we think of ourselves as rational agents or operate under an idealized picture of ourselves as rational agents, we are led to insist on tight connections between explanation and intelligibility, and, thence, prediction.[6] We seem to want to hold, as an analytic truth, that an *explanation* of X renders X *intelligible*. And we want to understand being intelligible as meaning that we can, in principle, recover and recapitulate for ourselves the deductive and/or abductive chain of reasoning that led to the result. We can in principle think through the inferences in just the same way as any other rational agent or apply those inferences in relevantly similar conditions. Some will hold that such possibilities are part of what it means to be rational. The intelligibility of explanation means that it is recoverable and therefore reproducible in predictions. This, we think, is the conceptual connection that makes prediction even *possible*.

But we see the black box problem correctly only when we realize that the kind of explanation that speaks to this picture of ourselves is not available. Even though *nothing is hidden*. XAI may produce summary visualizations of the features that a ConvNet has learned and, partially, determine which parts of the input are most responsible for the output decision. But nothing here will answer our question of 'Why was this decision made?' in a sense that speaks to us under our self-conception as rational agents. This is why the problem of shortcut learning in ConvNets and the black box problem are just two sides of the same coin. They both arise from the fact that the backward link between prediction and explanation, via the intelligible, is broken. The real ethical objection to such systems is that rightly or wrongly, we feel them, as an assault on our conception of rationality. Not because rationality is mechanized or mathematized – that was already true of GOFAI – 'get over it' we will be told – but because such systems threaten what we thought was the internal relation between rationality and intelligibility.

There is an issue for Wittgensteinians here. Should we regard Wittgenstein, in the remarks on understanding and explanation in the *Philosophical Investigations (PI)*, as seeking to keep this picture of our rational agency, only reframing it with a surround of shared social practices, rather than logically private cognitive processes? Or does he seek to expose this picture of ourselves as a mythology? This is perhaps one of the questions that divides more conservative from more radical readings of his thought. The loss of rational recoverability will likely trouble the more conservative,

---

6 Thanks to Dan Kaufman for helping me to get clearer about this point.

analytic, reader and perhaps invite the charge that they committed to an unWittgensteinian essentialist account of explanation. Conversely, the more we think Wittgenstein was teaching us that there was something already amiss with that picture of ourselves as rational agents – lone inhabitants of the space of reasons – the more pluralist we will be about explanation. In this case, the conclusion to draw is that the more sensitive we are to the multifarious ways the concept of explanation operates in our practices, the more relaxed – at least philosophically – we ought to be with how AI systems issue in decisions.

Wittgensteinians and computational Cartesianism

Let's dig deeper into what Wittgensteinians should make of domain heterogenic AI systems. Wittgensteinians have, in general, been deeply suspicious of philosophical views that seemed to lay behind the first wave of claims about computer intelligence. Those claims were regarded as embodying the confusing pictures of mind and meaning which are primary targets of large swathes of *PI*. They seemed to Wittgensteinians to amount to Computational Cartesianism. Should a Wittgensteinian-inflected response to the new wave of claims be modelled on the earlier response? After all, it might be said, the most sophisticated AI system still runs on servers and GPUs running symbolic code. Are, for that reason, objections to claims about GOFAI 'representational engines' at the same time, objections to AI domain heterogenic systems?

The two main lines of Wittgensteinian critique of the first wave of claims about machine intelligence will be familiar, but they are summarized here with a particular inflexion that serves the current aims.

The common ground of praxis

One line of attack focuses on our use of psychological concepts. The objection is that we would not, in fact, ever treat machines, or something that looked like one, or even things that did not look like machines but which we knew we had designed as machines as if they were agents. The keystone passage here is:

> Only of a human being and what resembles (behaves like) a living human being can one say: it has sensations; it sees; hears; is deaf; is conscious or unconscious.
>
> <div align="right">(<i>Wittgenstein 2009, §281</i>)</div>

This is usually understood as a remark about, in the Wittgensteinian sense, grammar: by which I understand a description of the microstructure of the practices which are the conditions of what we are able, meaningfully, to say, inside such practices. The thought is that such concepts only have an application where we are standing with others on a common ground of praxis: and a rough ground too – one whose surface gives traction to sense through shared embodiment, expressive interactions, hinge commitments, attitudes towards each other as souls and indeed whatever else we want to pack into the notion of a shared form of life. We do not in fact share this with machines and, scientific fantasy notwithstanding, never will. So psychological concepts do not and cannot gain application to what we also regard as machinery. We will return to this objection at the end, linking it to a more general thought, common amongst Wittgensteinians, about the role of the concept of life as an explanation-terminal, spade turning, concept. We should note for now though that this objection is, in no small measure, a general methodological one. It depends on an acceptance of a general account of how concepts gain and maintain meaning and then applies to the case of (nonsensical) psychological ascriptions to machines.

Regress arguments and PI

A second but, I think, the main line of Wittgensteinian critique against Computational Cartesianism is more specific in its focus. It applies to the GOFAI computer case, the regress shaped arguments of the *PI*. Across many remarks, Wittgenstein painstakingly explores the links between mindedness and meaning, normativity and agency. Near the heart of his investigations are the rule-following considerations and their application to psychological concepts including sensations, in the form of the private language remarks. Wittgenstein establishes here the link between the possession of psychological concepts and normativity, articulating the conditions under which a concept can be applied correctly or incorrectly and thus applied at all. The point to emphasize now is that though Wittgenstein is here concerned with the meaning of psychological concepts in a language, the argument is part of an attack on a bigger target: the idea of intrinsic representational states, intrinsic intentionality. Well, but aren't his central examples here – sensations, especially pain, paradigm examples of non-representational states; not *about* anything? Wittgenstein's rationale is that, for his opponents, concepts of inner sensations serve as a model of how a being represents the outer world to itself. So, if there is a problem about inner representations of the inner, there will certainly be one about inner representations of the outer. Seen this way, the private language considerations are of a piece with a slew of remarks and reminders, rebuttals and rejoinders all of which have the general form of regress objections. They are all attacks on what Wittgenstein sees as our tendency to impose mechanisms, states or objects – working either as intermediaries or lying, hidden, behind the phenomena in question – which are meant to do the explanatory heavy lifting in making the philosophical idea of intrinsic intentionality intelligible. The intermediate or hidden phenomena all turn out to require the very thing they were invented to explain.

Early in the *PI*, Wittgenstein couches the regress objection in terms of language acquisition, pointing out that we should not seek to explain a human child's learning to talk as if it were the acquisition of a second language (Wittgenstein 2009, §32). The implicit argument is that this would require an explanation of how the first language was acquired. And so on. The same kind of objection is applied to a gamut of putative intrinsic content vehicles: images, pointing, projection schema, names and descriptions, and, of course, rules. In this last case, the regress comes in the form of the apparent paradox about how we follow rules. To be acted upon, a rule requires that we interpret it. But any such interpretation can itself be regarded as a rule, one for the use of the first rule, and so on. The problem is how to stop the regress, without sneaking in intrinsic intentionality via the back door.

It is worth noting that very similarly shaped concerns to Wittgenstein's regress arguments crop up later in the philosophy of computing literature, though in ignorance of Wittgenstein's distinctive insights and certainly without Wittgenstein's ruthless follow-through on the issues. Thus, explaining the 'symbol grounding problem', the AI researcher Stevan Harnad asked:

> How can the semantic interpretation of a formal symbol system be made intrinsic to the system, rather than just parasitic on the meanings in our heads? How can the meanings of the meaningless symbol tokens, manipulated solely on the basis of their (arbitrary) shapes, be grounded in anything but other meaningless symbols?
>
> *(Harnad 1990, 335)*

The problem here is how, at some level of description of a system's states – at the lowest, the electrical states of transistors in a computer system – do those system states gain meaning, independently of *our* assigning values, such as 0 and 1, to them? Of course, *we can treat* any such system *as if* its states were semantic and very usefully so too. But, of course, in the only half of the problem that Harnad sees, if the meaning of the states of such systems is always parasitic on *our* semantic ascriptions, then they do not have such meaning in themselves. Such systems cannot manifest AI but only proxy intelligence or, better, *prosthetic* intelligence (Harre 1988).

The half of the problem that Harnad does not see concerns the 'meanings in our heads' upon which the 'meaningless symbol tokens' are parasitic. The 'meanings in our head' are taken to be intrinsic. Harnad fails to see the regress problem that Wittgenstein allows us to identify: that if there is a problem about how the system states of a machine can have semantics, then *so long as we are conceiving meaning in just the same way*, that is, as logically private and intrinsically intentional, there is equally a problem, about such meanings in our heads. (It is perhaps moot whether a Wittgenstein reader should take logical privacy to be a necessary *condition* or a necessary *consequence* of intrinsic intentionality.)

In the same year as Harnad's piece, Searle's much discussed Chinese Room Argument (Searle 1990) concluded that the physical world, including the physical states of a computer system but, presumably, not including the human brain, objectively contains neither syntax nor semantics. How then can syntax and semantics arise at all? For Searle, it must be just a fact that some special parts of the natural world – mental states and their neural correlates – are intrinsically intentional and, arguably, therefore logically private.

The regress objection to intrinsic, logically private meaning has been more recently, and rather more exactly, stated by Floridi as the Zero Semantic commitment condition for avoiding the Symbol Grounding Problem (SGP) for Artificial Agents (AAs):

> The requirement to be satisfied by any strategy is the zero semantic commitment condition (henceforth Z condition). According to the Z condition, no valid solution of the SGP can rely on forms of innatism, since no semantic resources (some *virtus semantica*) should be presupposed as already pre-installed in the AA's; and externalism, since no semantic resources should be uploaded from the 'outside' by some deus ex machina that is already semantically-proficient.
>
> Of course, a valid solution draws on an AA's own capacities and resources (e.g. computational, syntactical, procedural, perceptual, educational resources, exploited through algorithms, sensors, actuators etc.) to ground its symbols. However, these should not already be semantic, as that would be begging the question.
>
> *(Floridi 2013, 137)*

Floridi's Z condition is, arguably, consonant with Wittgenstein's arguments, at least to the extent that it consistently pursues the regress all down the line.

Finally, we see Radical Enactivists deploying a regress-style objection. For Hutto and Mylin:

> Naturalistic theories with explanatory ambitions cannot simply help themselves to the notion of information-as-content, since that would be to presuppose rather than explain the existence of semantic or contentful properties.
>
> *(Hutto and Myin 2013, sec. 1269)*

The point here is to debunk the following line of argument. First model meaningful, semantic, intentional content onto information content. Second, model that conception of information content onto Shannon-defined information. Third, define increasingly more narrowly specified neural and/or machine states in terms of decreasingly complex Shannon-defined information 'content'. Finally, claim that we have successfully explained how neural and/or machine states contain intentional content. The Radical Enactivist objection is that the second step equivocates on the conception of content and already assumes the existence of the intrinsic intentional content it was supposed to explain. (For Radical Enactivists, it is simply impossible to explain intentional content at all since the very idea of such content is incoherent, but we need not pursue that here.)

Regress arguments and AI

The main line of Wittgensteinian critique of the earlier wave of claims about computational minds takes then the structure, variously refined, of a regress objection. In ascribing intrinsic meaning to machine states, we presuppose the very idea of meaningful content we are supposed to be explaining. A GOFAI machine intelligence is then understood as a rule which carries its own interpretation along with it. And that is precisely what Wittgenstein's arguments reveal as a mythology.

We can now ask: Is such a regress-style objection effective against the AI systems under discussion? And does the Wittgensteinian means of avoiding the regress mean the rejection of claims about the conceptual possibility of AAs constituted by such systems?

The answer to the first question is clearly 'no'. The regress objection is meant to expose the notion of intrinsic intentionality, mythologized here into intrinsically meaningful rules of code, as a mythology. But the domain heterogenic systems we are interested in here simply do not appeal to intrinsically meaningful rules. The Black Box is, in the relevant respect, empty. There is no beetle.

What then of the second question? A Wittgensteinian may maintain that, after all, putative AAs still run, at least at present, on symbolic machines to which the regress arguments do apply. Moreover, in the training of the system, the decisions still have to be checked back against the data, and even if that process is itself handled by another ConvNet then at least that data, had, at some point, to be correctly tagged and bagged by actual human agents. So, doesn't the charge of parasitism on genuine agents, and hence the Wittgensteinian regress objection, still stick?

I think the Wittgensteinian needs to tread carefully here. Recall Wittgenstein's response to the regress. That there must be a way of taking the rule that is not an interpretation. His response is the concept of a practice, of living agents, interacting with each other and the world, going on in the same way, obeying the rule 'blindly' (Wittgenstein 2009, §219), of consonance in our 'form of life' (Wittgenstein 2009, §241).

Note here that if a practice or form of life is something defined by the participation of human *linguistic* agents, the move would be question-begging. Floridi's Z condition follows Wittgenstein here. It cannot be, for example, that we establish and engage in such meaning practices – insofar as they play a foundational role in the account – (by *convention* for the question would then be, '[…] and how do those conventions have meaning?' and the regress bites again.

Wittgenstein, of course, warns against the mistake by saying that the possibility of language as a means of communication is a matter of agreement not only in definitions but also in judgements (Wittgenstein 2009, §242). It is obvious that relying on definitions alone would fall to a regress argument. But here we should not – *cannot* – understand judgements on the basis of their semantic content. For so long as the regress objection is in play, that would fall foul of the Z condition. We could say that what matters is only *the fact* of judging the same way. Where the judgement is made manifest not in its semantic content but through action and shared action: through sheer consonance.

Animals like us *go on in the same way*. But even here the '*same* way' cannot be something subject to criteria of sameness, and thus *already* an intentional object for subjects *already capable of meaning*. For that involves remaining caught in the regress with which the argument began.

How *are* we to avoid the regress then?

At this point, some Wittgensteinians are prone to say, 'In the beginning was the deed'. But whatever its merits as a useful summary slogan, *if we take this route as a means of stopping the regress*, we seem still to owe a regress-avoiding explanation of what distinguishes deeds from mere movement. We cannot offer the regress-vulnerable move: that deeds are movements plus intentionality. What we need to give traction to the concept of deed is the dynamic of active engagement with the environment including the reciprocal and reflexive engagements of others.

What this comes to is that if Wittgensteinians are to avoid being caught by the regress arguments that we deploy against others, we must take the idea of the non-propositional, non-semantic, non-intentional *primitive*, both within and without human life, *seriously*.[7]

Now at this point, it is moot whether such a strategy is a means of stopping the regress with a 'solution' or one of avoiding the regress by rejecting the question which invites it. This latter is certainly a plausible, 'therapeutic' reading of Wittgenstein.[8] On this view, the various and particular regress arguments in the *PI*, about the content of sensation memories, images, rules, names and so on, are merely deployments, in particular philosophical contexts of a much more general thought for the truth of which they may be supposed to constitute cumulative evidence. This general claim – a meta-claim – is that the very demand for a general explanation of how meaning gets going is a mistake from the off and one from which we must free ourselves. In fact, there is no way to 'explain' intentional content, meaning, symbol grounding and correlates, in terms which involve getting underneath, outside or sideways onto intentional content, meaning, grounded symbols and correlates. This is the reason why the regress always bites and is, it will be suggested, what Wittgenstein was really trying to show us. There can be *descriptions*, diverse, detailed and deep, of *what* we mean. And really paying attention to those descriptions will, to some extent, allay our sense *of a need* for explanation. But there is no such thing as an explanation, *tout court*, of *how* we mean. If pressed to ask, what, precisely, is illegitimate about the demand for an explanation, a therapeutic reader of Wittgenstein has more than one option.

They may ask us to try our 'explanations', one by one, and then learn the lesson when the regress, in each particular case, is pointed out.

We may be offered an account of the meaning of 'explanation', one which notes the disparity between philosophical explanation of our concepts and reductive explanations of physical phenomena. Though that distinction will now need to be appropriately grounded and, to be true to Wittgenstein, will need to avoid essentialism about the concept of explanation.

Finally, it might be contended it is not the concept of explanation that is causing the problem but that of meaning and its correlates. On this view, it is just a mistake, from the off, to think that there is something called meaning, detachable from the weft and weave of species life, standing in need of explanation.

---

7 Compare: 'Our spontaneous linguistic expressions are not (vertical) derivations but (horizontal) extensions of our primitive, spontaneous language-games [...]. There is a use of words which does not grammatically differ from nonlinguistic, indeed from animal, behaviour' (Moyal-Sharrock 2000).

8 My thanks to Marie McGinn (in discussion) and especially Peter R. Murray (in correspondence) for forcing me to think much harder about this point.

This therapeutic reading of Wittgenstein and the regress arguments is a legitimate one. But in the current context, where we are faced with new territory where we really don't know our way about and don't know what to say about the 'decisions' of discriminative AI systems, the therapeutic response – 'shut up and contemplate' – seems not just unsatisfactory but risky. We do after all have to come to some kind of societal, legal and ethical response to our advancing technology. So, whether we regard the regress arguments as solutions, resolutions or dissolutions of the problem about meaning, we still have to say something about how we conceptualize the 'decisions' of domain heterogenic AI. A generous scattering of scare quotes will not do the necessary work.

When we recognize this, the question is what should now prevent us, philosophically, from regarding domain-heterogenic, non-representational and therefore non-semantic artificial 'agents', as, for all their technological sophistication, in the relevant regress-avoiding sense, *primitive*? The dilemma then, at least for some Wittgensteinians, who want their natural scepticism about techno-hype to have some philosophical heft behind it, is how to set the bar of the primitive *low* enough to avoid falling foul of the regress arguments whilst *high* enough to make AI claims about non-living machines and systems implausible or nonsensical. The claim here is that regress objections to the conceptual possibility of synthetic cognition are unavailable to the Wittgensteinian whether the regress arguments are taken as solutions or as dissolutions.

The suggestion here then is that to stop *or* avoid the regress, the idea of the primitive must be set at a level that is low enough to leave us naturally sceptical about more extravagant AI claims but in a way that is philosophically weightless regarding the conceptual possibility of machine cognition. We can hold that serious general AI is not just a hundred years away but, as Jack Schwartz has said, a hundred Nobel Prizes away (Mitchell 2019, 19) but welcome the change in thinking *about thinking* that thinking about AI brings. So, Wittgensteinians should be intensely relaxed about domain heterogenic system cognition. It is our representationalist opponents (and in the case of generative systems like ChatGPT, formal semanticists) who should be stressed.

Two positive observations: Judgement and historicity

Two positive observations may offer further support to the thought that Wittgensteinians should be intensely relaxed about AI.

The first concerns the nature of judgement. The Platonic tradition contends that all judgements are, if proper, founded in valid deduction from principles. The first Cognitive and Computer 'revolutions' inherited this High Church Rationalism: since rational cognition involved the normatively governed, rule-based, manipulation of symbols then, since a machine can (be said to) manipulate symbols, a machine could rationally (be said to) cognize too.

By contrast, the Aristotelian tradition's emphasis on *Phronesis* – practical wisdom – contends that judgements can be sound, defeasible but still pragmatically reliable, without deductive, propositional underpinning. In the background lies yet another regress objection. It will always be an issue how we can judge that *this* principle applies in *this* particular case. Behind every principle, stands another one. The Aristotelian tradition escapes this regress by contenting that sound judgements are possible as a result of an agent being shaped by their experience to make precisely such judgements. We call such shaping, habits. And in the dimension of ethics and character, virtues: habits of the heart. It is not surprising that ethical and especially aesthetic judgement, in which principles are either elusive or unwelcome, have offered the best examples for this tradition.

It is, I hope, obvious that Wittgensteinians are on the Aristotelian side of this divide about judgement. But it seems plain that the rationale for AI systems is too insofar as such systems are shaped by a history of training and supervised learning. Of course, we should baulk at using the 'experience' here, but the shape of the approach to cognition is the same. As that excellent Wittgensteinian SF writer – Ted Chiang – writes, echoing an earlier thought by Turing, enabling an AI to make decisions about things that actually matter is 'not going to happen by loading the works of Kant into a computer's memory; it's going to require the equivalent of good parenting' (Chiang 2020).

Does this have an impact on the ethical objection to Black Boxes? Now whether we are comfortable about what tech corporations get up to all is a different matter, but this should make Wittgensteinians at least a little less philosophically uncomfortable about accepting the 'decisions' of such systems where no domain homogenous answer is available. Why not regard the 'judgements' that a ConvNet makes in the same way that Wittgensteinians regard the term in the notion of 'agreement in judgements', as non-semantic and rationally non-recoverable? This, of course, runs right against the grain of modern Western culture: where transparency, defensibility and auditability of the reasoning process are of paramount value. Contemporary culture is deeply suspicious about the idea of trusting people with relevant experience, judgement or taste who, if asked, may be quite unable to offer a defensible principle behind their opinion, instead drawing attention to particular details, proffering more examples or, perhaps in desperation, citing long experience.

Such expert agents are, in this respect, very like Black Boxes. There is here something deeply ironic: at a time when our culture has become, in respect of judgement, so Platonic, our leading-edge technology has become exquisitely Aristotelian.

There is a second affinity between Wittgensteinian approaches and the AI approach. Though this is less easy to find justification for in Wittgenstein's writings, it aligns with what one school of thought has gone on to do with a broadly Wittgensteinian inheritance: Enactivism.

Note first that the significance of what representational Turing machines do is constituted by the (parasitic) meanings of the rules and the order in which they are applied. Whether these rules are applied once or a million times is irrelevant, and whether in the past, now or the future is irrelevant too. An instance of a representational engine – GOFAI– is defined semantically not temporally. Aside from tenseless order of the rules, they are essentially atemporal and ahistorical. It may be evident now that this is why such systems are *transparent*. And this is why such systems could not be agents.

But this is not in principle true of the relevant kind of AI systems. They are shaped by the history of the cascade of iterative interactions and weighting adjustments they took in response to the data they were trained on. Even marginally different data sets could, in principle, produce a different pattern of iterative adjustments and different results. It matters exactly how these interactions happen in real time – what iterates over what and when – so that the relevant systems are sustained over and through time. Counterfactuals are true of such systems in a way they could not be of classical representational engines. Seen this way, AI systems are paths laid down in pattern finding and pattern making. Now compare:

> REC (Radical Enactive and Embodied account of Cognition) are also committed to the Developmental-Explanatory Thesis, which holds that mentality-constituting interactions are grounded in, shaped by, and explained by nothing more, or other, than the history of an organism's previous interactions. Sentience and sapience emerge through repeated processes of organismic engagement with environmental offerings. For organisms capable of learning, it is this, and nothing else, that determines which aspects of their worlds are significant to them. Nothing other than its history of active engaging structures or explains an organism's current interactive tendencies.
>
> *(Hutto and Myin 2013, 59)*

What changes, philosophically, here if we replace 'organism' with 'AI System'? Seen this way, artificial systems (of the relevant sort) are (or at least could be) *primitive, radically enactive, cognitive agents*.

The critical point is this: seeming, to a degree, opaque – being, to an extent, a Black Box – comes with being an essentially historical, temporal perspectival agent. Even so, nothing is hidden. Except, as it were, the history of everything. Seen in this light, the mystery of the hidden 'inner' is the result of hypostatizing history. The history of an agential organism's 'active engaging structures'.

This is not to say that AI Black Boxes are temporal perspectival agents. Only that temporal perspectival agents are, to a degree, Black Boxes. AI Black Boxes are historically conditioned. Again, that is not to say they are temporal – in time. Historicity is not the same as temporality. What we lack is any philosophical grip on whether it is being temporal that gives us, and creatures like us, a history – or instead that having a history is essential to or productive of our being temporal. We do not know, therefore, whether it is historicity or temporality which is fundamental to agency. Nor is it clear whether having a history which is algorithmic rather than causal makes a philosophical difference. Wittgenstein can help us think, honestly and carefully about such questions. But it is not evident that we can go to him for answers here. What he does give us is the constraint, that we must avoid trying to make those connections by smuggling concepts of consciousness and intrinsic intentionality which, magically, will do all the work needed.

In summary, Wittgensteinians ought to be intensely relaxed about the claims associated with AI. The suggestion in this discussion is that there are no clashes with central insights of Wittgenstein's thought since informed claims about such AI are not vulnerable to the regress argument about intrinsic intentionality. And a therapeutic take on the regress arguments cannot issue in a denial of the conceptual possibility of synthetic cognition. On the positive side, the emphasis on a system/agent's decisions being shaped as cognitively rational – as intelligent – by the history of its particular interactions with the environment is a good conceptual fit with the kind of Wittgensteinian position which is honest and serious about avoiding the regress about meaning and mind with which *PI* charges representationalism. Finally thinking about Wittgenstein and AI in this way connects, very smoothly, with current developments in thinking about enactive embodiment though it remains to be seen whether enactivism is escaping or merely reframing the difficulties that face us.

Beasts

A Wittgensteinian may still object. Systems are still *machines*. They are not embodied. Many Wittgensteinians, even if they accept that the standard regress arguments are irrelevant in this context, will draw their red line here.

Reverting to Wittgenstein's thought – what resembles a human being and so on – they will hold that this is only a pointer to a more general insight – that the more general concept of biological life, rather than an entirely anthropocentric one, is the foundational, or better, the keystone concept which allows our psychological and agential concepts to hang together. Isn't even the wriggling fly (Wittgenstein 2009, §284) a better candidate for the application of a concept of agency than the most advanced AI we can conceive?

But can it be enough for the Wittgensteinian to say, 'Well, what matters is being alive! Artificial agents are machines and so are not alive and there's an end to it'? At this point, some Wittgensteinians are likely to go quiet or at least revert to meta-philosophical remarks, dark and *sotto voce*, about what it means to offer philosophical explanations here. Or talk about where it is we stand when we do philosophy. From as it were sideways on or from within the weft of the biosphere. Here the spade turns. We talk as we do and our language games and practices exclude the overlap of living agency and stochastic machinery.

The questions here for the Wittgensteinian are whether the keystone status of the concepts of life, the living and the biosphere commits us to an essentialist account of such concepts and the extent to which this status makes such basic concepts immune to evolution and change. On the one hand, in 1949, Wittgenstein writes of our basic concepts – at least some of which are in play in discussions about artificial intelligence:

> The basic concepts are interwoven so closely with what is most fundamental in our way of living that they are themselves unassailable.
>
> *(Wittgenstein 1992 LW II, p. 43f.)*

On the other hand, as James Klagge points out:

> Just as one should not be an essentialist about the nature of concepts at a time, one should not be an essentialist about the nature of concepts over time.
>
> *(Klagge 2017, 200–201)*

The question is whether is it compatible with the role of the 'basic concepts' to develop say the 'neocognitive' as a new member of the family, related in some ways and not others, to our existing concepts, connected not in virtue of meeting some common properties that all members share but, at some remove, via some overlapping strands, *fibrously* (Vazquez 2020). Defending his use of the term 'soul', Wittgenstein writes:

Am I saying something like, 'and the soul is merely something about the body'? No. (I am not that hard up for categories).

(Wittgenstein 1994, §690)

The question then is: When it comes to our conceptual response to developments in AI, just how hard up are we for categories?

Conclusion

In the debate about these issues, there may be a danger that Wittgensteinians are perceived as offering easy slogans in place of the more detailed looking and seeing, and the learning of differences, that Wittgenstein himself recommended as a means of ridding ourselves of misleading pictures, in particular about the very notion of intelligence. Where to learn such differences?

When we look at the natural world, in all its diversity, then as the ethologist, Frans De Waal notes, 'there is no single form of cognition and there is no point in ranking cognitions from simple to complex' (Waal 2016). There is not a 'Rubicon' between ourselves and the rest of minded nature that 'no brute will dare to cross' (Müller 1862, 360). It is much more of a boggy marsh divided by rivulets and streams and the occasional floodplain in which different kinds of minded species find themselves more or less connected and more or less isolated, shaped in unique ways by processes that arise out of the landscape as a whole.

It is surely contrary to a Wittgensteinian approach to say that there are no novel conceptual problems here. That we know, already, *what it makes sense to say* about such phenomena: about corvid cognition (Taylor 2014), cetacean communication (Sayigh 2013), the olfactory world of the dog (Horowitz 2010) or the voltage world of the eel (Catania 2019), the distributed cognition of the octopus ('ISCRI: An AI Programmed By An Octopus' 2020) 28/02/2023 09:49:00 the collective sensory response thresholds of eusocial insects (Gal and Kronauer 2022) or the extraordinary route-finding talents of the humble slime mould. Or, indeed, something really surprising from an AA.

Instead of looking for a general theory that covers all intelligent cognition on the planet, an account both Wittgensteinian and properly scientific should treat everything as a case study. It should seek connections but, also 'teach us differences'. We need fibrous concepts which allow for the continuity, gradation and enormous diversity that we see in the natural world. Should we seek to offer a univocal account of intelligence that will account or discount for the orangutan and the octopus, the bee and the bear, the cat and the coelacanth, the human and, now, the artificial? This may well be a metaphysical prejudice of which systematic empirical investigation, aided by Wittgensteinian therapy, will cure us.

With that in place, perhaps the best strategy on AI issues for Wittgensteinian philosophers is to find a tenable holding position. One which says not, AAs cannot be minded because they are not alive but that AI systems, might, perhaps some time far off, become, akin to very primitive *digital animals*.

Coda

Anything more than a holding position at this stage will mean building on but beyond the thought of Wittgenstein. We need, I think, to map the area of a triangle whose vertices are agency, intentionality and temporality.

None of these three can be foundational without the risk of regress. Wittgensteinians will certainly want to insist that there is no intentionality without agency: embodied interaction in a world. But agency presupposes the idea that we are temporal beings. That we live in and through time. Yet many in analytic philosophy will ask how we can be temporal beings without a foundational intentionality: so that there is a world in time *for* us.

How, in the life of an organism, agency, intentionality and temporality can stand up together, we don't know. What we especially do not understand is whether living embodiment is doing the philosophical graft here with the consequence that the very idea of unembodied AAs is a conceptual non-starter. Should Wittgensteinians say that it is the fact of embodiment – and its intractable mix of activity and passivity – which makes the difference? Or rather that it is what embodiment *does or enables* that is doing the work? If the latter, then it remains open that there are other ways in which those phenomena can come together to produce the agential and the perspectival. In assaying these other possibilities, the field of ethology – the close study of very different kinds of animals laying down their own paths in living – can play a vital role. It is also likely that progress – and failures – in AI will open up new lines of sight on the same triangle of connections. Both fields require us to continue the Wittgensteinian project of shifting for ourselves so that we can see the world aright.

References

Bary, Emily. n.d. 'How Artificial Intelligence Could Replace Credit Scores and Reshape How We Get Loans'. *MarketWatch*. Accessed 25 April 2022. https://www.marketwatch.com/story/ai-based-credit-scores-will-soon-give-one-billion-people-access-to-banking-services-2018-10-09.

Catania, Kenneth C. 2019. 'The Astonishing Behavior of Electric Eels'. *Frontiers in Integrative Neuroscience* 13. https://doi.org/10.3389/fnint.2019.00023.

CCLSNLUJ. 2020. 'Analysing the Use of Artificial Intelligence in Criminal Sentencing through the Loomis Decision'. *The Criminal Law Blog (blog)*. 14 April 2020. https://criminallawstudiesnluj.wordpress.com/2020/04/14/analysing-the-use-of-artificial-intelligence-in-criminal-sentencing-through-the-loomis-decision/.
Chiang, Ted. 2020. *Exhalation*. Main Market edn. London: Picador.
Dror, Itiel E. and Marcelo Dascal. 1997. 'Can Wittgenstein Help Free the Mind from Rules? The Philosophical Foundations of Connectionism'. In Johnson, D. M. and Erneling, C. E. (eds), *The Future of the Cognitive Revolution*. New York: Oxford Academic.
Floridi, Luciano. 2013. *The Philosophy of Information*. Reprint edn. Oxford: Oxford University Press.
Gal, Asaf and Daniel J. C. Kronauer. 2022. 'The Emergence of a Collective Sensory Response Threshold in Ant Colonies'. *Proceedings of the National Academy of Sciences* 119 (23): e2123076119. https://doi.org/10.1073/pnas.2123076119.
Gregory, Andrew. 2022. 'AI Tool Accurately Predicts Tumour Regrowth in Cancer Patients'. *The Guardian*, 23 April 2022. https://www.theguardian.com/society/2022/apr/23/cancer-ai-tool-predicts-tumour-regrowth.
Harnad, Stevan. 1990. 'The Symbol Grounding Problem'. *Physica D* 42 (1–3): 335–46. https://doi.org/10.1016/0167-2789(90)90087-6.
Harre, Rom. 1988. 'Wittgenstein and Artificial Intelligence'. *Philosophical Psychology* 1 (1): 105–15. https://doi.org/10.1080/09515088808572928.
Horowitz, Alexandra. 2010. *Inside of a Dog: What Dogs See, Smell, and Know*. A. Kindle IPad edn. Scribner.
Hutto, Daniel D. and Erik Myin. 2013. *Radicalizing Enactivism: Basic Minds without Content*. Kindle iPad version. MIT Press.
'ISCRI: An AI Programmed By An Octopus'. 2020. *Etic Lab (blog)*. 16 September 2020. https://eticlab.co.uk/an-artificial-intelligence-programmed-by-an-octopus-iscri/.
Klagge, James. 2017. 'Wittgenstein, Science, and the Evolution of Concepts'. In Beale, J. and Kidd, I. J. (eds), *Wittgenstein and Scientism*. London: ;Routledge.
Mitchell, Melanie. 2019. *Artificial Intelligence: A Guide for Thinking Humans*. Illustrated edn. London: Farrar, Straus and Giroux.
Müller, M. 1862. Lectures on the Science of Thoughts. London: Longman, Green, and Co.
Moyal-Sharrock, Daniele. 2000. 'Words as Deeds: Wittgenstein's "spontaneous Utterances" and the Dissolution of the Explanatory Gap'. *Philosophical Psychology* 13 (3): 355. https://doi.org/10.1080/09515080050128169.
Nguyen, Anh, Jason Yosinski and Jeff Clune. 2015. 'Deep Neural Networks Are Easily Fooled: High Confidence Predictions for Unrecognizable Images'. In *Proceedings of the IEEE Conference on Computer Vision and Pattern Recognition*, 427–36.
O'Neil, Cathy. 2017. *Weapons of Math Destruction: How Big Data Increases Inequality and Threatens Democracy*. 1st edn. London: Penguin.
Sayigh, Laela. 2013. 'Cetacean Acoustic Communication'. *Biocommunication of Animals* 275–97. https://doi.org/10.1007/978-94-007-7414-8_16.
Searle, John R. 1990. 'Is the Brain a Digital Computer?' *Proceedings and Addresses of the American Philosophical Association* 64 (3): 21–37. https://doi.org/10.2307/3130074.
Taylor, Alex H. 2014. 'Corvid Cognition'. *Wiley Interdisciplinary Reviews. Cognitive Science* 5 (3): 361–72. https://doi.org/10.1002/wcs.1286.
Trager, Rebecca. 2022. 'AlphaFold Has Predicted the Structures of Almost Every Known Protein'. *Chemistry World*. 2022. https://www.chemistryworld.com/news/alphafold-has-predicted-the-structures-of-almost-every-known-protein/4016033.article.

Vazquez, Arturo. 2020. 'Wittgenstein and the Concept of Learning in Artificial Intelligence'. University of Bergen. https://bora.uib.no/bora-xmlui/bitstream/handle/1956/22980/Master_Thesis___Arturo_Vazquez___Wittgenstein_and_AI.pdf?sequence=1&isAllowed=y.

Waal, Frans de. 2016. *Are We Smart Enough to Know How Smart Animals Are?*. *London:* Granta Books.

Weizenbaum, Joseph. 1976. *Computer Power and Human Reason: From Judgement to Calculation.* New edn. San Francisco: W. H. Freeman & Co Ltd.

Wittgenstein, Ludwig. 1981. *Tractatus Logico-Philosophicus. German and English* edn (Trans. C. K. Ogden). Abingdon: Routledge.

Wittgenstein, Ludwig. 1992. *Volume 2 Last Writings on the Philosophy of Psychology: The Inner and the Outer, 1949–1951.* Oxford: Wiley-Blackwell.

Wittgenstein, Ludwig. 2009. *Philosophical Investigations. 4th edn* (Trans. Hacker and Schulte). Oxford: Wiley-Blackwell.

Chapter 7

LANGUAGE MODELS AND THE PRIVATE LANGUAGE ARGUMENT: A WITTGENSTEINIAN GUIDE TO MACHINE LEARNING

Giovanni Galli

Introduction

Wittgenstein's ideas are a common ground for developers of Natural Language Processing (NLP) systems and linguists working on Language Acquisition and Mastery (LAM) models (Mills 1993; Lowney et al. 2020; Skelac and Jandrić 2020).[1] In recent years, we have witnessed a fast development of NLP systems capable of performing tasks as never before. NLP and LAM have been implemented based on deep-learning neural networks, which learn concept representation from rough data but are nonetheless very effective in tasks such as question answering, textual entailment and translation (Devlin et al. 2019; Kitaev, Cao, and Klein 2019; Wang et al. 2019). In this chapter, I will debate some Wittgensteinian concepts that impact the architectures of many NLP deep-learning systems. I will focus, in particular, on the attempt to build a specific kind of architecture to model a private language. The discussion, I think, helps extract philosophical assumptions leading the research and development of AI systems capable of language modelling. In this chapter, I will address some of the main features of NLP systems[2] used for word embed-

---

[1] I would like to thank the Organizing Committee for the excellent result of the British Wittgenstein Society Conference, Wittgenstein and AI, held in London in July 2022. I want to thank Ian Ground for his valuable contribution and all the panel participants for the insightful discussion.
[2] For a discussion about LAM models, see Poveda and Vellido (2006). In these pages, the focus will be on the only NLP models.

ding and one proposal to manipulate through a neural network a form of private language (Lowney et al. 2020).

In 'The Private Language Argument', I will reconstruct the complex path of the private language argument (PLA). In 'Connectionist Language Models in NLP', I will discuss connectionist language models and introduce notions about NLP systems' architecture. An overview of this kind of model is helpful to introduce the work of Lowney et al. (2020). They submit that their model can respond to the issues raised by Wittgenstein in the famous PLA. This argument unexpectedly turned out to be relevant not only for the philosophy of language but also for NLP and LAM modellers. I will describe the language game concept in NLP, how it is embedded, and its role in inductive systems development. This central concept in Wittgenstein's work is relevant to describe the role of context in understanding the meanings of words. In 'Wittgenstein and Connectionism', I present the Wittgensteinian main concepts at play in the connectionist paradigm. I argue that the connectionist theoretical framework can better catch the dependency of word meaning on context. There seems to be a correlation between Wittgenstein's invitation to look, an invitation to dismiss the aim of theorizing about languages, and the absence of theory-ladenness in deep-learning technologies involved in NLP. In 'The Beetle in the (Black) Box', I criticize Lowney et al.'s claim, whose model does not successfully capture Wittgenstein's Beetle-in-the-box case. Moreover, I argue that even if we can distinguish a strong and a weak definition of a private language, Wittgenstein's argument also holds for deep-learning models, and his worries are still a good guide for NLP developers.

The Private Language Argument

In this section, I present the PLA and characterize it as a language game. The PLA is one of the most famous contributions of the later Wittgenstein. According to Fogelin (1976, 153), PLA is Wittgenstein's most debated argument. The debate sparked by PLA, already broad in the 1970s, even increased over subsequent years and is still one of the most discussed aspects of Wittgenstein's philosophy to date. This issue raises an intriguing point that connects many crucial turning points in the history of philosophy. It begins with Gorgia's nihilism about the possible connection between language and the world. It continues with Galilei's discussion about the secondary quality (SQ) of objects in *Il Saggiatore* (1623). Moreover, of course, it also touches on Wittgenstein's work (Wittgenstein 1914–1916; 1978). According to Galilei,[3]

---

3 See Galilei (1623, 28).

The doctrine of SQs differs from that of primary accidents, such as size, shape, motion, rest and location. Galileo claimed that primary accidents exist in external bodies to which we attribute them. We give public ontology to the primary accidents in accordance with the use of a public language. On the other hand, we assign a private ontology to the SQ since these qualities 'appear to exist in the objects we perceive around us and actually reside only in us' (Fisher 2009, 93). If the SQs reside *exclusively* in us, they can be considered private objects in a Wittgensteinian sense. Wittgenstein criticized the concept of a private ontology, offering an alternative perspective on how language operates in relation to ourselves and the world. In PI §256 and §258–60 Wittgenstein claims that a private language, in which meanings are derived by ostensive internal relation to private objects, is impossible. The conclusion is that a meaningful discussion about private sensation is impossible.

The expressions of individual sensations seem to imply privacy of language; this is the 'primitive seduction of the private language' (Fogelin 1976, 156). Furthermore, Wittgenstein in the *Philosophical Investigations* (PI) offers two main scenarios: the first is the example of the diary of the occurrence of a private sensation (PI, §258), and the other is the monster fame case of the beetle-in-the-box (PI, §293). The argument sketch is presented in PI §243: 'The words of this [private] language are to refer to what only the speaker can know – to his immediate private sensations. So another person cannot understand the language.' His attack on the idea and the possibility of a private language is contained in the passages of PI §§244–71, even if we need to consider the broader context of §§243–315 to follow the main ramifications of the PLA. It is not here the place to disentangle the exegetical complexity and the interpretative genealogy of the PLA. It is highly controversial whether there is, or there at least *could* be, a specific PLA to be found in Wittgenstein. Someone claims to find some prolegomenon to it in the lines of the *Tractatus Logico-Philosophicus* (TLP).[4] Someone else sees it as a specific dialectic move of post-*Tractatus*[5] Wittgenstein. It is not here the place to explore a synoptic synthesis of the positions and interpretations found in the literature. However, it will be enough to cite the main four positions: orthodox, Kripkean, substantial and resolute. While the orthodox way[6] claims that the PLA is a *reductio*

---

[4] See Diamond (2000, 283).
[5] See Backer and Hacker (1984).
[6] Norman Malcom is one of the founders of the PLA (see Malcom 1954) and one of the defenders of what lately was called the *orthodox view* of PLA. That is the idea that the paragraphs §§244–71 contain embedded an argument in the form of *reductio ad absurdum*.

ad absurdum argument, Kripke[7] argues that the PLA is the consequence of the discussion on rule-following. Moreover, according to the substantial way, PLA is impossible. The resolute way instead defends the idea that PLA is possible, and that it is nonsensical to limit the possibilities of language. The first three perspectives agree that creating a private language is not possible. The first perspective views it as a deductive argument, while Kripke highlights the sceptical paradox when someone tries to develop a private language. Finally, the substantial perspective interprets Wittgenstein's work literally. The resolute reading rejects the idea that we cannot achieve a private language. In particular, the resolute readers argue that language has unlimited creative power. In fact, according to Mulhall (2007, 18), the idea of limitation is simply nonsense: no sense can be given to the idea of a philosophically substantial private language.

From §134 to §242, privacy has its central spot as a philosophical issue concerning private objects. In this chapter, I will focus on one of the famous passages: the beetle-in-the-box. According to Stern (2011, 255): 'Wittgenstein's treatment of private language has received more attention than any other aspect of his philosophy.' The pages about the beetle-in-the-box became famous in philosophical literature, as much as the image of Plato's cave in *The Republic* (Stern 2007), and it is even the protagonist of a title of recent philosophical text by Martin Cohen *Wittgenstein Beetle and Other Classical Thought Experiments* (2005). Let us consider the argument on its own merits, regardless of the specific Wittgensteinian style in which it was presented. Although this style is deeply rooted in his dialectic, many interpretations have emerged over the last few decades that have depicted different forms and objectives of the argument. According to Hacker, the PLA is one of 'the most original and significant philosophical reflections of the twentieth century. If the line of argument pursued in them is valid, their implications, both within philosophy and without, are considerable. Modern philosophical logic, theoretical linguistics, as well as branches of empirical psychology, would stand in need of re-evaluation' (Hacker 2001, 209).

Moreover, perhaps we can also add branches of artificial intelligence today. Lowney et al. (2020) intentionally selected the beetle-in-the-box as a case study to demonstrate the integration of contextual information into a language model, even if it is sourced from a private ontology.

---

7 Kripke argued that Wittgenstein introduced a new sceptical problem to which he gave a Humean solution. According to Kripke, PLA is connected to the logical and epistemological character of following a rule. I agree instead with Hacker's interpretation of the PLA (Baker and Hacker 1984, and Hacker 2001) and Alai's description (Alai 2021)

After presenting the notion of private language, I will now describe Wittgenstein's beetle-in-the-box case, one of the most well-known PLA scenarios:

> If I say of myself that it is only from my own case that I know what the word 'pain' means – must I not say the same of other people too? And how can I generalize the one case so irresponsibly?
>
> Now someone tells me that he knows what pain is only from his own case! — Suppose everyone had a box with something in it: we call it a 'beetle'. No one can look into anyone else's box, and everyone says he knows what a beetle is only by looking at his beetle. — Here it would be quite possible for everyone to have something different in his box. One might even imagine such a thing constantly changing. — But suppose the word 'beetle' had a use in these people's language? — If so it would not be used as the name of a thing. The thing in the box has no place in the language-game at all; not even as a something: for the box might even be empty. — No, one can 'divide through' by the thing in the box; it cancels out, whatever it is.
>
> That is to say: if we construe the grammar of the expression of sensation on the model of 'object and designation' the object drops out of consideration as irrelevant.
>
> *(Wittgenstein 2009: PI §293)*

The private object to which Wittgenstein refers is not a simple invention. The beetle is there – it is an issue of private experience and how to address it. It is an example of a private experience. It could be a private sensation, a private definition or a private object (Candlish 2004). In the background, there is a reference to the Russellian characterization of private language. Wittgenstein does not explicitly refer to the philosophy of logical atomism by Russell, but this lecture has likely been one of the targets addressing the PLA. Wittgenstein's target in PI could also be the metaphysics (a piece of plain nonsense?) involved in the Russellian logical atomism:

> The results of philosophy are the discovery of some piece of plain nonsense and of bumps that the understanding has got by running up against the limits of language. They – these bumps – make us see the value of that discovery.
>
> *(Wittgenstein 2009: PI §119)*

I believe that §293 of Wittgenstein's work can be interpreted as a scenario defining the limit for language games. Wittgenstein describes language in the form of language games, and I think it is possible to argue that there is a specific limit to language and language games. The PLA identifies this limit, precisely the example of the beetle-in-the-box case. In fact, he says: 'The thing [beetle] in the box has no place in the language-game at all; not even as a something: for the box might even be empty.' The 'thing in the box', or perhaps the same box being empty, falls outside the boundaries of the context in which we can find the meaning of the words we use. Moreover, the *fil-rouge* tying privacy to the limit of language games we also find in PI:

> As things are I can, for example, invent a game that is never played by anyone. – But would the following be possible too: mankind has never played any games; once, however, someone invented a game – which no one ever played?
> (Wittgenstein 2009: PI § 204)

The PLA aims not to limit the possibility of expressing one's autobiographical sketch or report. The game is extensive in that regard. The PLA issues do not impact autobiographical literature and reports. Writers have access to their interiority, and with creative acuity, they shape their private sensations, passions and feelings, which can be shared with the public. Even though from Caesar to Valéry, Pessoa and Gide, some of the best writers of autobiographical records, it could be inferred that reaching the autobiographical truth is impossible unless the paper does not wrinkle or burn from the touch of a pen on fire (Poe 1968), it does not mean that PLA issues play a role in it. To illustrate the boundless nature of literary creativity, consider Bernardo Soares' fictional autobiography in *The Book of Disquiet* by Pessoa, published posthumously in 1982. In writing an autobiography, the author has the freedom to present a realistic account of their life, such as Caesar's, or a poetic diary that reflects their personal experiences and emotions, like Pessoa's during the dictatorship in Portugal. Regardless of the approach taken, the autobiography serves as a private record of the writer's thoughts, feelings and creative desires. The autobiography case demonstrates that the PLA does not intend to deny the existence of what are commonly known as private experiences that individuals have in various contexts. This clarification helps to identify the primary targets of the PLA, which are the ontological and semantic aspects of private objects.

Taking a synoptic view of the PI, we can see that the PLA plays a central role in the overall dialectic of Wittgenstein's work. The discussions and claims that Wittgenstein presents throughout the book lead to the PLA, which is a complex argument that aims to summarize the previous discussions. Wittgenstein's dictum about language games, meaning as use, family resemblance, context and the tenets of connectionism all have similarities, and the powerful and flexible concepts discussed in PI lead to PLA being the primary hotspot of the discussion. Therefore, using PLA to understand the connection between Wittgenstein's work and connectionism is more relevant, rather than succumbing to simplistic interpretations. In the upcoming section, I will examine the connection between Wittgenstein's concepts and connectionism. I will specifically concentrate on two major NLP models, one used for word embedding and the other used to simulate the beetle-in-the-box scenario.

Connectionist Language Models in NLP

What is a proposition? This is the central question that TLP, PI and NLP connectionist methodologies aim to answer. Wittgenstein writes in the *Notebook*, 'My *whole* task consists in explaining the nature of the proposition' (T, 22.1.15). From this line, we must begin to trace back to the work of Wittgenstein to enlighten the contemporary exercise of connectionist methodologies for natural language. Wittgenstein's main objective was to explain the nature of propositions in his work. However, it is essential to note that the nature or essence of a proposition should not be conceived as a platonic feature of an item existing in a detached realm of beings, happenings and words and statements we express. Instead, the nature of a proposition is interwoven in the use of words in our language. This is why the first connection point between Wittgenstein's philosophy and connectionism can be found in *Notebook* and TLP, even before PI.

The first connectionist NLP method to be studied under Wittgensteinian light is Word2Vec.[8] It is a group of models based on neural network systems that produce word embeddings. Word embedding is a process in which semantic structures, such as words, phrases or similar entities from a specific vocabulary, are mapped to and mathematically modelled as Euclidean vectors of real numbers. It has a variety of applications, and it is helpful to generate text similarity, sentiment analysis and recommendation systems. The system deploys vectorial distribution to assign a specific value to a word analysed in a context, a specific *corpus*. It will be likely to find in the vectorial space the word 'cat' near 'dog, pet, kitty, purr, paws, meow', with a value far from a word that could be defined as an alcoholic drink, which defines the surrounding of, say, 'wine' and 'beer'. Word2Vec can utilize either of two model architectures to produce a distributed representation of words. The representation of words defines the collocation of words and their interlinguistic connections. The two models in play are continuous bag-of-words (CBOW) and continuous

---

8 One of the leading researchers who implemented firstly Word2Vec is Tomáš Mikolov, who introduced this technique in NLP in Mikolov, Chen, Corrado and Dean (2013).

Skip-gram. The CBOW model predicts the current word from a window of surrounding context words. The order of context words does not influence the prediction, and this is the bag-of-words assumption. The Skip-gram model is the reverse. It uses the current word to predict the surrounding window of context words (Mikolov, Chen, Corrado and Dean 2013).

The CBOW model is similar to a feedforward neural network. It aims to predict the current word from an output set of context words. If we input 'The beetle is in the box', choose the target word 'beetle' and our context words to be ('The', 'is', 'in', 'the', 'box'), this model will deploy the distributed representation of context words to predict the target word.

Instead, Skip-gram is a simple neural network with one hidden layer trained to predict the probability of a given word being a context word when given a specific input word. It works as the reverse of CBOW. The Skip-gram model takes the current word and predicts the words before and after it to form its context. Given some *corpus*, the starting move is to select a target word over a rolling window. The researchers use pairwise combinations of the target word and all other words in the window to have a set of training data. After the training, the model assigns the probability of a word to be a context word for the given target. If we take the *corpus* 'The beetle is in the box' and we select the target word 'beetle' in a rolling window of, say three words ('The', 'beetle', 'is'), the model will predict the probability of 'The' and 'is' before and after the target word 'beetle'.

We can appreciate how the notion of context[9] is crucial in such an NLP system. When analysing a corpus of texts, it is important to consider the context in which the language is used. This includes both the collocation of words and the extra-linguistic practices that shape our language. From Frege to Wittgenstein and modern linguistics, it is clear that both linguistic and contextual features are essential in forming the meaning of words in our language. I will dig a little into the notion of context in the next paragraph, but for now, it is important to highlight the limitations of NLP systems in relation to the context. In the Word2Vec system, every word is assigned a unique vector which codifies all its collocations and thus represents its meaning. Consequently, if two words are such that there is a context in which one of them cannot be substituted with the other, their Word2Vec vectors will be expectedly different. Another limitation concerns cases of synonymy relative to a context. Word2Vec does not operate with the notion of meaning in a

---

9 The attempt to formalize contextual information and reduce it computationally is the crucial point of NLP systems developers; see Gayler (2003); Church (2007); Brézillon, Turner and Penco (2017).

particular context. Instead, it identifies the meaning of a word with a list of contexts conceived as collocations of words. An example could be run by taking some statements containing the most polysemous words, such as 'run', 'go' or 'set'. The system will be struggling to predict the definition of the target word, that could be the same in different contexts and have different meanings which cannot be captured by the NLP models.

The second model to be scrutinized is the VSA, which Lowney et al. (2020) used to model the beetle-in-the-box case. VSA stands for Vector Symbolic Architecture; that is a connectionist model using high-dimensional vectors to encode systematic and compositional information as distributed representations (Kanerva, 1994; Plate, 2003; Rasmussen and Eliasmith, 2011). VSA family of models follows the connectionist framework of Smolensky extending it into high-dimensional vector space. (Lowney et al. 2020: 652) set up a formalism comprising three operations on vectors: multiplication, addiction and permutation. According to them 'VSA provides a principled connectionist alternative to classical symbolic systems (predicate calculus, graph theory) for encoding and manipulating a variety of useful structures'. In fact, they suggest that 'The biggest advantage of VSA representations over other connectionist approaches is that a single association (or set of associations) can be quickly recovered from a set (or larger set) of associations in a time that is independent of the number of associations'. In that way, 'VSA thus answers the scalability problem raised by classicists with regard to biologically plausible real-time processing' (Lowney et al. 2020, 654). They choose this kind of model to capture statements similar to those of the beetle case in PI. Their choice relies on the fact that 'VSAs use multidimensional vectors and numerical weights, randomly assigned at the most basic level, in the actual processing of the networks constructed'. The flexibility they attribute to the model is based also on the fact, which is actually the Wittgensteinian tenet against the ostensive relation to private objects, that 'There is no one-to-one correspondence to an entity or item for representation. A symbol is represented in signs/vectors that are distributed across a vector space, and operations with symbols, in turn, use these distributed representations to establish proximity relations that model thought and language use' (Lowney et al. 2020, 654). To recognize the meaning of a word as a symbol that does not have an ostensive and one-to-one 'correspondence to an entity or item for representation' is specifically to rely on the idea that 'for Wittgenstein there is not typically an atomic content or correspondence that one can point to in order to explicate the meaning of a term' (Lowney et al. 2020, 654). The meaning of a word, a symbol, is a product of 'a complicated network of similarities overlapping and criss-crossing' (PI, §66; see also Mills 1993, 139). Following Goldfarb (1997), Strawson (1954) and Hintikka & Hintikka (1986), Lowney and the other researchers agree with the Hintikkas' way of thinking, who believe that 'Wittgenstein was not denying the possibility to referring to sensations nor a private language outright' (Lowney et al. 2020, 659). They use connectionism to shape a formalism in which Wittgensteinian assumptions about the nature of language are satisfied, namely that the VSA can capture some language features without assuming the connection with objects for meaning. However, the limitation of the beetle case remains fixed if we model it with a neural network model as VSA. Connectionist models cannot explain language and its meanings insofar as – as Wittgenstein stressed – we cannot give theories of language, but only descriptions. Connectionist models, as mind models, can 'help guide inquiry into the workings of the phenomena and can dispel some misconceptions, but as close as it may come to analogically portraying some important features, it should not be mistaken for the only or the actual way that language works' (Lowney et al. 2020, 668). Perhaps it is better to say that the VSA proposed to model the beetle case does not resolve the beetle puzzle, even if it models the case following the line of the Hintikkas's and Hacker's interpretation, according to which there is no literal claim against the possibility of using the language to talk about private objects, as private sensations. Still, it is possible to talk about these private items using a language made by public meanings construed through interactions in extra-linguistic contexts. These contexts are not yet encoded in systems such as Word2Vec or the Smolensky vectors. With these corrections to Lowney et al. proposal, I agree with their conclusion that

> by respecting Wittgenstein's insights and providing a VSA account that displays linguistic compositionality, integrates soft symbols, and develops analogical structures that can be systematic and advance productively, we have shown how twenty-first-century connectionism can address what appeared to be limitations in the functionality of its operation, limitations in learning, and limitations in biological plausibility that might have thwarted connectionism's ability to be a better mind-model for language and cognitive science.
>
> *(Lowney et al. 2020, 668)*

In this section, I have presented Word2Vec and the VSA proposed by Lowney et al. (2020). The two systems have underlying philosophical assumptions that were developed by Wittgenstein. Consequently, they show how Wittgenstein's ideas are deeply embedded in the deep-learning NLP models, and how his ideas are integral to the breakthrough of AI language models. In the following section, we will explore how Wittgenstein's conceptual tools are closely linked with the main connectionist principles.

Wittgenstein and Connectionism

Between the 1960s and the mid-1990s, two main approaches concerning LAM were predominant: the connectionist and the symbols and rule approach. There are two main approaches to explaining cognition. The first considers it as an ability that can be understood through a neural network. The second approach, the symbolic or rule-based approach, views the mind as an information processing system similar to a computer. In this view, language is seen as a collection of symbols that are governed by rules, similar to how programming languages are used in computers. At the time the symbols and rule approach was predominant, Mills (1993) stated some important similarities between Wittgenstein's later philosophy and connectionism. Building on this view, Lowney et al. (2020) specify the affinity between Smolensky's (1991, 1995) distributed representation connectionist approach and Wittgenstein's main philosophical notions, such as symbol constitution, language games, family resemblance, rule-following, logic and language learning. According to them, there is a possible path connecting Wittgenstein and connectionism.

The last decades have witnessed an upswing in the debate between the classical approach and connectionism, and many scholars have made an important effort to disentangle the Wittgensteinian roots of connectionism and deep-learning models. According to Stern (1991), Mills (1993), Goldstein and Slater (1998), and Elman (2014), connectionism provides an understanding of mind and language use that can be traced back to the so-called later Wittgenstein. Connectionism states that cognition is an emergent property relying on associations and activation of patterns following parallel processing. Dating back to Skinner's work, Chomsky, Fodor and Pinker proposed an alternative to connectionism through the renewed classical symbolic approach (Fodor and Pylyshyn 1988). Now, we could recast connectionism as a cognitive science movement working on deep-learning models. Recently, it has been noticed the importance of Wittgenstein's work for both NLP systems and connectionist theoretical frameworks, in particular deep-learning neural networks. NLP and LAM models rely on deep-learning neural networks in both cases. The use of deep-learning models to analyse the Wittgensteinian concepts in NLP and LAM offers a perspective that helps clarify the underlying assumptions in current connectionism ideas.

Connectionism, as an alternative to classical approaches and as a family of concepts and methodologies, is much more effective than symbolic AI. According to Mitchell (2019, 38), 'A symbolic AI program's knowledge consists of words of phrases (the "symbols"), typically understandable to a human, along with rules by which the program can combine and process these symbols in order to perform its assigned task'. It was thanks to the back-propagation, a general learning algorithm, towards which Misnky and Papert (1969) were sceptical, that multilayer neural networks played a crucial role in the foundation of modern AI and led to the rise of Machine Learning (ML). Back in the 1980s, at the University of California, San Diego, there was the most known team working on neural networks led by psychologists David Rumelhart and James McClelland. This team is well-known today for the writing of *Parallel Distributed Processing* (1986), recognized as the 'bible of connectionism' (Mitchell 2019, 39). According to them, the 'symbolic systems such as those favoured by Minsky and Papert' (Rumelhart, McClelland, and the PDP Research Group 1986, 113) would fail to catch the human-like abilities such as perceiving objects, understanding language and retrieving information from memory. According to Mitchell, 'What we now call neural networks were then generally referred to as connectionist networks, where the term *connectionist* refers to the idea that knowledge in these networks resides in weighted *connections* between units' (Mitchell 2019, 39).

Connectionism has been defined as a neurologically inspired architecture: 'connectionist nodes and networks were said to model neurons and the synapses created through the connection of axons and dendrites. Connectionism thus showed promise for unifying brain biology and perception with higher cognitive activities such as thought and language' (Lowney et al. 2020, 645). Connectionism implies consequences about how we understand the language and the mind that early Wittgenstein figured out in his later work (Stern 1991; Mills 1993; Dror and Dascal 1997; Goldstein and Slater 1998; Elman 2014). In fact, according to Mills (1993, 145) connectionist training is very similar to the network experiencing the proper use of the words, in particular language games. Connectionist models rely on both the notion of language games and contextual features to develop powerful tools.

Wittgenstein's transition from TLP, through *The Blue and Brown Books* (BB), to PI, is fundamental for the conceptual redefinition of these concepts. In the pages of BB, language games are conceived as primitive forms of language complete in themselves, yet imagined as evolving in changed circumstances into new and more complex ones. Moreover, in BB, a language game is defined as a *Satzsystem*. The language game is thought of in analogy with an axiomatic system. It involves a large-scale semantic holism. It will be in PI that the concept of *Sprachspiel* updates the preview developments. Here the language games are analogous to games in which the meaning of words is inextricably tied to the speakers' non-linguistic practice – 'the whole, consisting of language and actions into which it is woven' (PI, §7). Here emerges the force of the universe of practice and actions, and especially the crucial role of the public context. The study of language in the 1950s is disciplined by linguistics, and Firth (Firth 1968) is one of the leading figures that pinpointed the role of context. He was convinced that the complete meaning of a word is always contextual, and no study of meaning apart from context can be taken seriously and coined the notion of collocation. Collocation is 'quite simply the mere word accompaniment, the other word-material is which [the word is] most commonly or most characteristically embedded' (Firth 1968, 180). According to him, context-collocation is a part of the word's meaning (Firth 1969). His fame followed the slogan, 'You shall know a word by the company it keeps' (Firth 1969, 179). As we have seen in Word2Vec and in VSA for the beetle, the context and the collocation are crucial issues for the connectionist models. Moreover, it is again the context to be the hinge of the Wittgensteinian concept of meaning-as-use. This is a contextual concept. Meaning is public and accessible insofar as words are contextualized (in a specific language game).

Given that understanding and mastery of a language is a practice and that the meaning of the words is the use we make of them, as Wittgenstein stated in the PI, it follows that the contexts of specific situations in which we learn, use and understand the language, is a key item in the analysis of NLP and LAM. According to Wittgenstein, the contexts in question have public features and are crucial for his description of language games. Hence it is not possible to develop linguistic abilities in a private context, such as those described in the case of the beetle-in-the-box. The conceptual role of contexts is crucial for both NLP and LAM. As concerns NLP, looking at the shallow neural network of Word2vec, a word vector representation (WVR) applied in a translation model built by Google, the concept of context is of recognized importance given the output the network must give. Moreover, Lowney et al. (2020) showed how VSA can resolve some limitations encountered by the previous connectionist approach concerning the private language. Even if we distinguish a strong and a weak sense of the argument of the private language, the concept of meaning as occurring within a public context is assumed by NLP. In conclusion, WVR and VSA neural networks are built with different purposes, the former for translation, the latter to explain LAM, but both are grounded on the assumption that the meaning of linguistic signs could change according to the contexts in which they are used.

To conclude, we could say that Wittgenstein paved the path for the computational study of language: that is a connectionist analysis of language. We have seen that connectionism employs Wittgenstein's ideas and it is coherent with the broad picture of philosophy: connectionism offers a way of describing the language – it is coherent with Wittgenstein's suggestion to stop the ambition of theorizing about meaning and therefore to describe. From the symbols and rules approach to connectionist models we see the evolution of Wittgenstein's work:

While the symbols and rules approach might provide an emergent level of description, we see a disjunction, though not a sharp one, at the level of symbols (as encapsulated representations or dynamic attractors) and then at the level of roles (in which rule-like features come from connectionist ability to build analogical structures). These transitions suggest a more fluid picture of language than the classical approach allows and suggest an emergent rather than a reductionist or implementational account.

(Lowney et al. 2020, 666)

Before moving on, let us summarize the relationship between Wittgenstein's ideas and connectionist models, such as Word2Vec, Smolensky models, BERT or GPT. We claim that all of these models are computational upgrades of language games. In the following section, I critique the idea that the VSA can simulate a private language and provide an instrument to simulate the reference of private objects. The precedence of context over linguistic practices in language games remains an insurmountable barrier to those who argue for the feasibility of a private language.

The Beetle in the (Black) Box

As Mills (1993) noted, for Wittgenstein there is not typically an atomic content or correspondence that one can point to explicate a term's meaning. This is what follows from the story of the sensation diary and the story of the beetle. In these two stories, there is a relation between a human being, an interior (private) object and the language. If we want to model this framework with computational tools and connectionist methodologies, we will have a relation between human language and a system of algorithms (running on a device). An analogy could exist between what happens in the Wittgenstein scenarios and in connectionist models. Indeed, if the connectionist model is a kind of analogue to the mind model implied in PLA, the two models share similar features. The most important one is the analogy between the inaccessibility of the private objects to the others in PLA and the inaccessibility of the black box in the algorithms of connectionist models. Due to a proprietary copyright shield, some algorithms are programmed to contain or shadow some processes within a black box (this is the case with Google search, Instagram and Netflix). In this case within the black box, the content is not private as in the beetle case. However, this could be an analogy for the beetle case and the solution proposed by Lowney et al. (2020). They propose a method to hide/shadow the meaning of an interior object, shifting it from one meaning to another so that my beetle could be different from your beetle. It does not resolve the problem highlighted by Wittgenstein. The problem of PLA cannot be solved and demarcates the limits of the language games. According to Rudin and Radin (2019, 2): 'In machine learning, these black box models are created directly from data by an algorithm, meaning that humans, even those who design them, cannot understand how variables are being combined to make predictions.' Take all the Xs as processes within a black box, which seems to behold to the 'privacy' of the machine – we cannot understand what is going on there. The analogy between Wittgenstein's scenarios and the black box property of algorithms does not want to play the role of anthropomorphizing the machines, 'it makes no sense to ascribe thought or thoughtlessness, understanding, misunderstanding or failure of understanding to machines' (Hacker 2001, 34), but to highlight similar features, similar boundaries in both cases. As Rudin and Radin say, the black box hides the algorithmic processes, so how the variables are combined cannot be understood to make the final prediction. Black boxes limit our ability to understand data processing. The black box contains information we cannot access, as in the beetle case. The VSA proposal we have seen does not overcome this limitation. Lowney et al. (2020, 655) recognize the inaccessibility of the private object: 'Together, the iterations encountered in social contexts provide us with common language-games about, e.g. beetles, but there need be no specific entity directly represented by a VSA symbol.' Again, they say that 'VSA's use of random vectors virtually guarantees that "my beetle" will be different from "your beetle", thus mirroring the variations in the uses of the word that we each have encountered'. Their model aims to capture the shifting nature of the meaning of the word 'beetle' in different contexts:

> Further, as the concept or symbol BEETLE evolves in the experience of an individual, or the world 'beetle' changes its use by that individual in different contexts, the random vectors that constitute the symbol itself may be 'constantly changing', but these differences, at what becomes the sub-symbolic level, do not interfere with the informative communication that can take place at the symbolic level due to the regularities in the use of the words.
>
> *(Lowney et al. 2020, 655)*

What must be specified is that it is not possible to capture the meaning of 'beetle' as in the Wittgenstein scenario. What can be done with the VSA model is capturing the use of 'beetle' in some language games, in a public context. Their proposal to develop an algorithm to catch some uses of BEETLE is thus a kind of language game. They propose a way to describe what we can do publicly with language. Better, they tell how we can play with a philosophical problem, namely PLA. Nevertheless, their argument works only if we take the weaker version of PLA, in which we can deal with different private objects with slightly different meanings and communicate about them to each other. Therefore, in their scenario, the privacy of the meaning disappears. Their proposal is coherent, though, with the suggestion to describe the language. Indeed, Wittgenstein claims that theorizing about language, including private language, is not a good philosophical practice.

Some scholars have worked on the importance of context for human reasoning and communication. In particular, Hollister, Gonzalez and Hollister (2017) extend the discussion about contextual reasoning in humans and how modelling it in a computer program can help to get closer to the ultimate intelligent machine: 'We strongly believe that to create systems that have the full range of human-like intelligence requires imbuing them with the ability to process context – giving the system an idea of when and where the information was previously encountered so that a solution might be found using the situational context' (Hollister, Gonzalez and Hollister 2017, 599). AI developers face a terrific challenge: implementing contextual intelligence in deep-learning systems. The assumption is that context precedes language game in action. The ability to understand and master a language is based on contextual experience. The context precedes the speakers' awareness of the linguistic experience. Lowney and his colleagues face a significant challenge: they want to represent a situation where we do not have any information about the beetle's owner's contextual experience as a private object when using VSA. In other words, we end up with an empty data set related to the beetle owner's contextual experience. To function effectively, VSA requires incorporating contextual information inherent to the language used by speakers. This approach validates Wittgenstein's PLA and reinforces that language is a shared activity rather than providing further support for the philosophical stance of resolute readers.

The beetle case, as explained by Wittgenstein and Lowney et al. (2020), highlights the importance of context in understanding the meaning of words. In the absence of context, words lose their meaning. Context plays a crucial role in explaining the meaning of words. Word2Vec, a sophisticated word embedding system created by humans, cannot capture the nuances of open concepts. The analogy of privacy illustrates the limitations of NLP systems in grasping the meaning of words. Word2Vec and VSA are language games lacking the contextual features inherent in our daily practices and form of life.

As we have seen, deep-learning models are a type of artificial intelligence that learns to perform tasks by analysing large amounts of data. These models are often used in NLP applications. Deep-learning models are trained on large data sets of text and code. The model learns to associate patterns in the data with specific outputs. Once a deep-learning model is trained, we can use it to perform tasks on new data. Indeed, deep-learning models have been very successful in many NLP tasks. However, they are not able to represent the contextual features of meaning that are essential for understanding the beetle-in-the-box case. The PLA does raise important questions about the ability of deep-learning models to understand the meaning of words and create private meanings. Overall, the PLA is a reminder that we need to be careful about making claims about the ability of AI to understand human language. While deep-learning models have succeeded in many NLP tasks, they still have limitations.

Wittgenstein's PLA shows that the meaning of a word is not determined by its private reference to some internal object or state of mind, but rather by its use in a particular language game. Deep-learning models are not able to represent the contextual features of meaning that are essential for understanding the limitations of the beetle-in-the-box case. Therefore, deep-learning models cannot be used to represent the PLA. They represent the limit of language games and the meaning that can be derived from them.

References

Alai, Mario. 2021. *La Filosofia Analitica del Linguaggio*. Milano: Mimesis.
Baker, Gordon P. and Hacker, Peter M. S. 1984. 'On Misunderstanding Wittgenstein: Kripke's Private Language Argument'. *Essays on Wittgenstein's Later Philosophy. Synthese*, 58(3): 407–50.
Candlish, Stewart. 2004. 'Private Objects and Experimental Psychology'. In *Wittgenstein Today*, edited by Coliva, Annalisa and Picardi, Eva, 297–317. Padova: Poligrafo.
Church, Kenneth. 2007. 'A Pendulum Swung too Far'. *Linguistic Issues in Language Technology*, 2(4): 1–26.
Devlin, Jacob, Chang, Ming-Wei, Lee, Kenton and Toutanova, Kristina. . 2019. 'BERT: Pre-training of Deep Bidirectional Transformers for Language Understanding'. In *Proceedings of the Conference of the North American Chapter of the Association for Computational Linguistics: Human Language Technologies (NAACL-HLT)*, 1–16. Minneapolis: Association for Computational Linguistics.
Diamond, Cora. 2000. 'Does Bismarck Have a Beetle in His Box?'. In *The New Wittgenstein*, edited by Crary, Alice and Read, Rupert, 262–92. London: Routledge.
Dror, Itiel, E. and Dascal, Marcelo. 1997. 'Can Wittgenstein help free the mind from rules?'. In *The philosophical foundations of connectionism*, edited by Johnson, D. and Erneling, C., 217—26). Oxford: Oxford University Press.
Elman, Jeffrey, L. 2014. 'Systematicity in the Lexicon: On Having Your Cake and Eating it Too'. In *The Architecture of Cognition. Rethinking Fodor and Pylyshyn's Systematicity Challenge*, edited by Calvo, Paco and Symons, John, 115–46. Massachusetts: The MIT Press.
Firth, John, R. 1968. *Selected Papers 1952–1959*. London and Harlow: Longmans, Green and Co Ltd.
Firth, John, R. 1969. *Papers in Linguistics 1934–1951*. London: Oxford University Press.
Fisher, Eugen. 2009. 'Philosophical Pictures and Secondary Qualities'. *Synthese*, 171(1): 77-110.

Fodor, Jerry, A. and Pylyshyn, Zenon, W. 1988. 'Connectionism and Cognitive Architecture: A Critical Analysis'. *Cognition*, 28(1–2): 3–71.
Fogelin, Robert, J. 1976. *Wittgenstein*. London and Boston: Routledge.
Galilei, Galileo. [1623] 1960. 'Two Kinds of Properties. Selection from Il Saggiatore'. In *Philosophy of Science*, edited by Danto, Arthur C. and Morgenbesser, Sidney.151–73. New York: Meridian Books.
Gayler, Ross, W. 2003. 'Vector Symbolic Architectures Answer Jackendoff's Challenges for Cognitive Neuroscience'. In *ICCS/ASCS International Conference on Cognitive Science*, edited by Slezak, Peter, 133–38. Sydney, Australia: University of New South Wales, CogPrints.
Goldfarb, Warren. 1997. 'Wittgenstein on the Fixity of Meaning'. In *Early analytical philosophy: Frege, Russell, Wittgenstein. Essays in honor of Leonard Linsky*, edited by Tait, William, W., 75–89. Chicago: Open Court.
Goldstein, Laurence and Slater, Hartley. 1998. 'Wittgenstein, Semantics and Connectionism'. *Philosophical Investigations*, 21(4): 293–314.
Hacker, Peter M. S. 2001. *Wittgenstein: Connections and Controversies*. Oxford: Clarendon Press.
Hintikka, Jaakko and Hintikka, Merrill B. 1986. *Investigating Wittgenstein*. Cambridge: Basil Blackwell.
Hollister, Debra L., Gonzalez, Avelino and Hollister, James. 2017. 'Contextual Reasoning in Human Cognition and the Implications for Artificial Intelligence Systems'. In *Modeling and Using Context*, edited by Brézillon, Patrick, Turner, Roy and Penco, Carlo, 599–608. Cham: Springer.
Kanerva, Pentti. (1994). 'The spatter code for encoding concepts at many levels'. In *ICANN '94, Proceedings of the international conference on artificial neural networks*, edited by Marinaro, M., and Morasso P. G., 226–229. London: Springer–Verlag.
Kitaev, Nikita, Cao, Steven and Klein, Dan. 2019. 'Multilingual Constituency Parsing with Self-attention and Pre-training'. *Proceedings of the 57th Annual Meeting of the Association for Computational Linguistics*, 3499–505.
Lowney, Charles W., Levy, Simon D., Meroney, William and Gayler, Ross W. 2020. 'Connecting Twenty-First Century Connectionism and Wittgenstein'. *Philosophia* 48: 643–71.
Malcolm, Norman. 1954. 'Wittgenstein's Philosophical Investigations'. *Philosophical Review*, 63(4), 530–559.
Mikolov, Tomas, Chen, Kai, Corrado, Greg and Dean, Jeffrey. 2013. 'Efficient Estimation of Word Representations in Vector Space', 5 May 2022, https://arxiv.org/abs/1301.3781.
Mills, Stephen. 1993. 'Wittgenstein and Connectionism: A Significant Complementarity?'. *Royal Institute of Philosophy Supplement*, 34: 137–57.
Minsky, Marvin and Papert, Seymour. 1969. *Perceptrons: An Introduction to Computational Geometry*. Massachusetts: The MIT Press.
Mitchell, Melanie. 2019. *Artificial Intelligence. A Guide for Thinking Humans*. New York: Farrar, Strauss and Giroux.
Mulhall, Stephen. 2007. *Wittgenstein's Private Language: Grammar, Nonsense, and Imagination in Philosophical Investigations, Sections* 243–315. Oxford: Oxford University Press.
Pessoa, Fernando. [1982] 2015. *The Book of Disquiet*. London: Penguin Classics.
Plate, Tony. 2003. *Holographic Reduced Representation. Distributed Representation for Cognitive Structures*. Stanford: CSLI Publications Lecture Notes.

Poe, Edgar, A. 1968. 'The Impossibility of Writing a Truthful Autobiography', In *The Portable Edgar Allan Poe,* edited by Van Doren Stern Philip, 521–30. New York: Viking Portable.

Poveda, Jordi and Vellido, Alfredo. 2006. 'Neural Network Models for Language Acquisition: A Brief Survey'. In *IDEAL Intelligent Data Engineering and Automated Learning,* edited by Corchado, E., Yin, H., Botti, V. and Fyfe, C., 1346–57. Berlin: Springer.

Rasmussen, Daniel and Eliasmith, Chris. 2011. 'A Neural Model of Rule Generalization in Inductive Reasoning'. *Topics in Cognitive Science*, 3: 140–153

Rumelhart, David, E., McClelland, James, L. and the PDP Research Group. 1986. *Parallel Distributed Processing: Explorations in the Microstructure of Cognition.* Cambridge, MA: The MIT Press.

Rudin, Cynthia and Radin, Joanna. 2009. 'Why Are We Using Black Box Models in AI When We Don't Need To? A Lesson From An Explainable AI Competition'. *Harvard Data Science Review*, 1(2): 1–10.

Skelac, Ines and Jandrić, Andrej. 2020. 'Meaning as use: From Wittgenstein to Google's Word2vec'. In *Guide to Deep Learning Basics. Logical, Historical and Philosophical Perspective*, edited by Skansi, Sandro, 41–53. Berlin: Springer.

Smolensky, Paul. 1991. 'Connectionism, Constituency and the Language of Thought'. In *Connectionism: Debates on Psychological Explanation* (Vol. 2), edited by MacDonald, Cynthia and MacDonald, Graham, 164–98. Oxford: Blackwell, 1995.

Smolensky, Paul. 1995. 'Reply: Constituent Structure and Explanation in an Integrated Connectionist/symbolic Cognitive Architecture'. In *Connectionism: Debates on Psychological Explanation* (Vol. 2), edited by MacDonald, Cynthia and MacDonald, Graham, 223–90. Oxford: Blackwell.

Stern, David, G. 1991. 'Models of Memory'. *Philosophical Psychology*, 4(2): 203–17.

Stern, David, G. 2007. 'The Uses of Wittgenstein's Beetle: Philosophical Investigations §293 and its Interpreters'. In *Wittgenstein and his Interpreters: Essays in Memory of Gordon Baker,* edited by Kahane, Guy, Kanterian, Edward and Kuusela, Oskari, 248–68. Malden: Blackwell.

Stern, David, G. 2011. 'Private Language'. In *Oxford Handbook of Wittgenstein*, edited by Kuusela, Oskari and McGinn, Marie, ;248–68 Oxford: Oxford University Press.

Strawson, Peter, Frederick. 1954. 'Wittgenstein's "Philosophical Investigations". *Mind*, 63, 70–99.

Wang, Alex, Pruksachatkun, Yada, Nangia, Nikita, Singh, Amanpreet, Michael, Julian, Hill, Felix, Levy, Omer and Bowman, Samuel, R. 2019. 'SuperGLUE: A Stickier Benchmark for General-Purpose Language Understanding Systems'. In *Advances in Neural Information Processing Systems 32 (NIPS 2019),* edited by Wallach, H., Larochelle, H., Beygelzimer, A., d'Alché-Buc, F., Fox. E. and Garnett, R., 3266–80. New-York: Curran Associates Inc.

Wittgenstein, Ludwig. [1921] 1961. *Tractatus Logico-philosophicus,* edited by Pears, David, F. and Brian, F., McGuinness. New York: Humanities Press.

Wittgenstein, Ludwig. 2009. *Philosophical Investigations*, 4th edn, edited by Hacker, Peter M. S. and Schulte, Joachim, Oxford: Wiley-Blackwell.

Wittgenstein, Ludwig. [1914–1916] 1969. *Notebooks 1914-1916*, edited by von Wright, Georg H. and Anscombe, Gertrude, E. M. New York: Harper Torchbooks.

Wittgenstein, Ludwig. [1933–5] 1958. *The Blue and Brown Books.* New York: Harper and Row.

Wittgenstein, Ludwig. 1978. *Philosophical Grammar,* edited by Rhees, Rhus and Kenny, Anthony. Berkeley: University of California Press.

Chapter 8

SIMPLIFICATION WITHOUT FALSIFICATION: THE PROBLEM OF RELEVANCE IN LOGIC AND AI

Oskari Kuusela

Introduction

The problem I discuss in this chapter, with reference to Ludwig Wittgenstein's later philosophy of logic, its development and AI, concerns the issue of how to simplify complex information without falsification. Two relevant modes of simplification are abstraction and idealization. When we abstract, we leave out some features of the actual cases. When we idealize, we make things neater, for example, more uniform or exact than they are. As I will explain, the problem of how to simplify without falsifying quickly brings us to the notion of relevance. What can be abstracted or idealized away without falsification is that which is not relevant (essential, important or significant), and in general simplification without falsification requires that whatever is relevant (essential, important or significant) is taken into account. However, the notion of relevance in turn assumes or involves the perception of things being significant; it presupposes that the acting or thinking agent or entity has goals, purposes or interests. Thus, to get an AI system to simplify without falsifying, and to make it able to handle complex information in an intelligent way in this sense, seems to require that its behaviour is informed by goals, purposes or interests.[1]

The assumption I am making about intelligent behaviour is worth making explicit: In what follows, I assume that simplification without falsification is

---

1 Interest is perhaps the broadest of these three notions, and not every sense of interest is relevant for my discussion. For example, sentient beings have an interest not to suffer, but interests in this kind of innate or instinctive sense are not relevant for my discussion. See 'The Later Wittgenstein on Abstraction and Idealization' for the relevant sense of goals, purposes or interests.

an essential aspect of intelligent behaviour, even though it does not exhaust it. This is what enables an intelligent agent or entity to pick out what is relevant from a wealth of information and to update its perception of what is relevant when needed. Accordingly, I assume that to create an AI system whose behaviour could be described as intelligent (whatever intelligence in general is or means) requires that the system is capable of simplification without falsification. This seems important also for AI systems that are specialized rather than generally intelligent and might be used, for example, for diagnosing illnesses, examining images to find a certain kind of object, and so on for a great number of possible tasks. Before an AI system can be relied on in performing such tasks without a human being checking whether it might have ignored something relevant, we must be confident that it can simplify without falsifying.

There are interesting parallels between the development of Wittgenstein's philosophy of logic in relation to the problem of simplification without falsification and the development of AI. I begin by outlining the development of Wittgenstein's philosophy of logic in order to provide a background for my discussion of the problem of simplification without falsification in connection with AI.

The Background: *Tractatus* on Logic and the Collapse of its Project

Wittgenstein's goal in his early *Tractatus Logico-philosophicus* was to give a formal description of all possible propositions. Given that Wittgenstein envisaged language as a totality of propositions, this was intended at the same time to constitute a formal description of all possible or sensible ways of using language, and to draw limits to language use (Wittgenstein 1951: TLP preface, 4.001, 4114–4.115). Wittgenstein's idea – adapted from Gottlob Frege and Bertrand Russell – was that such a determination of the possible uses of language could be given through the explication of the underlying logical rules governing the use of language assumed to be common to all possible languages. This would then, to put it in Frege's and Russell's terms, amount to the clarification of the principles governing all thought that aims at truth. Further, this formal description of language was intended to constitute the foundation for logical analysis. Provided a successful formal description of all possible propositions, any proposition whatsoever could be analysed in accordance with this view of propositions by translating it into the logical language introduced in the *Tractatus* and designed by Wittgenstein in accordance with this conception of propositions. (Rather than expressed by means of theses, Wittgenstein's early account of logic is codified into the structure of his logical language.) In this way, Wittgenstein thought, a universally applicable method of logical analysis would be established that could be used to analyse any possible proposition – or anything that can be sensibly said in language.[2]

More specifically, Wittgenstein attempted to articulate this formal description of all possible propositions in terms of his notion of 'the general propositional form' which he describes as constituting the essence of propositions or language (Wittgenstein 1951: TLP 4.5, 5.47ff.). In this view, every proposition is a true/false representation of a possible state of affairs, whereby complex propositions are analysable into truth-functions of simple propositions consisting of logically simple, not further analysable names (Wittgenstein 1951: TLP 4.2, 4.22, 4.24, 5). As for the philosophical aims of this project, a key idea was that, once in place, this method of analysis could be employed to solve any philosophical problem whatsoever, assuming with Russell and Wittgenstein following him, that philosophical problems would be logical problems, that is, problems resulting from or involving logical unclarities (Russell 1914/1926, 42; cf. 68; Wittgenstein 1951: TLP 4.112, 6.53).

Believing that he had successfully completed this task of establishing the foundations for logic, Wittgenstein envisaged all philosophical problems to have been solved 'in essentials' (Wittgenstein 1951: TLP preface). Once the right method was in place, that is to say, all that was needed was to apply it. Since this could be left to others once the method was established, Wittgenstein went on to do other things. However, as he realized upon his return to philosophy, after a roughly 10-year hiatus that followed the completion of the *Tractatus*, truth-functions do not always work as he had set out. Even though this account of truth-functions in terms of the logical connectives continues to be treated as standard in logic, there are propositions that do not function in this way. For example, the conjunction 'A is green all over and A is red all over' is false, when conjuncts are true. Here it is important for understanding the problem for logic that, on the one hand, formally speaking nothing excludes the possibility of both conjuncts being true: the conjunction is not formally a contradiction. On the other hand, to appeal to the content of the propositions to explain contradiction, or the exclusion of the possibility of the conjunction being true, compromises the formality of logic, because this constitutes an appeal to something beyond the logical rules for conjunction. The logical behaviour of this complex proposition therefore does not correspond to the standard truth-tables, whereby a conjunction is true when the conjuncts are true. Indeed, the same problem arises in many other cases too,

---

2 For the project of the *Tractatus*, its background in Frege and Russell, and the justification of the interpretation assumed here, see Kuusela 2019, Chapters 1–3.

for example, with propositions about physical magnitudes like length, mass, temperature, speed, acceleration, time and so on. Thus, if the temperature in this room is 25 °C, anyone who knows what this means, knows it is not 30 °C. The proposition 'the temperature in this room is 25 °C and the temperature in this room is 30 °C' is always false, and thinkers and language users familiar with relevant concepts know this without any need to examine the situation, that is, a priori, as Wittgenstein explained this notion in the *Tractatus*.[3] Consequently, as Wittgenstein was forced to admit, '[...] what I said in the *Tractatus* doesn't exhaust the grammatical rules for "and", "not", "or" etc.; there are rules for the truth functions which also deal with the elementary part of the proposition' (Wittgenstein 1998: PR §82, p. 109; cf. Wittgenstein 2000: MS 108, 31). Wittgenstein's attempt to clarify the essence of propositions, language and thought by abstracting away anything contingent, leaving in place only their essential core codified into the rules governing his notation, had thus failed (Wittgenstein 1951: TLP 3.34–3.3421; Wittgenstein 2009: PI §§97, 108, 114–15; for more detailed discussion, see Kuusela 2023).

The conclusion in the last quote is highly significant. It indicates that, contrary to what Frege, Russell and the early Wittgenstein following them had assumed, it is not the case that the same logical rules govern thinking in all areas of thought regardless of what is thought or spoken about. As the point that there are logical rules that 'deal with the elementary parts of the proposition' can be understood, the rules governing the behaviour of the logical connectives are sensitive to what is spoken of. Logic therefore is not topic-neutral, to put the point as a first approximation.[4]

Indeed, the complexities of logic do not end here. Similar issues arise, for example, in connection with logical accounts of generality. Contrary to what the early Wittgenstein had assumed, and as logicians standardly do, there is not just one notion of 'all'. As Wittgenstein writes in the early 1930s, 'Generality is as ambiguous as the subject-predicate form. // There are as many different "alls" as there are different "ones". [...] // So it is no use using the word "all" for clarification unless we know its grammar in this particular case' (Wittgenstein 2000: TS 213, 328; cf. Wittgenstein 1974: PG, 269). That

---

3 For the early Wittgenstein's account of the a priority of logic, see Kuusela 2019, 63–64.

4 If logic is not topic-neutral, there is also no neat distinction between questions regarding the foundations of logic or establishing the method of logic on the one hand and philosophical logic or the application of logic on the other hand, contrary to what Wittgenstein assumed following Russell, whereby the purpose of philosophical logic (Russell) or the application of logic (Wittgenstein) was the analysis of specific propositional forms or concepts, and the clarification of the nature of whatever we speak about in terms of language (cf. TLP 5.557–5.5571; for discussion see Kuusela 2019, Chapter 5.1).

is, just like what counts as one object or instance depends on what is spoken/thought about (see next paragraph), so too the function of 'all' is sensitive to what the objects of thought are. Whilst, for example, all weekdays can be enumerated or listed, all real numbers cannot.[5] 'All' therefore behaves logically differently in the two kinds of cases. This counts as a formal difference in that it pertains to the use of relevant expressions and can be described without appealing to the content or meaning of what is spoken of. In other words, whilst 'all' can sometimes be explained through the formal procedure of giving a list, it cannot be explained in this way in other cases.

As for Wittgenstein's point about 'one' (see preceding quote), this and its significance can be explained as follows. Whilst the notion of numerical identity applies, for instance, to books and musical instruments in the sense that two people can have exactly the same but numerically different books or instruments, it does not apply to colours or thoughts. If two books have the same colour, the colours are not merely indistinguishable whilst still numerically different, but the two books share the same colour. Likewise, in order for two people to disagree about the truth of 'Wittgenstein was 165 cm tall' they must disagree about the truth of one and the same thought, not somehow each be concerned with their own thought. Thus, what it means for there to be one colour and one book is not the same. Although the point about the shareability of thoughts was emphasized by Frege in his criticisms of psychologistic accounts of logic, he did not recognize, or perhaps merely not regard as relevant for logic, that 'thought' can be used in more ways than this, some of which are not governed by this principle about shareability (Frege 1979, 127, 132–34). This is exemplified by thoughts in the sense of conscious events, as when a thought occurs to someone. Although someone else might have the same thought, its occurrence is a separate conscious event in each case (cf. Wittgenstein 2000: MS 145, 25). This latter point is significant in that, as it indicates, logic is even more fine-grained than is captured by saying that it is topic-sensitive or not topic-neutral. Logic is also context-sensitive in that different rules may govern the use of words as the expression of certain concepts, for example, the concept of thought, on different occasions.[6] Importantly, that I can later share with you the thought that occurred to me shows that we are not dealing here with an ambiguity of the word 'thought', as if we were

---

5 Symbolizing all natural numbers by $\aleph_0$ is likewise different from listing them, but here issues relating to the notion of infinity and the philosophy of mathematics arise that are beyond the scope of this chapter. Let me therefore simply emphasize that by 'listing' I mean listing relevant items one by one.
6 I am speaking of logic here in a broad sense that includes Russellian philosophical logic.

speaking of thoughts in some different sense when speaking about thoughts as conscious events, that is, as mental occurrences of a certain kind. Importantly, when I share a thought with you, I do not share a mental occurrence; I cannot pass on my psychological states to you. But the possibility of sharing a thought that I had presupposes that we are talking about thoughts in the same sense when speaking of thoughts as mental occurrences and as something that can be shared, even though the use of 'thought' is governed by different rules on the two occasions. (A thought is all of this; the concept of thought covers all these cases.)

Put generally, Wittgenstein reached the conclusion that 'Language is much more complicated than the logicians and the author of *Tractatus* have imagined' (Wittgenstein 2000: MS 152, 47; cf. Wittgenstein 2009: PI §23, Wittgenstein 1980: RPP I §920). Importantly, however, as Wittgenstein emphasizes, the *Tractatus*' formal description of possible propositions was not entirely wrong. Many propositions do behave as indicated by the standard truth-tables; logicians employing this kind of logic are not wrong in any straightforward sense. Rather than wrong, the *Tractatus*' account was incomplete and simplistic: it only covered part of the function of the notions of generality and logical connectives, and thus did not provide a correct account of all possible propositions. As Wittgenstein comments later, 'The rules for "and", "or", "not" etc., which I represented by means of the T-F notation, are a part of the grammar of these words, but not the whole' (Wittgenstein 1998: PR §83, p. 111).

Wittgenstein's Failed Attempt at Solution and the Parallel with the Development of AI

Forced to abandon the notion of the general propositional form as an account of all possible propositions, or of the formal unity of propositions, language and thought (cf. Wittgenstein 2009: PI §108), Wittgenstein tried to address this problem pertaining to the clarification of the logical rules governing thought and language by introducing the notion of propositional systems. This was an attempt to identify propositions as belonging to discrete systems that may behave according to different logical rules – and to get a handle on the variety of the logical rules governing language and thought in this way. The adoption of this new approach also required Wittgenstein to revise his early account of linguistic representation in the *Tractatus*, the so-called picture theory of propositions.[7] Rather than representing the possible states of affairs of the world individually, as Wittgenstein had assumed, propositions represent

---

7 See Kuusela 2022 for discussion of the picture 'theory'.

together as a system, similarly to a clock whose hands indicate time by pointing to certain positions on the clock face as opposed to others (cf. Wittgenstein 1974: PG, 131; Wittgenstein 2000: MS 114, 126). As Wittgenstein explains using measuring rods as his example:

> The fact that *one* measurement is right automatically excludes all others. I say automatically: just as all the graduation marks are on *one* rod, the propositions corresponding to the graduation marks similarly belong together, and we can't measure with one of them without simultaneously measuring with all the others. – It isn't a proposition which I put against reality as a yardstick, it's a *system* of propositions.
>
> *(Wittgenstein 1974: PR §82, p. 110)*

This applies to propositions about colour in an apparently straightforward way. If I say of object A that it is red all over, I am herewith also saying that it is not green, blue, brown, orange, and so on, all over, and this is how colour concepts work together as a system. (I will return at the end of this section to the sense of 'apparently', and how what I just said is problematically simplistic.) Likewise with propositions about temperature, speed and other earlier mentioned examples. Each of these types of propositions functions together with others of the same type as a system. Further, as indicated by the preceding points regarding 'all' and 'one', there may be differences between how 'all' and 'one' work in connection with different propositional systems.

One might thus say that Wittgenstein adjusted the task of providing a complete formal description of all possible propositions, or of language and thought as a whole, by limiting his descriptions to specific propositional systems. What one needs to do, on this approach, to have an overview of the logic of language and thought is to achieve an overview of the function of different propositional systems. This limits the scope of what logical descriptions have to account for in that instead of accounting for all of logic at once, which assumes that its rules function uniformly across different areas/topics of thought or language use, one can now focus on different propositional systems separately. This suggests that one might try to build up a complete account of the logic of language and thought from accounts of its separately described sub-parts. – But already here a problem arises. Can we assume that language/thought as a whole constitutes a system? If language or thought does not constitute a systematic whole but is a mere aggregate or collection of different propositional systems or uses of language, there is no criterion of completeness for determining when the logical rules of language or thought have been overall completely accounted for. As Kant emphasizes, in the case of a mere aggregate, unlike a systematic whole, it is not possible to tell whether we have accounted for all its components or accidentally left some out (see Kant 1999, A832-833/B860-861, cf. A64-65/B89, A645/B673).[8]

Irrespective of the last difficulty, however, we can see here a parallel between the development of Wittgenstein's philosophy of logic and the history of the development of AI. Similarly to Wittgenstein's attempt in his middle period to account for logic by describing narrower sub-parts of language and thought, AI researchers, after their failure to achieve their original goal of developing systems that could respond to the world in a generally intelligent way, turned to developing systems dealing with more manageable and narrowly determined micro-worlds, such as the blocks world of Terry Winograd's SHRDLU. The hope was to build up from such elements of intelligent behaviour a generally intelligent system that would be eventually capable of dealing with the real world (see Winograd 1972 and Dreyfus 1997 for discussion).

Abstractly speaking the problem that arose for the development of AI therefore is the same as or in any case analogous with Wittgenstein's problem. Rule-based AI systems need to understand whatever worldly items they are dealing with in order to be able to do whatever they are supposed to do. When the real world turned out to be too complex to deal with on the basis of the rules governing the behaviour of such systems, AI researchers narrowed the world down to simpler micro-worlds to make manageable the task of codifying into rules what the system needs to do. Wittgenstein's original aim was similarly to codify the logical rules governing language and thought into the structure of his logical language, thus accounting generally for all possible uses of language all at once. (This involved abstracting away different more specific propositional forms which, according to the original idea, were then to be accounted for later through the application of logic.) When the uses of language turned out to be more complex than Wittgenstein could account for all at once, he narrowed the uses down to discrete systems to make manageable his task of clarifying the logic of language.

But as Wittgenstein quickly realized in the case of logic, this approach faces serious problems. It seems difficult or impossible to determine the logical behaviour of propositions in terms of propositional systems, because this

---

8 The later Wittgenstein maintains that there is no such criterion of completeness for language: '[...] ask yourself whether our own language is complete and whether it was so before the symbolism of chemistry and the notation of the infinitesimal calculus were incorporated into it; for these are, so to speak, suburbs of our language. (And how many houses or streets does it take before a town begins to be a town?) Our language can be regarded as an ancient city: a maze of little streets and squares, of old and new houses, of houses with extensions from various periods, and all this surrounded by a multitude of new suburbs with straight and regular streets and uniform houses' (Wittgenstein 2009: PI §18).

requires that the use of propositions is limited to or contained within specific discrete systems. Problems such as the following arise: Is it possible to keep the propositional systems distinct, so that we can describe relevant uses of language separately and completely? If a certain proposition plays a role in more than one system, how do we know what rules ought to govern its use in a particular case? For example, if I tell you that the traffic light is green, have I excluded it being blue, as suggested by the idea of colour propositions constituting one system? Might it next be blue? Hardly, since the colours of traffic lights are limited to red, yellow and green, as anyone with a driving licence is required to know. If I describe someone looking white as a sheet, am I describing their face as having the colour or a clean white sheet? No, as the Cambridge English dictionary explains, 'if someone is (as) white as a sheet, their face is very pale, usually because of illness, shock, or fear.' Similarly, if someone's lips are blue from cold, this doesn't mean that their lips are the blue of the French tricolour, and neither does a red sky match the colour of the red in the French flag. Thus, colour ascriptions, to take a 'simple' example, do not function uniformly across the board, but they interact in a variety of ways with the objects of colour attribution and involve in this sense knowledge regarding the world.[9] The system of colour propositions, in other words, is not self-contained, but the rules for the use of colour concepts are context-sensitive. (For further examples of the context-sensitivity of colour attributions, see Travis 2008, 111.)

Thus, the risk of falsifying simplifications persists, even if we give up the goal of accounting for logic as a whole all at once. This explains why Wittgenstein, after moving on from the failed attempt to account for logic in terms of propositional systems to his mature view, keeps emphasizing that the purpose of language games in his later philosophy is not to build up from them (an account of) the actual complex uses of language. Rather, language games in the later Wittgenstein are models that can be used to clarify aspects of language use by comparing actual uses with the simpler language games employed as models:[10]

> When I describe certain simple language games, this is not in order to describe on their basis [MS 113 45v and TS 213, 202r: to build up from them] the

---

9 Adjectives generally aren't always used predicatively, as exemplified by attributive uses such as 'big mouse' and 'small horse', where the sense 'big' and 'small' depends on the object, as illustrated by the fact that small horse is bigger than a big mouse. Note, though, that there are examples relating to colour, such as red and white wine, white coffee and white chocolate, that are not descriptions but names, even though they look confusingly similar to descriptions.

10 For the method of language games, see Kuusela 2019, Chapter 5.

processes of our actual developed language, which would only lead to injustices. (Nicod & Russell.) Rather, we let the language-games be what they are. They should only emanate their clarifying effect on our problems.

(Wittgenstein 2000: MS 115, 81; my square brackets; cf. Wittgenstein 2009: PI §130–31)

Thus, Wittgenstein concluded that the logical rules governing the function of propositions cannot be accounted for in terms of propositional systems. The different uses of language, embedded into our actions in the world in their various contexts, have to be understood in the broader context of language as a whole. In other words, language cannot be divided into micro-languages in order to build up language proper out of them. 'It is only in a language that something is a proposition. To understand a proposition is to understand a language' (Wittgenstein 1974: PG, 131; Wittgenstein 2000: MS 114, 126).[11]

Now, what about AI? Is it possible to build up a generally intelligent system capable of dealing with the real world out of systems that can deal with micro-worlds, without the system, for example, losing sight of what micro-world corresponds to what part of the real world, and consequently failing to respond intelligently to the real world in an appropriately contextualized way? As noted, such projects of developing a generally intelligent AI system out of more narrowly intelligent systems were attempted, but without success. Historically, the development of AI therefore seems to mirror the development of Wittgenstein's philosophy of logic with regard to this failure too, not merely with regard to the respective strategies of Wittgenstein and AI researchers to simplify their original tasks. Just as Wittgenstein's attempt to account for the logic of language and thought in terms of simpler propositional systems failed, being able to cope with micro-worlds turned out not to be a step towards coping with the real world (see Dreyfus 1997). As I explain in the final section, Wittgenstein's mature philosophy of logic, and his account of how to simplify without falsifying, can help to understand what the problem here is, and what is required for simplification without falsification. This can help to understand what is required for being able to pick out what is relevant in whatever one is dealing with and to ignore what can be safely ignored.

---

11 For a more detailed account of the development of Wittgenstein's philosophy of logic, the notion of propositional systems, and how one might still employ propositional systems consistently with Wittgenstein's mature later methodology, see Kuusela 2023.

The Later Wittgenstein on Abstraction and Idealization

The key to Wittgenstein's later response to the problem of simplification (abstraction and idealization) without falsification is abandoning the abstract notion of complete descriptions of language use he assumed earlier.[12] Basically, when and whether a logical clarification of the use of language is complete depends on what unclarities or problems one is dealing with. There is no such thing as a complete description in an abstract and general sense, but whether a description is complete depends on the purpose for which it is given. This seems true of descriptions in general. The question when and whether a description of a room is complete is devoid any clear sense, unless we specify what the purpose of the description is. Is it relevant, for instance, how many books there are in the bookshelves? Is it relevant which books are in the shelves? Is the colour of their covers relevant? What about the number of pages in each book? Or does it suffice to say merely that there are books in the bookshelves? Next, what about there being cat in the room? Should this be included in the description like the bookshelves? And so on. As this indicates, there are no absolute or general criteria for the completeness of a description, but completeness depends on the purpose for which a description is given. (Typically, an understanding of such purposes is assumed implicitly, and indicated by the context, so that questions like the preceding are not often explicitly asked.) As another example consider descriptions of actions for the purposes of morality. What is relevant to include in order to correctly judge a case depends here on moral concerns, and someone might be mistaken about what counts as relevant, for example, due to their moral corruption. (Is it the only morally relevant feature of a certain action that it constituted an action of stealing, or is it also morally relevant that the person stole in order to feed starving children?) As this indicates, what counts as relevant is not always a matter of contingent, optional interests, as in the first example.

It is now easy to explain Wittgenstein's later conception of simplification without falsification in the case of logical descriptions. One can abstract and idealize in logic without falsification as long as the description accounts for whatever is relevant for the clarificatory task at hand. Correspondingly, anything irrelevant for the task can be safely left out without any harm and without saying anything false. This means that the completeness and correctness of logical descriptions or clarifications is relative to particular clarificatory tasks or purposes. What is relevant for a clarification depends on what exactly

---

12 See Kuusela 2019, Chapter 4 for a more detailed discussion of relevant points in Wittgenstein and the justification of the interpretation assumed here.

needs to be clarified. A logical description is complete insofar as it accounts for whatever needs to be accounted for in order to deal with the problems or unclarities at hand. This also means that two clarifications might describe the very same uses of language differently. This is fine, and does not involve any falsification, as long as each description meets its specific clarificatory goals. (Similarly in everyday language use, if I tell someone about my holiday, I will adjust my account to what I expect to be of interest to my listener. Consequently, two people might hear very different accounts of my holiday, whilst both accounts are nevertheless true.)

Accordingly, when speaking of his philosophical task in general terms as one of ordering our knowledge regarding language use, Wittgenstein emphasizes that, contrary to the *Tractatus*, there is not anything like *the* arrangement of this knowledge. 'We want to establish an order in our knowledge of the use of language: an order for a particular purpose, one out of many possible orders, not *the* order' (Wittgenstein 2009: PI §132). Thus, there can be different logical orderings of our knowledge of language use each serving their own purposes of clarification relating to the solution of particular philosophical problems. What needs to be said about certain uses of language in response to one set of problems might differ from what needs to be said about the same uses in response to another set of problems (analogously to telling different people about a holiday).

Wittgenstein makes a related point also in criticizing the notion of a complete logical analysis in the *Tractatus*. In short, whilst a logical analysis will always abstract away certain features of actual language use, it should nevertheless account for whatever is essential for the analysis. But what is or counts as essential? There is no absolute or general answer to or criterion for this, and therefore no such thing as a complete analysis of a proposition that accounts for every possible unclarity relating to the concepts or uses of language in question in the sense of Tractarian complete analyses. (New unclarities or problems can always arise, and they have no determinate limit.) Wittgenstein illustrates this in the *Investigations* by asking what is essential in a lamp. As this brings out, there is no single privileged answer, but what is essential depends on our interests or concerns. If our interests are, for example, aesthetic rather than practical, different 'features' of the lamp may be essential or important.

> one may say of certain objects that they have this or that purpose. The essential thing is that this is a lamp, that it serves to give light – what is not essential is that it is an ornament to the room, fills an empty space, and so on. But there is not always a clear boundary between essential and inessential.
>
> *(Wittgenstein 2009: PI §62)*

What these considerations bring to view is the dependence of what is relevant, important, significant or essential on our interests or concerns.[13] Nothing is relevant, important, significant or essential as such or in general in an abstract sense, but this depends on what is at issue or at stake, that is, what is of interest to one or what one is concerned with. As explained, in the case of logical descriptions, what is relevant and ought to be included in a description so that it is complete, depends on the specific task of clarification at hand. As noted, this explains how it is possible to simplify (abstract or idealize) without falsification. What this account of simplification without falsification then leads us to, is the notion of relevance that has caused trouble for AI. Hubert Dreyfus comments on the notion of relevance and AI:

> I was particularly struck by the fact that, among other troubles, researchers were running up against the problem of representing significance and relevance […].
>
> *(Dreyfus 2008, 332)*

> Minsky, unaware of Heidegger's critique [of a Cartesian conception of the mind], was convinced that representing a few million facts about objects, including their functions, would solve what had come to be called the common sense knowledge problem. It seemed to me, however, that the deep problem wasn't storing millions of facts; it was knowing which facts were relevant in any given situation. One version of this relevance problem was called the frame problem. If the computer is running a representation of the current state of the world and something in the world changes, how does the program determine which of its represented facts can be assumed to have stayed the same, and which would have to be updated?[14]
>
> *(Dreyfus 2008, 332; my square brackets)*

The point I wish to make is the following. Regardless of whichever way we try to explain relevance, that is, whether we attempt to do so in terms of the structure of care that is constitutive of Dasein's understanding of being according to Heidegger, as Dreyfus would recommend, or whether we attempt to do so in

---

13 In order to avoid confusion, it might be worth noting that I am not (and Wittgenstein is not) speaking of relevance either in the sense of the relevance theory relating to communication and Gricean philosophy of language, nor in the sense of relevance logic that deals with certain odd inferences licenced by classical logic that everyday thought/language does not recognize.

14 Similar problems also affect contemporary deep neural networks whose capacity to identify objects may be affected by small changes in images presented to them as input that may be imperceptible to or not picked out as relevant by humans (see Szegedy et al. 2014; Eykholt et al. 2018).

some different way, for example, with reference to the Socratic idea of human action as oriented towards the good or what is perceived as good, something like this, that is, that things matter for the acting or thinking agent, seems to be required to account for relevance. For a disinterested agent or entity anything or nothing is relevant. Thus, for instance, if my own good does not matter to me, I might just as well walk under a bus; an approaching bus will not count as anything relevant to avoid when crossing a street. Accordingly, as John Haugeland has argued, that things matter is relevant for understanding language too. Understanding a story may require one, for instance, to keep track separately of what is said from the perspective of another person, that is, what they care about and are trying to do, and from one's own perspective (Haugeland, 1998, 52–54). It may also require having a sense of oneself and even clarity about what really matters, for example, in what way having a child matters, without which the point of a story may be lost, even though one understands all the words and sentences in it (Haugeland 1998, 55–59). Accordingly, as Haugeland puts the point, 'The trouble with Artificial Intelligence is that computers don't give a damn' (Haugeland 1998, 47). Consequently, Haugeland maintains that when it comes to designing artificial intelligence with the purpose of understanding human psychology (a.k.a. mind design), 'No system lacking a sense of *itself* as "somebody" with a complete life of its own (and about which it particularly cares) can possibly be adequate as a model of human understanding' (Haugeland 1998, 3).

Similarly, implicit in Wittgenstein's account of how to simplify without falsification, or more abstractly how to deal with complex information in an intelligent way, is the notion of goal, purpose or interest. Logical clarification, which was Wittgenstein's concern specifically, is a human activity that serves specific human interests (see Floyd 2016). Accordingly, Wittgenstein speaks of 'our real need' and of 'turning our whole inquiry around' 'on the pivot of our real need' when explaining the methodological repositioning he believed was required to address the problem of false simplification in his early philosophy (Wittgenstein 2009: PI §108).[15] I presume that by 'our real need' Wittgenstein means here our need for clarity in philosophical thinking or more generally the need for clarity in thinking in general, given his emphasis (in a letter to Norman Malcolm) that the purpose of philosophy is not merely to enable one to talk about 'some abstruse questions about logic, etc.' but to 'improve your thinking about the important questions of everyday life' (Malcolm 2009, 93).

---

15 For a discussion of what Wittgenstein means by turning the inquiry around, see Kuusela 2008, Chapter 3 and Kuusela 2019, Chapter 4.

Here, I believe, something important comes to view about what it is or means to have goals, purposes or interests.

Wittgenstein's goal or purpose in developing methods of logic and philosophy that would enable one to think clearly was motivated by an underlying commitment to clarity and clear thinking, the aspiration for which informed his philosophical work throughout. It was for the sake of this commitment that he was ready to dismantle his early philosophy as well as to abandon his intermittent attempt to address its problems by means of the notion of propositional systems when these methods turned out not to enable one to analyse or clarify the uses of language up to a standard required by philosophy. Indeed, Wittgenstein did all this, despite the unusual level of recognition that his early work received, and without knowing whether he could ever solve his problems regarding logical methodology or whether he might merely be destroying what he had achieved. This commitment made him willing, in other words, to tolerate high levels of stress and to resist the comfort of fame brought by his early work, which would have already been enough to secure his name in the history of philosophy. This reveals something important about having goals, purposes or interests, as can now be explained.

Having goals, purposes or interests in any serious sense is not merely a matter of setting out – or being programmed – to do certain things, for example, to analyse the uses of language by means of such and such a method. It involves as an essential component preparedness to revise and question what one is doing with a view to achieving the goals and purposes in question, or to satisfy one's interests. This same structure of commitment that I illustrated with reference to Wittgenstein is discernible also in morality which, if one takes it seriously, may require one to question and revise one's moral views for the sake of remaining true to one's commitment to morality. This is so, at any rate, if we accept the Aristotelian conception that only the good (virtuous) can really know what is good or what goodness involves, which implies that one may be required to revise one's views about the good and how one lives and acts, as one makes progress towards becoming good. (Morality on such a view is impossible to codify into any moral rules.) Having goals or purposes and being willing to do what is required to achieve one's goals or purposes is therefore not merely a matter of setting out to do something one thinks will enable one to achieve those goals and purposes. It also involves the capacity to critically examine and change what one is doing, which is required for staying true to one's commitment to one's goals and purposes. Without this kind of commitment, self-criticism and capacity to change one's approach, the activities undertaken to achieve one's goals and purposes risk becoming spurious, merely done for the sake of form and in order for one to appear to be doing something to achieve the goals and purposes in question. (This problem seems to plague many human institutions once they have become established, if they are not constantly renewed with the purpose of ensuring that they serve the purposes for which they were originally set up.)

The question then is whether it is possible to design AI systems that are capable of having goals, purposes and interests in the outlined sense, whereby having goals, purposes or interests depends on a genuine commitment to them as something that matters to the agent or entity that has them. As I have argued, the capacity of an agent or entity to simplify without falsification is dependent on an ability to discern what is relevant. This, in turn depends on having goals, purposes or interests, whilst having genuine goals, purposes and interests involves or requires a commitment to do whatever it takes to achieve those goals, purposes or interests, including criticizing, questioning and rejecting what one has done up to now in their pursuit. Is this possible for AI? Insofar as the capacity to simplify without falsifying is necessary for generally intelligent AI systems, is it possible to design such systems? I do not know and do not think my guesses would be of much value. What I have tried to do is to outline certain minimal conditions that a generally intelligent AI system would have to meet.[16]

References

Dreyfus, Hubert. 'From Micro-Worlds to Knowledge Representation: AI at an Impasse'. In John Haugeland (ed.), *Mind Design II*. Cambridge, MA: MIT Press, 1997, pp. 143–182.

Dreyfus, Hubert. 'Why Heideggerian AI Failed and How Fixing it Would Require Making it More Heideggerian'. In Philip Husbands, Owen Holland, and Michael Wheeler (eds.), *The Mechanical Mind in History*. Cambridge, MA: The MIT Press, 2008, pp. 331–372.

Eykholt, Kevin, Evtimov, Ivan, Fernandes, Earlence, Li, Bo, Rahmati, Amir, Xiao, Chaowei, Prakash, Atul, Kohno, Tadayoshi, and Song, Dawn. 'Robust Physical-World Attacks on Deep Learning Visual Classification'. *arXiv:1707.08945v5 [cs.CR]*, 2018: 1–11. https://doi.org/10.48550/arXiv.1707.08945.

Floyd, Juliet. 'Chains of Life: Turing, *Lebensform*, and the Emergence of Wittgenstein's Later Style'. *Nordic Wittgenstein Review* 5 (2) 2016: 7–89.

Frege, Gottlob. *Posthumous Writings*. Oxford: Blackwell, 1979.

Haugeland, John. *Having Thought: Essays in the Metaphysics of Mind*. Cambridge, MA: Harvard University Press, 1998.

---

16 I am grateful to Peter Murray for comments on an earlier draft, the face/sheet example, discussion of what it is to have the goals or purposes, and some references to recent AI literature. My thinking about what it is to have goals or purposes is also influenced by Haugeland's 'Truth and Rule-following' (in Haugeland 1998; 2002), although I am uncertain about how to connect my ways of speaking with his.

Haugeland, John. 'Authentic Intentionality'. In Matthias Scheutz (ed.), *Computationalism: New Directions*. Cambridge, MA: MIT Press, 2002, pp. 159–174..

Kant, Immanuel. *The Critique of Pure Reason*. Indianapolis: Hackett, 1999.

Kuusela, Oskari. *The Struggle against Dogmatism*. Cambridge, MA: Harvard University Press, 2008.

Kuusela, Oskari. *Wittgenstein on Logic as the Method of Philosophy*. Oxford: Oxford University Press, 2019.

Kuusela, Oskari. 'Wittgenstein's *Tractatus* without Paradox: Propositions as Pictures'. *Revista de Filosofia Aurora*, 34 (63) 2022: 85–104.

Kuusela, Oskari. 'The Colour-exclusion Problem and the Development of Wittgenstein's Philosophy of Logic'. In Florian Franken-Figuiredo (ed.), *Wittgenstein's Philosophy in 1929*. New York: Routledge, 2023, pp. 61–79..

Malcolm, Norman. *Ludwig Wittgenstein: A Memoir*. Oxford: Clarendon Press, 2009.

Russell, Bertrand. *Our Knowledge of the External World*. London: George Allen and Unwin, 1926 (originally published in 1914).

Szegedy, Christian, Zaremba, Wojciech, Sutskever, Ilya, Bruna, Joan, Erhan, Dumitru, Goodfellow, Ian, and Fergus, Rob. 'Intriguing Properties of Neural Networks'. *arXiv:1312.6199 [cs.CV]*, 2014: 1–10. https://doi.org/10.48550/arXiv.1312.6199.

Travis, Charles. *Occasion Sensitivity: Selected Essays*. Oxford: Oxford University Press, 2008.

Winograd, Terry. 'Understanding Natural Language'. *Cognitive Psychology* 3 1972: 1–191.

Wittgenstein, Ludwig. *Tractatus Logico-Philosophicus*. London: Routledge & Kegan Paul, 1951. (TLP)

Wittgenstein, Ludwig. *Philosophical Grammar*. Oxford: Blackwell, 1974. (PG)

Wittgenstein, Ludwig. *Remarks on the Philosophy of Psychology, Vol 1*. Oxford: Blackwell, 1980. (RPP I)

Wittgenstein, Ludwig. *Philosophical Remarks*. Oxford: Blackwell, 1998. (PR)

Wittgenstein, Ludwig. *Wittgenstein's Nachlass: The Bergen Electronic Edition*. Oxford: Oxford University Press, 2000. (References by Manuscript/typescript number.)

Wittgenstein, Ludwig. *Philosophical Investigations*. Oxford: Wiley, 2009. (PI)

Chapter 9

MODELLING ANALOGICAL REASONING: ONE-SIZE-FITS-ALL?

Ioannis Votsis

Introduction

A key type of reasoning in everyday life and science is reasoning by analogy. Roughly speaking, such reasoning involves the transposition of solutions that work well in one domain to another, on the basis of pre-existing analogous properties between the two domains. If we are to automate scientific reasoning with artificial intelligence (AI), then we need adequate models of analogical reasoning that clearly specify the conditions under which good analogical inferences can be made and bad ones avoided. Two general approaches to such modelling exist: universal and local. In this chapter, we assess the merits and demerits of both approaches. We concede that there are substantial obstacles standing in the way of the universal model view, but that these may be mitigated to some extent by supplementing existing models with additional criteria. One such criterion is defended, particularly against a challenge due to Wittgenstein. We argue that this challenge can be met and thus that there is hope for a one-size-fits-all model in the study of analogical reasoning.

The structure of the chapter is as follows. The section titled 'Philosophical Models of Analogical Reasoning' provides an overview of the main philosophical models of analogical reasoning, identifying some of their strengths and weaknesses. The next section, titled 'AI Models of Analogical Reasoning', briefly looks at one model of analogical reasoning that originates in the symbolic AI tradition, and offers some very general remarks about the prospects of modelling analogical reasoning with neural AI. Following that, the section titled 'Norton's Material Challenge' sets out the key issue of concern for this chapter, namely whether a universal model of analogical reasoning can be constructed. In the section titled 'Relevant Conceptual Uniformity', we consider one promising route towards a universal model via the supplementary criterion that the concepts involved are relevantly uniform. The subsequent section, titled 'A Wittgensteinian Spanner in the Works?', presents a challenge to this route that can be found in Wittgenstein's family resemblance metaphor, whose ultimate target is the rejection of concept uniformity. An attempt is made to meet this challenge by arguing that some concepts in natural science are uniform, or at least more uniform than others, but also that scientific inquiry strives towards, and manages to increase, uniformity. The ensuing section, titled 'Testability and Computational Implementation', highlights the testability of the proposed criterion as well as the relative ease with which it can be computationally implemented, raising the overall prospects of automating the process of scientific discovery. The section titled 'Conclusion' contains a summary of the main points but also a parting attempt to answer the question why analogical reasoning works at all.

Philosophical Models of Analogical Reasoning

In this section, we explore some of the main models of analogical reasoning, particularly as they are applied to the sciences. The models are taken from the philosophical literature. Let us begin the discussion with some useful terminology. Analogical reasoning is reasoning that exploits analogies. Performing such reasoning first requires some known or accepted similarities between the properties and/or relations – henceforth, simply 'properties' – of two domains, which we may call 'source' S and 'target' T. These similarities ground the analogy, which is then employed to infer an additional similarity between S and T. The additional similarity concerns a property known or accepted to hold in S, but heretofore not known or accepted in T. Darwin posited his theory of evolution by natural selection by, among other things, drawing inspiration from two sources: (1) artificial selection and (2) Malthus' principle of population growth. Artificial selection involves the breeding of animals or plants to suppress or accentuate certain traits. During Darwin's time, for example, pigeons and other birds were bred for exhibition purposes by making their beaks smaller and their chests bigger. This was accomplished by successively mating birds that exhibited the desired traits, which were then inherited in the next generation, leading to a slow but steady tendency towards those traits. Malthus's principle of population growth was an attempt to model what happens to the size of a human population when the availability of resources varies. In times of plenty, and other things being equal, such populations grow. At some point, however, the growth outpaces the availability of resources, leading to competition and a struggle for existence, including war and population reductions. Using analogical reasoning, Darwin argued that nature places similar selection and resource pressures on animals and plants. These pressures suppress or accentuate traits depending on whether or not possessing them provides advantages or drawbacks in the struggle for survival and reproduction. In his own words:

> [w]hy may I not invent hypothesis of natural selection (which from the analogy of domestic productions [i.e. artificial selection], & from what we know of the struggle of existence [i.e. Malthus' principle] & of the variability of organic beings, is in some very slight degree, in itself probable) & try whether this hypothesis of natural selection does not explain (as I think it does) a large number of facts.
>
> *(Letter to J. S. Henslow, quoted in Darwin [1860] 1967: 204)*

Analogical reasoning is typically construed in argument form. The premises assert known/accepted similarities between the properties of S and T as well as some additional property that S is known/accepted to possesses. That additional property is then inferred in the conclusion to be true of T. As an example, we may turn to the abovementioned analogy, whose corresponding argument may be formulated as follows (where AS is Artificial Selection, NS is Natural Selection, MP is Malthus' Principle):

1. AS is similar to NS in that selective reproduction affects which traits are inherited.
2. MP is similar to NS in that there is competition for resources.
3. AS selection pressures affect survival and reproduction rates.
4. MP resource pressures affect survival and reproduction rates.
5. Therefore, NS selection and resource pressures affect survival and reproduction rates.

Stated thus, the argument is best characterized as either inductive or abductive in form. Still, it can be turned into a deductive argument by finding and stating the missing premises. Two questions arise here. One is descriptive: What form of arguments are involved in analogical reasoning as it is practiced? The other is prescriptive: What form of arguments should be involved in such reasoning? We shall not wade into this debate. For simplicity, and unless otherwise noted, the analogical arguments presented hereafter are cast in broadly inductivist terms.

Another important issue that comes up in this literature concerns the role of analogical arguments. Sometimes such arguments are utilized to provide support for a conclusion, thereby playing a justificatory role. Indeed, as Bartha notes: 'In fields such as archaeology, where we lack direct means of testing, they may provide the strongest form of support available' (2010: 2). More frequently, however, they are utilized to provide some initial plausibility, thereby playing a discovery or heuristic role. The former role is typically thought to be more demanding than the latter. As a result, models of analogical reasoning that are geared towards justification are also employed for discovery but not vice versa. In what follows, we are focusing more on discovery rather than full-blown justification. This stance is not meant to prejudice our attitude towards the debate over the proper role for analogical reasoning. To make this clear, whenever possible, we will employ the neutral term 'admissible' to denote the various roles such arguments may play. That is to say, admissibility may be enunciated in different ways. For example, initial plausibility, probability, and so on.

Let us explore some philosophical models of analogical reasoning. The first such model is simplistic but useful in that it conveys some basic ingredients that go into modelling analogical reasoning:

The Simple Schema (TSS)

An analogical inference from S to T in relation to feature Q is admissible if and only if:

'(1) S is similar to T in certain (known) respects.
(2) S has some further feature Q.
(3) Therefore, T has the feature Q, or some feature Q* similar to Q'. (Bartha 2010: 13)

This is a no-frills version of analogical reasoning. The key question is whether Q, the additional feature of S asserted in premise 2, is also a feature of T. Given the analogy between S and T established in premise 1, we are allowed to conclude that it is also a feature of T. Note that, strictly speaking, the inferred feature need not be identical but may just be merely similar to Q – hence the reference to Q*.

TSS is clearly too liberal. Almost any S–T pairing can be deemed to be analogous and therefore ripe for an extended analogy to a corresponding feature Q. That's because the only requirement TSS brings to the table is the existence of some similarities between S and T, and these are rather easy to come by. Here's a made-up example that illustrates how this liberality can lead to absurd results:

1. Diamonds and chalk are made up of carbon-based molecules.
2. Diamonds have a hardness rating of 10 on the Mohs scale.
3. Therefore, chalk has a hardness rating of 10 on the Mohs scale.

This is obviously a bad inference to draw as chalk is a very soft rock. It is made up of calcite, which actually has a rating of 3 on the Mohs scale, where 10 is the hardest and 1 the softest.

Another philosophical model, one that seeks to plug the holes left behind by TSS, is Hesse's (1966) causal model. The model is meant to establish justification for the inferred similarity by imposing three restrictions on analogical arguments. First, the known/accepted similarities between S and T that set up the basic analogy must be observational (the observational condition). Second, the properties in S that form part of the basic analogy must be causally connected to the additional property in S that forms part of the extended analogy (the causal condition). Third, there must not be essential or causal properties in S that are known to be dissimilar with essential or causal properties in T (the no essential dissimilarity condition). This model is typically presented in tabular form:

Hesse's Causal Model (HCM)

Similarities / Domains	S	T
Known Observational Similarity	Property Q_1	Property Q_1 (or Property Q_1^*)
	...	...
	Property Q_n	Property Q_n (or Property Q_n^*)
Inferred Observational Similarity	Property Q_{n+1}	Property Q_{n+1} (or Property Q_{n+1}^*)

The known similarities, which establish the basic analogy, are conceived of as horizontal relations (denoted by the double-headed arrow) between the observational properties $Q_1, ..., Q_n$ of S and those of T. The causal relation between $Q_1, ..., Q_n$ and Q_{n+1} is conceived of as a vertical relation (denoted by the single-headed arrow). Finally, the inferred similarity is property Q_{n+1} (or Q_{n+1}^*), which is located under T at the very bottom on the right. The last row establishes the extended analogy between S and T. Applying this model to the diamond–chalk case, we can block the inference that chalk has a hardness rating of 10, because the property of being made up of carbon-based molecules on its own does not *cause* an object to have that level of hardness.

Despite generally acknowledged as a step in the right direction, HCM is seen as ultimately inadequate. One common accusation is that it is too strict because it requires a causal connection between $Q_1, ..., Q_n$ and Q_{n+1}, where (presumably) sometimes a mere correlation can serve just as well. As an example, Bartha (2010) gives Benjamin Franklin's inference that (metal) rods attract lightning in the wild just like they attract electrical fluid in the lab, which Franklin bases on several existing similarities between electrical fluid and lightning: '1. Giving light. 2. Colour of the light. 3. Crooked direction […] 10. Melting metals. 11. Firing inflammable substances. 12. Sulphureous smell' (Franklin 1941: 334). This was a good analogical argument, Bartha argues, even though '[t]here was no known causal connection between the twelve "particulars" [the known similarities] and the thirteenth property [the inferred similarity], but there was a strong correlation' (2010: 44).

An altogether different philosophical approach puts probability front and centre, seeking to quantify the goodness of analogical arguments. In a nutshell, known/accepted similarities increase the overall likeness between S and T, thereby lending more support to the inferred similarity. The idea goes back to John Stuart Mill ([1843] 1973), who argued that 'There can be no doubt that every such resemblance which can be pointed out between B [read: T] and A [read: S], affords some degree of probability, beyond what would otherwise exist, in favour of the conclusion drawn from it' (p. 556). The properties that those resemblances are about, he explained, 'must not be properties known to be unconnected with it' (p. 555). That is, they must not be properties that are not known to be irrelevant for the extended analogy. We can give this model a modern formulation, interpreting probabilities as rational degrees of belief, a.k.a. 'credences', as follows:

Mill's Probability Model (MPM)

The admissibility of an analogical inference from S to T in relation to property Q_k increases if and only if: (a) $S(Q_k)$ and (b) for any property Q_i that is distinct from Q_k, $P(T(Q_k) \mid (S(Q_i) \approx_s T(Q_i)) \& B) > P(T(Q_k) \mid B)$.

where:

$P(\cdot \mid \cdot)$ stands for a conditional probability function

$\Phi(Q_i)$ stands for domain Φ possessing property Q_i

$\Phi(Q_i) \approx_s \Psi(Q_i)$ stands for domains Φ and Ψ being similar with respect to property Q_i, which is not recognized as irrelevant

B stands for background knowledge.

Applying this model to the electrical fluid-lighting case enables us to draw the inference that (metal) rods attract lightning in the wild just as they attract electrical fluid in the lab, provided the similarities Franklin cites do indeed increase our credence in the inferred similarity. Questions can of course be posed about the credence-inducing credentials of those similarities, but we will not pursue them here.

MPM may overcome the restrictiveness that presumably afflicts HCM, but it does so by being more generous in its attribution of goodness to analogical arguments. As such, it opens itself up to accusations of being too liberal. Similarities that are not known to, but may actually, be irrelevant are allowed to increase credence in T possessing that additional property. As an example, take the *Ligularia fischeri* (S) and the *Caltha palustris* (T) plants. These plants look very much alike and are often mistaken for one another. Suppose that for a given individual X, S is known to be edible, but they do not know if T is edible. Suppose, moreover, that X does not know whether the properties involved in the phenotypical similarities are actually irrelevant for the edibility of the plants. Following MPM, X may then tragically draw the inference that T is edible, even though it is not only inedible but poisonous. Alas, this is not just a fabricated case. Every year several people in Korea get poisoned this way.

The final philosophical model to consider here can be found in Bartha (2010: Ch. 4). His model is designed to play only a heuristic role. Moreover, the conditions it imposes are meant to be sufficient, but not necessary, for initial plausibility:

Bartha's Articulation Model (BAM)

An analogical argument meets the requirements for prima facie [i.e. initial] plausibility if:

1. *Overlap.* $\phi^+ \cap P \neq \emptyset$ (where $\emptyset$ is the empty set).
2. *No-critical-difference.* $\phi^C \cap N = \emptyset$. (Bartha 2010: 101)

The symbols are articulated as follows: P denotes all the properties in the positive analogy (i.e. the known similarities between S and T), N denotes all the properties in the negative analogy (i.e. the known dissimilarities between S and T), ϕ^+ denotes the properties in S that causally or merely correlationally contribute to the presence of the additional property in S, and ϕ^C denotes the properties in S that are critical factors, that is, 'those elements of the prior association [i.e. the known similarities] represented as playing an *essential* part *in the circumstances*' (100) [original emphasis]. What Bartha seems to mean by the first condition is that at least one property in S used in the positive analogy between S and T must be causally or merely correlationally connected to the additional property in S. This condition is clearly made in the image of HCM's vertical relation, but a bit looser to allow for correlational, not just causal, connections. What he seems to mean by the second condition is that no property in S that plays a critical role in that connection should be part of the negative analogy between S and T. BAM is further developed in the same chapter to deal with arguments that employ multiple analogies. Moreover, in a subsequent chapter (Ch. 8), Bartha offers an adaptation of his model in probabilistic terms, which he calls 'non-negligible prior probability'. As the details of this adaptation are quite involved, we refrain from its exposition here.

The model is not without its critics. One objection concerns the sanctioning of both causal and correlational connections between the base analogy properties and the property in the extended analogy. Although BAM's inclusion of correlational cases appears to be a step forward when compared to HCM's outright prohibition, it is still unclear why we should admit all correlational cases when making such inferences. If only some correlational cases pass muster, we need criteria that distinguish the good ones from the bad ones. Put otherwise, BAM appears to be too liberal in its conception of analogical reasoning.

AI Models of Analogical Reasoning

Let us now discuss, albeit briefly, AI models. These are often accompanied by computational implementations and come in roughly two flavours: symbolic and neural.[1] The symbolic models include the structure-mapping engine (SME) (Falkenhainer, Forbus and Gentner 1986) and the active-symbol architecture (Hofstadter 1995). The neural models include the wild relation network (Barrett et al. 2018), and the emergent symbol binding network (Webb, Sinha and Cohen 2020). In what follows, and due to space limitations, we consider only one symbolic model, the SME, but also make some general remarks about what can be expected from neural models.

The SME is a computational model that implements Gentner's (1983) structure-mapping theory of analogical processing in cognition. The model restricts similarities to structures, that is, the relations between elements and even the relations between relations, of the domains in question. In more detail, neither the elements nor the monadic properties of T need to resemble the elements or the monadic properties of S, but some relations in T must be similar to relations in S. Although not explicitly expressed in terms of analogical inference admissibility, we may provide such a formulation for ease of comparison with the foregoing models:

---

[1] Mitchell (2021) provides a useful and up-to-date overview of AI models and divides them into three types: symbolic, deep learning and probabilistic program induction.

Structure-Mapping Engine (SME)

An analogical inference from S to T with respect to relation R_k is admissible if (and only if?): (a) R_k is a relation in S, (b) there is a systematic mapping between some set of relations R^S in S and some set of relations R^T in T, where $R_k \notin R^S, R^T$ and (c) in case there is more than one such mapping, the one with the highest systematicity is prioritized as a basis for the inference.

Note that it's not clear whether the conditions in this model are envisioned to be merely sufficient, or also necessary. Note, moreover, that the critical concept in those conditions is *systematicity*. This, in effect, means that the mapping between relations must include higher-order relations, that is, relations between relations, because these (presumably) indicate that the knowledge in a given domain is connected.

It's worth considering a few details about the implementation, which consists of three steps. The first step, roughly, involves the search for all possible individual relation and object pairings between S and T. The relations are described in a logical or quasi-logical language that contains constants and predicates. These predicates are nested in a tree-like structure to form expressions. To understand what's going on, let us adapt an example from Falkenhainer, Forbus and Gentner (1986). Suppose that the domains in question are the solar system S and the Rutherford atom T. S is described in terms of the following nested two-place predicates: (i) Causes(And, Revolves_Around()), (ii) And(Attracts(), Greater_Mass()), (iii) Greater_Mass(Sun, planet), (iv) Attracts(Sun, planet), and (v) Revolves_Around(planet, Sun). T is described in terms of the following two-place predicates: (vi) Greater_Mass'(nucleus, electron) and (vii) Attracts'(nucleus, electron). Two object pairings can be established in this case: nucleus – Sun and electron – planet. These pairings are suggested by the mass inequality relational pairing, expressed by the similarly named predicates Greater_Mass() and Greater_Mass'(), and the attraction pairing, expressed by the similarly named predicates Attracts() and Attracts'(). The second step, roughly, involves the construction of all possible global mappings. These are mappings that merge individual pairings into a coherent whole. Finally, the third step, involves an evaluation of global mappings to select the one that scores highest on systematicity. In the case at issue, assuming no other pairings can be produced, SME will suggest that the other predicates in S also apply in T. For example, Revolves_Around(electron, nucleus). More crucially, it will suggest that 'the [mass] inequality, together with the mutual attraction of the nucleus and the electron, causes the electron to revolve around the nucleus' (275). This is, roughly, what happened in the history of atomic physics, when the Rutherford-Bohr model of the atom was proposed. According to this model, which has since been superseded, electrons are kept in orbit around the nucleus of an atom with an electrostatic force, just like planets are kept in orbit around the Sun with a gravitational force.

One objection to the SME model is that a lot hinges on the choice of predicates. Not only is that choice difficult to make, but there are also questions about the effects it has on the drawing of analogical inferences. The latter issue generalizes into a problem that afflicts various areas of philosophy and beyond. That judgements concerning such issues as the ordering of theories on the basis of verisimilitude or simplicity may be affected by linguistic choices is a decades-old problem (Miller 2017). This problem is further compounded by the fact that SME does not provide any guidance on how to choose or indeed construct predicates, but assumes that these have already been supplied. Additional problems with SME are discussed in Bartha (2010: Ch. 3), who complains that systematicity is neither necessary nor sufficient for good analogical inferences.

It is now time to turn to some general remarks about neural net models of analogical reasoning. Neural net approaches to AI have been on the ascendancy in recent years. A big part of the reason why is the fact that deep neural nets, unlike symbolic systems, are more readily able to handle data that are not fully structured. As Kautz (2022) stresses, deep neural nets obviate 'the need for manually engineered features [machine learning speak for variables]' (112). This opens opportunities that were once unavailable. Still, one major obstacle in the way of neural models of analogical reasoning is that neural nets are not particularly good at reasoning. Their hidden layers of nodes, where the computation occurs, are notoriously difficult to interpret. In fact, not only do those computations fail to resemble human reasoning, but they also often require vast amounts of data to draw simple inferences.

Despite these obstacles, recent attempts at making headway on the problem of computationally modelling analogical reasoning have leaned heavily on neural nets. On this approach, analogy making is something that needs to be learned. This involves feeding neural nets with relevant training data. For example, correct and incorrect analogies. To address the problem that the data needs to be orders of magnitude higher than the available correct and incorrect analogies, AI theorists and practitioners have resorted to the automatic generation of data. In some areas, this process is easier to carry out than in others. Non-verbal analogical reasoning tasks involving shapes whose attributes (e.g. colour and shape) vary, known as Raven's progressive matrices, are now routinely explored with neural nets, precisely because the production of vast amounts of training and testing data can be automated.

Although neural nets trained on such sets are gradually getting better at drawing the right analogies, deep disagreements have emerged (Barrett et al. 2018; Hu et al. 2021; Zhang et al. 2019) over whether the automatically produced data are diverse enough to give rise to sufficiently stringent tests of the resulting models. Moreover, and as already indicated above, not all reasoning tasks are easily amenable to the artificial generation of data. Given the generally higher complexity of analogical inferences in science (vs. in non-verbal tasks), one would expect that artificial data would be harder to synthesize *ab initio*. As such, analogical reasoning in science presents a significant challenge for those advocating neural net approaches. There is also a more general reason to doubt the amount of mileage we can get out of neural nets. If we had a method to produce diverse data that provide sufficiently stringent tests for our models, then we wouldn't really need (to test) those models because the method itself would presumably generate the desired model or something like it.

It is not our intention here to say that neural net models face insurmountable problems as regards the modelling of analogical reasoning in science. Rather, we just wanted to highlight some genuine difficulties. To end on a more positive note, we would like to point out that neuro-symbolic approaches to AI are increasingly being adopted to solve problems that require the complementary strengths of neural nets and symbolic methods. Kautz (2022), for example, insists that 'the next big scientific advance in AI' will involve such hybrid systems. We expect a similar tendency in the area of analogical reasoning in science, raising the prospects of a fully automated approach to scientific discovery.

We conclude this section with some big picture remarks on the analogical reasoning models, both philosophical and AI, on offer. Such models are prescriptive in that they do not merely, or primarily, concern themselves with the actual practice of discriminating between good and bad analogical reasoning. Some of them are explicitly qualitative (TSS, HCM, non-probabilistic BAM), while others are quantitative (MPM, probabilistic BAM, SME). Some are merely heuristically oriented (BAM, SME), hoping to establish initial plausibility claims about inferred similarities. Others play both a heuristic and a justificatory role (TSS, HCM, MPM), hoping to also establish support towards those claims. All of them encounter counterexamples, which allege either that they are too liberal (TSS, MPM, SME, BAM) or too stringent (HCM).[2] Despite these drawbacks, nothing of what we said here prevents

---

2 Although we have not discussed this point earlier, it is worth noting that some models have been accused of being too strict in some respects and too liberal in others.

their amelioration through a modification (addition, deletion or both) of their stated conditions. The section following the next offers one such additional criterion that can be bolted on to any of the above models. Before we get to that section, however, a general challenge awaits.

Norton's Material Challenge

An easy way out of having to deal with counterexamples is to deny that any such models, even when they are modified, cover all (and only) instances of good analogical reasoning. This is tantamount to denying the existence of a universal model of analogical reasoning, and it is a route that several scholars have taken. Some (Currie 2013; Reiss 2015; Toulmin 1958) have suggested that different fields of research require different models. Others, like Norton (2003, 2011, 2021), have suggested a more fine-grained approach, claiming that different research questions, even when these emanate from the same field, require different models. In this section, we consider a general challenge against those who wish to analyse analogical modelling in terms of a one-size-fits-all, that is, a universal model.

The challenge is due to Norton and is based on the claim that inductive inferences are only good in so far as they are licenced by local facts. His argument is based on an ingeniously simple example. Compare the following two inductive inferences:

	Inference 1	**Inference 2**
Premise:	Some samples of bismuth melt at 271 °C.	Some samples of wax melt at 91 °C.
Conclusion:	All samples of bismuth melt at 271 °C.	All samples of wax melt at 91 °C.

Although the two inferences are structurally identical, only the first one is good. That's because all samples of bismuth do melt at 271 °C, but not all samples of wax melt at 91 °C. On Norton's view, the goodness of an inductive inference is 'grounded in matters of fact that hold only in particular domains' (2003: 647). Thus, there are facts about bismuth, but not about wax, that make it the case that all of its samples behave in the same way.

Unsurprisingly, Norton extends this attitude to analogical reasoning, which he considers to be a species of inductive reasoning. In doing so, he repudiates the universal model of analogical reasoning:

> If analogical reasoning is required to conform only to a simple formal schema, the restriction is too permissive. Inferences are authorized that clearly should

not pass muster [...] The natural response has been to develop more elaborate formal templates that are able to discriminate more finely by capturing more details of various test cases [...] elaborations cannot escape the inevitable difficulty. Their embellished schema [is] never quite embellished enough. There is always some part of the analysis that must be handled [...] without guidance from strict formal rules.

(2021: 119–20)

In other words, he takes the whole project of attempting to construct models like the above as doomed from the outset. Such models seem to face the impossible (to him) task of trying to catch all the counterexamples with the introduction of more and more qualifications. Expressed a different way, modellers may be facing the impossible task of trying to find an elusive balance between just the right amount of permissiveness and just the right amount of restrictiveness.

The compelling force of the bismuth-wax example notwithstanding, it is worth asking whether the process of adjusting models of analogical reasoning has no end in sight. Is the trade-off between maximizing correct analogies and minimizing incorrect ones necessarily unavoidable? To definitively answer questions like these in the affirmative is no trivial matter, and would require an impossibility proof. No such proof has been given. At best, what Norton presents us with is an inductive case (whose own licencing fact is not entirely justified) for pessimism vis-à-vis universal models of analogical reasoning. In the sections that follow, we want to give some hope to the optimists by motivating an additional criterion of admissibility for analogical reasoning. This criterion may be combined with any of the aforementioned models.

Relevant Conceptual Uniformity

In this section, we claim that relevant conceptual uniformity is a fruitful, potentially even necessary, additional criterion for the determination of good from bad analogical arguments. To set up this criterion, we first need to say something about relevance, uniformity, and the relation between them.

To say that a concept is unqualifiedly uniform is to say that the things/tokens it represents are homogeneous with respect to *some* of their natural properties. The uniformity required is not total homogeneity of the tokens, that is, sameness of all their properties, for the simple reason that that would result in only one token per concept. Moreover, conceptual uniformity is not to be used in isolation from, but rather in tandem with, relevance constraints. It should be clear, from the diamond–chalk example, that to avoid drawing unsuitable analogical inferences, such constraints must be in place. These, as we have seen above, may take the form of causal or correlational conditions relating the properties (and concepts) in the base analogy to the property (and concept) in the extended analogy. A set of properties (and its corresponding set of concepts) is unqualifiedly relevant for another set of properties (and its corresponding set of concepts) if and only if the former set of properties completely and non-redundantly determines the presence (and any values) of the latter. As such, the former can be employed to genuinely explicate lawlike behaviour relating to the latter. For example, certain genetic properties of *Ligularia fischeri* as well as those of humans are presumably causally relevant in genuinely explicating that plant's edibility by humans. The claim we would like to put forward here is that if the former properties and concepts are unqualifiedly relevant to the latter properties and concepts, then those concepts must be unqualifiedly uniform. Another way of expressing this relationship is that unqualified conceptual uniformity is a necessary, but not sufficient, condition for unqualified conceptual relevance.

Focusing only on unqualified conceptual uniformity ignores the fact that various concepts are gainfully employed in scientific reasoning but are not entirely uniform – the concept of species is a well-known example. Indeed, as we will see in the next section, scientific concepts may start life as fairly dis-uniform, and gradually build towards increased uniformity. That means it is worth considering the extent to which a concept is uniform. Similarly, focusing only on unqualified property/conceptual relevance ignores what we have already implicitly conceded, namely that it is worth considering the degree to which a property/concept is relevant to another property/concept. This is obvious in cases where the base analogy properties/concepts may be imperfectly correlated with the extended analogy property/concept – think of the electrical fluid-lightning case. Taking these observations into account, we may say that the concepts featuring in the analogy between S and T must be restricted to those that are *relevantly uniform*. That is, they must be concepts whose tokens exhibit a certain degree of homogeneity vis-à-vis some of their natural properties, with the properties involved in the base analogy at least partly determining the presence (and any values) of the property in the extended analogy. Other things being equal, increasing the strength of that determination relation should lead to a corresponding increase in the degree of homogeneity between the tokens. Based on these ideas, we can then define the following criterion:

Relevant Conceptual Uniformity Admissibility: Other things being equal, the more relevantly uniform those concepts, the higher the admissibility of the analogical inference.

To see the usefulness of the notion and corresponding criterion of relevant conceptual uniformity, we need go no further than Norton's bismuth-wax example. Ironically, Norton's analysis of what really goes on in this example brings out the importance of this notion to the surface. In his own words: 'All samples of bismuth are uniform just in the property that determines their melting point [...] Wax samples lack this uniformity in the relevant property, since "wax" is the generic name for various mixtures of hydrocarbons' (2003: 650). In other words, it's no wonder that the inference from some to all tokens of bismuth is reliable, but the one from some to all tokens of wax is not. Bismuth, qua a chemical element, is highly uniform with respect to several properties, including, most relevantly, those that result in the lawlike behaviour of melting points.[3] In more detail, melting points are decided by how much energy is needed to overcome the intermolecular forces that make up the internal structure of a substance. Since the internal structure of different bismuth tokens is identical, the energy required is the same in all cases. By contrast, wax is not a relevantly uniform concept, at least not with respect to the internal structure of its samples. As such, no inference to the melting point of all its tokens can be secured from some of them. Indeed, even the subordinate concept of paraffin wax, represents tokens whose melting points vary considerably because the corresponding intermolecular forces vary considerably (Himran, Suwono and Mansoori 1994).

The proposed relevant conceptual uniformity admissibility criterion can be integrated into any of the existing models of analogical reasoning. We only have space for two quick demonstrations here, so we restrict most of our comments to the TSS and MPM models. For expedience, we may speak directly of concepts being relevantly uniform with respect to other concepts, dropping the reference to properties being relevantly uniform. Moreover, we here treat the additional criterion as necessary, though this need not be the case. We may thus aptly modify these accounts as follows:

---

3 The periodic table of elements, of which bismuth is a member, contains some of the most uniform concepts found in nature, second only to the uniformity that exists across subatomic particle concepts.

TSS (with relevant conceptual uniformity)

(1) S is similar to T in relation to properties $Q_1, ..., Q_n$, which are encoded by concepts $C_1, ..., C_n$.
(2) S possesses some further property Q_{n+1}, encoded by concept C_{n+1}.
(3) Concepts $C_1, ..., C_n$, are relevantly uniform vis-à-vis concept C_{n+1}.
(4) Therefore, T possesses property Q_{n+1}, or some property similar to Q_{n+1}.

MPM (with relevant conceptual uniformity)

The admissibility of an analogical argument from S to T in relation to property Q_k increases if and only if: (a) $S(Q_k)$ and (b) for any concept C_i (corresponding to property Q_i) that is distinct from, but relevantly uniform with respect to, concept C_k (corresponding to property Q_k), $P(T(Q_k) \mid (S(Q_k) \approx_{s^*} T(Q_i)) \& B) > P(T(Q_k) \mid B)$.

The subscript s* in the modified MPM account signifies that S and T are similar to each other, without needing to specify that the similarity must not be known to be irrelevant. That's because the relevant conceptual uniformity admissibility criterion now carries the burden of determining relevance.

Before we bring this section to a close, it is worth appraising what it is we have addressed in the challenge posed by Norton. First of all, we must grant that uniformities cannot simply be stipulated. They must be discovered. So, Norton is right in asserting that facts of the matter enter the determination of analogical inference admissibility. Having said this, the relevant conceptual uniformity admissibility criterion is blind to the specific research question (or field) pursued. As such, it is not a local, but a universal, condition, or at least aspires to be one provided a version of it works in all cases. If such a version does indeed work in all cases, then, by integrating it into existing models of analogical reasoning, it brings us one step closer to universality. Less polemically, such models are perhaps not as local as Norton would have us believe.

A Wittgensteinian Spanner in the Works?

One major obstacle to the above approach has its origins in Wittgenstein's *Philosophical Investigations* (PI), where we are urged to move away from the view that terms or concepts possess essences, which can be captured by formal definitions given in terms of necessary and sufficient conditions. Language, on Wittgenstein's view, doesn't work like that. Taking the concept of games as an illustration, he argues that there is so much variation in its tokens, for example, ball games, board games, card games, and so on, that it is pointless to try to find a definition. But that doesn't mean that different tokens of games are not more similar to each other than they are to other things. Using this claim as a basis, he then asserts that: 'I can think of no better expression to characterize these similarities than "family resemblances" [...] "games" form a family' (Wittgenstein 1953: PI §67). Norton's and Wittgenstein's rationales are similar as they both seem to claim that we philosophers are unhealthily preoccupied with 'generality', and, in so doing, omit practice, which is often grounded in local peculiarities – in the present case, facts about the usage of concepts and terms.

Wittgenstein's anti-definitional/anti-essentialist stance is in stark contrast to the requirement of (relevant) conceptual uniformity, for his view effectively denies the uniformity of concepts. On this view, tokens at best exhibit varying degrees of similarity to one another, and concepts are thus less than perfectly uniform. This presents a challenge to the limit case of the relevant conceptual uniformity admissibility criterion, that is, the case where the concepts involved are perfectly uniform, as it judges it to be unsatisfiable. In what follows, we consider what can be said to address this challenge.

Let us start by conceding that much of what goes on in language is as Wittgenstein describes it. Many of our concepts have meanings and extensions with unclear boundaries and are best treated in terms of graded membership. Just because many concepts are like this, however, doesn't mean that all concepts, including scientific ones, should be treated this way. That is to say, we must not infer that all concepts are dis-uniform or less than perfectly uniform from the (admittedly reasonable) claim that many everyday concepts do exhibit varying degrees of dis-uniformity. This would be as bad an inference by analogy, as the ones that the analogical reasoning modellers are so desperate to avoid.

More positively, we can, in fact, argue for uniformity from within, that is, by following Wittgenstein's own methodology. On this methodology, membership in a concept is decided through language use. That some concepts in science, particularly those in natural science, are uniform is evidenced by such use. Definitions are demanded, given and consistently followed in science. Some of the best-known examples concern the base concepts employed in the International System of Units (SI): metre, second, mole, ampere, kelvin, candela and kilogram. Incidentally, Wittgenstein (1953: §50) is unconvinced by these concepts and launches the following complaint about the standard metre. It is meaningless, according to him, to ask if the standard metre is a metre long, because the standard metre is a physical object and thus cannot be laid next to itself. This complaint is obviously outdated. At the time, the standard metre was defined against a physical object, namely a platinum-iridium bar. Today, all seven base units concepts are given definitions in terms of fundamental physical constants and each other. The standard metre is defined thus: 'The meter is the length of the path travelled by light in vacuum during a time interval of 1/299 792 458 of a second' (NIST).[4]

Some uniformity in nature is necessary. Without it, our world would be too much of a jumble to make any sense of and predict. In fact, even Hume, who suggests that causal relations and inductive inferences are but mere projections of the mind, assumes some uniformities. For, without some (restricted) uniformity of B following A, it would be impossible to form a habit of the mind that B follows A. If the world had no uniformity whatsoever, we wouldn't even be able to communicate with each other, as all categories, including sounds and words, would contain a random selection of tokens with unique features. In such a world, we would be unable to accomplish anything, unless we did so by chance.

Assuming that there are natural categories out there, as our best (most successful) science seems to indicate, the process of accurately representing them with concepts cannot but be gradual. That's because, as with any other epistemic investigation, victories are hard-earned. Concepts must be successively refined, which, as we have already argued, involves a tendency towards greater uniformity and lawlike relevance. The fact that the SI base units, as well as various other concepts, have changed over the years, and the way they have changed, reflects this toiling process. The standard metre, for example, has changed from being equal to 1/10,000,000 of the distance that separates the equator from the North Pole to a platinum-iridium bar held at very specific temperature and pressure vacuum conditions to the contemporary vacuum traversing length of light definition. Despite these changes, and the orders of magnitude reduction in the uncertainties involved, a metre 200 years ago is still approximately the same as a metre today, at least in relation to macroscopic scales and even down to optical microscope scales.

An important consequence of refining definitions towards relevant uniformity is that doing so increases the truth(-likeness) of proposed generalizations. The generalization expressed by the sentence 'All neutrinos interact with matter to produce electrons' has some truth content in that electrons are indeed produced in neutrino interactions with matter. But it is not entirely true or even close to the truth. That's because, as it turns out, there is not just one type of neutrinos, but three: electron, muon and tau neutrinos. Only the former interact with matter to produce electrons. Thus, if we replace the

---

4 Indeed, the last remaining bastion of sample-centric standards was the standard kilogram, a platinum-iridium cylinder kept at the International Bureau of Weights and Measures in Sèrves, France. Even this however was replaced by a definition in 2019.

concept 'neutrinos' in the above generalization with the more uniform and relevant concept 'electron neutrinos', then we end up with a generalization that is significantly more truthlike: 'All electron neutrinos interact with matter to produce electrons.' Note that the postulation of, and experimental confirmation that, neutrinos come in three different types was gradual, spanning about seven decades.

Testability and Computational Implementation

One beneficial aspect of the overall approach recommended in this chapter is that it is testable. Recall that the goodness of analogical reasoning, according to this approach, depends partly on the degree of relevant conceptual uniformity. As such, and other things being equal, analogical inferences are less likely to succeed when the concepts involved are less relevantly uniform. This is a prediction that drops out of the proposed approach and can be tested by running experiments with human subjects. We could, for example, assign subjects the role of discovering extended similarities on the grounds of basic similarities between different domains. If we vary the relevant conceptual uniformity levels of concepts across the subjects, we may find that higher levels are more or less helpful in making those discoveries. The puzzles could involve scenarios inspired by real scientific discoveries made with analogical reasoning, in which case it's best to select subjects with no prior knowledge of science.

Another way to test the prediction is through computational methods. One such method is agent-based simulations. Artificial agents can be placed in a simulated environment, equipped with information about similarities that hold between domains with stipulated properties, and instructed to draw analogical inferences about further similarities. Once again, varying the relevant conceptual uniformity levels of concepts across agents, and checking the success of the resulting inferences, would allow us to determine whether the proposed criterion is fertile, at least as a proof of concept. Another computational method that may be employed here is machine learning. We can train several competing neuro-symbolic models with analogical reasoning data. For example, we can train them with correct and incorrect analogies. The data should be such that the input features of different models correspond to concepts with different levels of relevant conceptual uniformity. Once the models are trained and tested on the existing data sets, we can unleash them on the world to see if any succeed, and indeed do better than the others, at making scientific discoveries.

It's important to note that, as far as we can see, no great obstacle stands in the way of computationally implementing the relevant conceptual uniformity admissibility criterion. For example, either via agent-based simulations or via a machine-learning neuro-symbolic model. If that is the case, and seeing as other aspects of analogical reasoning have already been successfully implemented *in silico*, it's safe to conclude that there are some grounds for hope in the assertion that analogical reasoning can be fully automated. Given the importance of analogical reasoning to heuristics, this, in turn, offers hope that scientific discovery, more generally, may one day be fully automated. Indeed, this is regardless of whether a universal approach to modelling analogical reasoning is feasible.

Conclusion

The foregoing discussion has, we hope, shed some light on analogical reasoning, its capabilities and limits. We began by exploring five major attempts (TSS, HCM, BAM, MPM, SME) at modelling analogical reasoning. Each of these made some headway towards that goal but also had some drawbacks. We then proceeded to outline an objection that affects all of them, namely Norton's argument that there is no universal model of analogical reasoning. We followed that up with an attempt to eliminate or at least reduce the objection's sting by positing an additional criterion for the goodness of analogical reasoning: the relevant conceptual uniformity admissibility criterion. We then questioned the satisfiability of this criterion with a challenge that has its roots in Wittgenstein's family resemblance metaphor. As a way of meeting the challenge, we argued that some concepts in natural science are indeed uniform, or, at least, more uniform than others, and that scientific inquiry strives towards such uniformity. We also tried to provide some initial motivation for the claim that analogical reasoning, in particular, and scientific discovery, more generally, can plausibly be automated.

One final thought is worth having. Bartha (2010) asks the very pertinent question 'what reason do we have to expect analogical arguments to work?' and immediately responds that '[t]he best answer I can give is that our models of analogical reasoning provide a forum that lets us debate about, and ultimately identify, the "right" critical factors, and hence the appropriate invariants for establishing symmetry between two domains' (303). This response leaves out the most important piece of the puzzle. The simple reason why analogical arguments work is because nature cooperates. Less metaphorically, nature contains considerable uniformity as well as repetition, and that is something that we can exploit. After all, bodies with mass attract each other, regardless of whether they are terrestrial or celestial. Masses and charges exhibit the same inverse square form of laws in the domains of gravitational and electrostatic phenomena. Selection and resource pressures determine survival and reproduction rates, irrespective of whether they were put in motion by the environment or by human hands. Newton's aphorism is highly instructive here: 'Nature is after all simple, and is normally self-consistent throughout an immense variety of effects, by maintaining the same mode of operation' (Letter to Dr William Briggs, reproduced in Turnbull 1960: 418).

References

Barrett, D., Hill, F., Santoro, A., Morcos, A., & Lillicrap, T. (2018, July). Measuring abstract reasoning in neural networks. In *International Conference on Machine Learning* (pp. 511–520). Stockholm:PMLR.

Bartha, P. (2010). *By Analogical Reasoning*. Oxford: Oxford University Press.

Campbell, N. R. (1957). *Foundations of Science*. New York: Dover.

Currie, A. (2013). Convergence as evidence. *The British Journal for the Philosophy of Science*, 64, 763–786.

Darwin, C. ([1860] 1967). *Darwin and Henslow: The Growth of an idea: Letters 1831–1860*, edited by Nora Barlow. London: Bentham-Moxon Trust and John Murray.

Drake, S. (1999). *Essays on Galileo and the History and Philosophy of Science* (Vol. 1). Toronto: University of Toronto Press.

FaIkenhainer, B., Forbus, K. D., & Gentner, D. (1986). The structure mapping engine. In *Proceedings of the American Association for Artificial Intelligence*, (pp. 272–277), AAAI Press: Philadelphia, PA–.

Franklin, B. (1941). *Benjamin Franklin's Experiments*, edited by I. Bernard Cohen. Cambridge: Harvard University Press.

Gentner, D. (1983). Structure-mapping: A theoretical framework for analogy. *Cognitive science*, 7(2), 155–170.

Heering, P. (1992). On Coulomb's inverse square law. *American Journal of Physics*, 60(11), 988–994.

Hesse, M. B. (1966). *Models and Analogies in Science*. London: Sheed and Ward.

Himran, S., Suwono, A., & Mansoori, G. A. (1994). Characterization of alkanes and paraffin waxes for application as phase change energy storage medium. *Energy Sources*, 16(1), 117–128.

Hofstadter, D. R. (1995). *Fluid Concepts and Creative Analogies: Computer Models of the Fundamental Mechanisms of Thought*. New York, NY: Basic Books.

Hu, S., Ma, Y., Liu, X., Wei, Y., & Bai, S. (2021, May). Stratified rule-aware network for abstract visual reasoning. *Proceedings of the AAAI Conference on Artificial Intelligence*, 35(2), 1567–1574.

Kautz, H. (2022). The third ai summer: AAAI Robert s. Engelmore memorial lecture. *AI Magazine*, 43(1), 105–125.

Kuhn, T. S. (1961). The function of measurement in modern physical science. *Isis*, 52(2), 161–193.

Lange, M. (1993). Natural laws and the problem of provisos. *Erkenntnis*, 38(2), 233–248.

Lovett, A. & Forbus, K. (2017). Modeling visual problem solving as analogical reasoning. *Psychological Review*, 124(1), 60.

Medin, D. L. & Schaffer, M. M. (1978). Context theory of classification learning. *Psychological Review*, 85(3), 207.

Mill, J. S. ([1843] 1973). *The Collected Works of John Stuart Mill (Books I–III)*, edited by John M. Robson. Toronto: University of Toronto Press.

Miller, D. (2017). *Out of Error: Further Essays on Critical Rationalism*. Oxon:Routledge.

Mitchell, M. (2021). Abstraction and analogy-making in artificial intelligence. *Annals of the New York Academy of Sciences*, 1505(1), 79–101.

National Institute of Standards and Technology (NIST). ;(2020). Definitions of SI base units. https://www.nist.gov/si-redefinition/definitions-si-base-units.

Newton, I. ([1687] 1999). *The Principia: Mathematical Principles of Natural Philosophy*. Berkeley: University of California Press.

Norton, J. D. (2003). A material theory of induction. *Philosophy of Science*, 70(4), 647–670.

Norton, J. D. (2011). History of science and the material theory of induction: Einstein's quanta, mercury's perihelion. *European Journal for Philosophy of Science*, 1, 3–27.

Norton, J. D. (2021). *The Material Theory of Induction*. Calgary, Alberta: University of Calgary Press.

Oppenheimer, R. (1956). Analogy in science. *American Psychologist*, 11(3), 127.

Reiss, J. (2015). A pragmatist theory of evidence. *Philosophy of Science*, 82(3), 341–362.

Rosch, E., & Mervis, C. B. (1975). Family resemblances: Studies in the internal structure of categories. *Cognitive Psychology*, 7(4), 573–605.

Rosenfeld, L. (1969). Newton's views on aether and gravitation. *Archive for History of Exact Sciences*, 6(1), 29–37.

Toulmin, S. (1958). *The Uses of Argument*. Cambridge: Cambridge University Press.

Turnbull, H. W. (Ed.) (1960). *The Correspondence of Isaac Newton* (Vol. II). Cambridge: Cambridge University Press.

Webb, T. W., Sinha, I., & Cohen, J. D. (2021). Emergent symbols through binding in external memory. In 9th International Conference on Learning Representations (ICLR). Piscataway, NJ: IEEE.

Wittgenstein, L. (1953). *Philosophical Investigations*, translated by G. E. M. Anscombe. New York: Macmillan Publishing Co., Inc.

Zhang, C., Gao, F., Jia, B., Zhu, Y., & Zhu, S. C. (2019). Raven: A dataset for relational and analogical visual reasoning. In *2019 IEEE/CVF Conference on Computer Vision and Pattern Recognition* (pp. 5312–5322). Piscataway, NJ: IEEE.

NOTES ON CONTRIBUTORS

Diane Proudfoot, Professor of Philosophy, University of Canterbury, New Zealand.

Tomi Kokkonen, Postdoctoral Researcher, University of Helsinki, Finland.

Ilmari Hirvonen, PhD Student, University of Helsinki, Finland.

Arturo Vazquez, PhD Student, University of Southampton, United Kingdom.

Éloïse Boisseau, PhD Student, University of Aix-Marseille, Gilles Gaston Granger Centre, France.

Laith Abdel-Rahman, Independent Researcher and Software Engineer, J.P. Morgan and Chase.

Ian Ground, Honorary Research Fellow in Philosophy, University of Hertfordshire, UK and Vice-President of the British Wittgenstein Society.

Giovanni Galli, Postdoctoral Researcher, University of Teramo, Italy.

Oskari Kuusela, Associate Professor in Philosophy, University of East Anglia, United Kingdom.

Ioannis Votsis, Associate Professor in Philosophy, Northeastern University London, United Kingdom.

INDEX

abstraction 124, 165, 165n1, 175
action 10–11, 19, 47–49, 49n3, 50, 50n5, 51–52, 54, 56–57, 62, 64, 74, 74n8, 75–76, 76nn9–10, 77–81, 86n3, 90–91, 91n7, 92–93, 95, 95n12, 96–97, 97n13, 98–100, 100n15, 101–2, 106, 111, 126, 134, 156, 160, 174–75, 178
affordance 51–52; environmental affordance 51
agency 49–50, 50n6, 52, 118, 128, 130, 139–40, 142
AI ethics 119
algorithm 46, 56, 70, 70n4, 73, 111n3, 114, 124, 132, 156, 158–59
analogical argument 185, 187–89, 195, 198, 202
analogical reasoning 14, 183–86, 190, 192–95, 197–99, 201–2; AI models of 183, 190; philosophical models of 183–84, 186; universal model of 183, 194, 202
analysis 7nn18, 20, 10, 55, 58, 66, 81, 110–13, 151, 157, 166–67, 168n4, 176, 195, 197
analytic pragmatism 110–11
animal 51, 74n8, 75, 135n7
anthropomorphism 29, 29n22; anthropomorphic 29n23; anthropomorphize 29n22, 108
Aristotle 93n9
artificial intelligence (AI) 1–2, 2n5, 3–4, 4n10, 5–6, 6n16, 7, 7n19, 8–14, 17–19, 22–28, 30, 32, 39–40, 44n2, 46–48, 51, 54, 54n9, 57, 61, 61n1, 62–63, 65–67, 69–70, 70n4, 71–72, 72n5, 73, 73n6, 74–76, 76nn9–10, 77–78, 80–82, 85, 88n5, 105, 105n1, 106–10, 112–20, 123, 123n1, 124, 124n4, 125, 127, 129, 131, 133, 136–42, 145, 145n1, 154–56, 160–61, 165–66, 170, 172, 174, 177, 180, 183, 190, 190n1, 192–93
artificial neural network (ANN) 116
attitude 8, 28, 30, 50, 52, 56, 77, 130, 186, 194
automaton 8, 26–27, 27n19, 54
autonomous discourse practice (ADP) 11, 106, 110–11, 113–15, 117, 119

Baker, Gordon Park 148n7
Bartha's Articulation Model (BAM) 189–90, 193, 202
Bartha, Paul 185–90, 192, 202
behaviour pattern 21, 50, 73, 74n7, 78–81
behaviourism 20–24, 107–10, 115, 117, 119, 126; behaviourist 8, 17, 20–21, 21n7, 22–24, 24n12, 25, 43–44, 108, 115; behaviouristic 44, 55; behaviouristic interpretation 44
Bennett, Maxwell 85, 87
bias 29, 127
black box 12–13, 70n4, 123–24, 124n4, 125–28, 133, 139, 158–59; black box problem 12, 70n4, 123–24, 124n4, 126–28
Block, Ned 25, 44
The Blue and Brown Books (BB) 2, 18–19, 25, 41, 53, 63–65, 87n4, 156
body 10, 24, 26, 43, 48, 50–51, 53, 67, 141, 147, 202
brain 8, 19, 20nn4–6, 31, 62, 66, 85–86, 86n3, 105, 105n1, 107–9, 118–19, 132, 156
Brandom, Robert 11, 105–6, 108, 110–15, 117–20
Brandomian vocabulary 111
bustle of life 27, 31

calculation 10, 23, 56, 68, 100–102; calculate 20, 41, 68, 77, 98–99, 101–2;

calculating 18, 54, 56, 67–68, 68n2, 75, 76n9, 80, 91, 98–101
calculator 20, 56, 90, 98–99, 101–2
Cambridge action 11, 95–98, 100n15
Cambridge agent 94
Cambridge change 94–95, 95n11, 96–98
Cambridge criterion 94
Carnap, Rudolf 24, 24n14, 25
Cartesianism 126, 129–30
causal 14, 49, 49n3, 52, 54–56, 62, 66, 68, 70n3, 73, 81, 125, 139, 187–90, 196, 200
ChatGPT 2, 39, 105, 118, 127, 127n5, 136
chess 20, 20n6, 29, 72–73, 73n6, 74–76, 76n9, 77–80, 101
Chiang, Ted 137
Chomsky, Noam 11, 105–6, 108–10, 112, 114–17, 119–20, 155
cognition 9, 12, 18, 22, 40, 51, 62, 67, 108, 110, 113, 116, 119, 136–39, 141, 155, 190
cognitive architecture 8, 31, 50–51, 57
cognitive process 48, 117, 128
computation 48–49, 62, 66, 74–75, 117, 192
computational implementation 184, 201
computationalism 31–32, 49; computationalist 21, 21n8
computer-imitates-human game 21, 23, 25
computing 4, 8, 17–21, 27, 44, 46, 62, 66, 68, 74n8, 75, 131
computing machine 17–18, 20, 27, 46, 62, 75
conceptual problem 10, 63, 65–67, 70n3, 71, 74, 74n8, 141
connectionism 4–5, 5n13, 146, 150–51, 154–57; connectionist 5, 12–13, 32, 146, 151, 153–58
consonance 134
convolutional neural network (ConvNet) 124, 126, 128
creativity 46–47, 116, 150
criterion 21–23, 25, 29–30, 42–43, 46, 48, 50, 53, 57–58, 63–66, 69, 70n3, 74n8, 77, 86n3, 94, 100–101, 117–18, 123, 126, 134, 171, 172n8, 175–76, 183–84, 190, 194–99, 201–2

Darwin, Charles 19, 19n3, 184–85
De Waal, Frans 141
deception 23
Dennett, Daniel 49, 74n7, 115
deontic 54

Descombes, Vincent 99
description 20, 29n23, 62, 73–74, 78, 80–81, 91, 94–96, 130–31, 135, 148n7, 154, 157–58, 166–67, 170–71, 173n9, 175–77
dichotomy 6n16, 10, 61n1, 62, 71, 81; dichotomous 10, 66, 71, 81
disposition 24n13, 47, 51, 52n7, 57, 68n2, 77; dispositional 49, 55
Dreyfus, Hubert 172, 174, 177

E-language 109
electronic brain 8, 19
Electronic Delay Storage Automatic Calculator (EDSAC) 20, 27
embodiment 47, 53, 120, 130, 139, 142
emotional concept 24
empathy 29
empirical problem 9, 65–66, 70n3, 72n5
empirical proposition 64
enactivism 9, 12, 40, 50–51, 53, 138–39; enactivist 9, 22, 40, 51–52, 56–58, 132–33
error 87n4, 114
ethics 1, 1n2, 77, 110, 119, 127, 137
evidence 2n5, 41, 44, 46, 64–66, 69, 70n3, 74n8, 119–20, 135
example 4–5, 5n14, 10–11, 13, 18–19, 21–22, 22nn9–10, 23, 25–26, 28, 29n23, 42, 44, 46, 49–50, 52–53, 55, 62–67, 68n2, 70nn3–4, 72–73, 73n6, 74–76, 76n9, 77n11, 79–81, 85, 85n1, 86, 89–92, 95, 95n11, 96–98, 102, 109, 111n3, 112, 116, 119, 123–24, 124n4, 127, 130, 134, 137, 147, 149–50, 153, 165, 165n1, 166–69, 171, 173–76, 178–79, 184–87, 189, 191–202
explainable AI (XAI) 70n4, 127–28
expressive bootstrapping 111–13, 118
external relation 55

facial expression 28, 28n21, 31, 74
family resemblance 2n3, 6, 14, 76n10, 150, 155, 184, 199, 202
feature 14, 28, 50–51, 62–63, 67, 69, 71, 73–74, 77, 79–81, 87, 96, 118, 128, 145, 151–52, 154, 156–61, 165, 175–76, 186, 192, 200–201
figurative expression 79
Floridi, Luciano 132, 134
folk psychology 49–50
form 2n3, 4, 8–9, 11, 13, 20, 22, 28, 30, 43, 57, 65–66, 86, 91–92, 95, 97–98,

112, 118, 120, 126, 130–31, 134, 141, 146, 147n6, 149, 152, 160, 167–68, 170, 179, 185–87, 191, 196, 199–200, 202
form of life 2n3, 43, 91, 118, 120, 130, 134, 160
Franklin, Benjamin 187–88
functional equivalence, classes of 99

Geach, Peter 94–95
general intelligence 117
Generative Pre-Trained Transformer (GPT) 11, 107, 116, 158
Gentner, Dedre 190–91
Good Old Fashioned Artificial Intelligence (GOFAI) 4, 12, 70, 70n4, 124, 126, 128–30, 133, 138
grammar 2n3, 23, 41, 64–66, 72, 75, 79, 81, 108–10, 130, 149, 168, 170; depth grammar 65; grammatical 10–11, 41, 55, 63, 68–69, 75, 80, 87, 89, 168; surface grammar 65–66, 81

Hartree, Douglas Rayner 19
Haugeland, John 4, 70, 70n4, 178
Hesse, Mary Brenda 187
Hesse's causal model (HCM) 187, 189–90, 193, 202
human 5, 6n16, 8, 10–12, 17–21, 23–29, 29n22, 30, 30n25, 31–32, 40, 42–44, 44n2, 45–48, 51–54, 56, 58, 61–62, 66–67, 69, 70n4, 71–72, 74, 74n8, 75–76, 76nn9–10, 77–78, 80–81, 85–86, 86n3, 89, 91–92, 92n8, 93, 101–2, 105–10, 114–19, 124, 127, 129, 131–32, 134–35, 140–41, 155–56, 158, 160–61, 166, 178, 180, 184, 192, 201, 203
human computer 18
Hume, David 55, 200
Hutto, Daniel 40, 51, 125, 132–33, 138

idealization 165, 165n1, 175
I-language 109
imitation game 8, 20–21, 23, 25, 25n15, 29, 31, 45
inductivist interpretation 44
inner and outer 26, 30
intellectual action 90–91, 91n7, 98–102
intention 51, 56, 115, 193; intentional 4, 9–10, 48, 50, 50n5, 51–52, 74, 74n7, 76, 76nn9–10, 79, 88, 90–91, 96, 97n13, 100, 132–35; intentional action 74, 76, 76nn9–10, 79, 90–91, 97n13, 100

intentional stance 74n7
intentionality 12, 50n5, 51–52, 62, 74n7, 97, 130–34, 139, 142
internal relation 54–55, 128, 147
interpretation 3, 8, 21, 23–25, 31, 41, 44, 46, 50, 53, 69, 70n3, 115, 131, 133–34, 148n7, 154, 167n2, 175n12
interpretationism 49

Johnson, Mark 85n2, 89

Kant, Immanuel 1n1, 137, 171–72
Kasparo Garry 73n6
Kautz, Henry 192–93
Klagge, James 140
Kripke, Saul 5n14, 54–55, 148, 148n7

Lakoff, George 85n2, 89
language 1, 2n3, 3, 6–13, 20, 43, 50, 54–55, 61–63, 67–69, 70nn3–4, 71–72, 72n5, 73, 73n6, 74, 74nn7–8, 75–76, 76n10, 77, 77n11, 78–82, 105–10, 111n3, 112–16, 124n4, 130–31, 134, 135n7, 140, 145–61, 166–68, 168n4, 170–72, 172n8, 173, 173n10, 174–76, 177n13, 178–79, 191, 198–99
language game 2n3, 13, 43, 69, 75, 116, 140, 146, 149–50, 155–61, 173, 173n10
language model 50, 148
large language model (LLM) 11, 105–6, 116, 124n4
Last Writings on the Philosophy of Psychology (LW) 26, 28, 31, 67, 78–79, 140
law 1, 1n2, 123, 123n3
learning 2, 12, 20n6, 45, 47, 52n7, 56–57, 70nn4, 8, 76, 76n10, 77, 80, 105, 107, 114, 124–25, 128, 131, 137–38, 141, 145–46, 154–56, 159–61, 190n1, 192, 201–2
Lectures on Philosophical Psychology (LPP) 18
Lectures on the Foundations of Mathematics (LFM) 2, 7, 17–18, 43
literal use 9, 62, 67, 72, 75, 77–80
logic 1, 6, 13, 62, 64, 67, 71, 81, 106, 117, 148, 155, 165–68, 168nn3, 4, 169, 169n6, 170–74, 174n11, 175, 177n13, 178–79
Lovelace, Ada 46–48
Lowney, Charles 5n13, 13, 31, 145–46, 148, 153–60

machine 2, 4–5, 8–12, 17, 17n1, 18–24, 24n12, 25–27, 27n16, 27nn18–19, 29, 29nn23–24, 31, 39–44, 44n2, 45–54, 56–58, 61–68, 68n2, 69–70, 70nn3–4, 71–74, 74n8, 75–77, 77n11, 78–82, 85, 85n1, 87–88, 88n5, 89–90, 90n6, 91, 91n7, 92, 92n8, 93, 98–102, 105, 107–9, 111n3, 112, 115–19, 124–25, 127, 129–30, 132–33, 136–40, 145, 156, 159–60, 192, 201–2
machine learning (ML) 2, 4, 12, 45, 47, 56, 70n4, 76, 105, 114, 124, 145, 156, 159, 192, 201
Malthus, Thomas Robert 184–85
meaning 2n3, 3, 8, 13, 41–42, 44n2, 45, 63–65, 71, 76, 76n10, 77–80, 86, 91, 107, 109, 111–13, 119, 126, 128–36, 139, 146, 150, 152–54, 156–61, 169
measure 21, 108, 130, 171
mental state 4, 11, 28, 49, 49n3, 50, 57, 62, 69, 132
mereological fallacy 85, 85n1, 86–87
merge 11, 109
metaphor 6, 67, 78n12, 89, 184, 202
metaphysical proposition 64, 74
metavocabulary 111, 111n3, 112–13, 118, 120
metonymy 87–90, 97
Mill, John Stuart 188
Mill's probability model (MPM) 188–89, 193, 197–98, 202
mind-reading 28–29
minimalist program 108–9, 117
miracle 127
mistake 11, 24, 40–41, 56, 58, 74n8, 85, 85nn1–2, 87, 91, 116, 134–35
Mountbatten, Louis 19
Mylin, Erik 132

natural language processing (NLP) 12, 70n4, 105, 145, 145n2, 146, 151, 151n8, 152, 152n9, 153–55, 157, 160–61
naysayer 23
neocognitive 140
neural network 20, 31, 31n28, 146, 151–52, 154–55, 157, 192–93
norm 9, 48, 56–57, 91, 100–2, 106, 110
normative 40, 54–56, 68, 80–81, 99–101, 110, 116–17
normativity 40, 43, 49, 53–54, 56–57, 130
Norton, John Daniel 14, 183, 194–95, 197–99, 202
notebooks 1914-1916 151

octopus 141
one-way power 93, 96–97
ontology of thinking 44, 48
originality 47
other minds 10, 28, 30, 126

pattern of behaviour 44, 73, 73n6, 74–75, 76n10, 78, 80–81
PavloIvan 43
perception 30, 51–52, 56, 156, 165–66
Philosophical Grammar (PG) 18, 32, 42, 168, 171, 174
Philosophical Investigations (PI) 3, 3n6, 5, 5n14, 12, 18, 21, 26, 28–29, 29n24, 42–43, 54, 61n1, 63, 65–67, 72, 72n5, 73–77, 77n11, 78n12, 79–81, 86, 90, 100, 128, 147, 149–50, 153, 156, 168, 170, 172n8, 174, 176, 178, 198–99
Philosophical Remarks (PR) 43, 55, 64, 168, 170–71
Philosophy of Pyschology: A Fragment (PPF) 74, 75n8, 77–78, 80, 125
Phronesis 137
physical predicate 86–87
Pinker, Steven 21, 62, 155
polysemy 76n10
practice 6, 10–11, 40, 45, 47, 49, 54, 56, 63, 67–68, 73, 77, 91, 101, 106–7, 110–11, 111n3, 112–15, 118, 120, 128–30, 134, 140, 152, 156–58, 160, 193, 199
pragmatic AI 113, 117–18
Pragmatically mediated semantic relations 111–12
pragmatism 110–12
prediction 45, 128, 152, 159, 201
primary meaning 79–80
primary use 79
primitive 12, 28, 31, 135, 135n7, 136, 138, 142, 147, 156
private 2n3, 12–13, 20, 25, 102, 128, 130, 132, 145–50, 153–54, 157–61
private language 2n3, 12–13, 130, 145–49, 154, 157–58, 160
propositional system 170–74, 174n11, 179
Proudfoot, Diane 2, 5, 8, 17, 17n1, 19, 21n8, 24–25, 28, 29n22, 30, 30n26, 31n28, 44–46, 53, 53n8, 54, 54n9, 108n2
psychological language 9–10, 61–63, 67–69, 71–73, 73n6, 74, 74n8, 75–77, 77n11, 78–82
psychological predicate 63, 68–72, 72n5, 75, 76n9, 77, 80–81, 86–87, 87n4, 90
public discussion 17, 20, 39

Ramsey, Frank 3
rationality 127–28
reading machine 116, 119
reason 2, 4, 9–10, 14, 19, 27, 31, 46, 48, 55, 57, 91n7, 92, 100, 107, 110, 119, 125, 129, 135, 192–93, 195, 202
regress 130–37, 139, 142
regularity 68
relevance 13–14, 98, 107, 165, 177, 177n13, 178, 195–96, 198, 200; Relevant, 4, 6, 8, 14, 63–65, 72n5, 81, 86n3, 91n7, 93, 123, 125–27, 133, 136–38, 146, 151, 165, 165n1, 166, 168–69, 169n5, 173–75, 175n12, 177, 177n14, 178, 180, 183, 192, 195–202
relevant conceptual uniformity 14, 183, 195, 197–99, 201–2
Remarks on the Foundations of Mathematics (RFM) 19, 55–56, 63, 68, 101–2
Remarks on the Philosophy of Psychology (RPP) 20, 27, 27n18, 28–30, 32, 41–43, 64, 69, 69n2, 72n5, 74–75, 76n9, 86n3, 87n4, 170
representationalism 48–49, 51–52, 139
resolute reading 3, 148; resolute reader 148, 160
response-dependence 25, 30; response-dependent 25, 30
robot 19n3, 40, 47, 52, 52n7, 53, 56, 58
robotics 39–40, 48, 51–53, 56–58
rule 2n3, 4–5, 5n14, 11, 20, 23, 29, 41, 54, 56, 62–63, 68, 70n4, 72, 74, 77, 80, 100–1, 110, 112, 125, 130–31, 133–35, 137–38, 148, 148n7, 155, 157–58, 166–74, 179, 195
rule-following 2n3, 5, 5n14, 54, 56, 80, 110, 130, 148, 155
Russell, Bertrand 5–6, 6n16, 19, 55, 110, 149, 166–67, 167n2, 168, 168n4, 174

sapience 106, 108, 113, 115–20, 138
Schwartz, Jack 136
scientific discovery 6, 184, 193, 202
Scientism, 120
Searle, John Rogers 4, 9, 12, 23, 61, 61n1, 62, 105, 105n1, 116, 132
secondary meaning 79–80
secondary sense 10, 43, 76n10, 79
secondary use 42, 79, 81
sensation 67–69, 135, 147, 149, 158
sentience 108, 113, 115, 117–18, 138
Shanker, Stuart 2–6, 22–24, 41
Silver, David 72, 74–77, 77n11, 78–79

the simple schema (TSS) 14, 186–87, 193, 197–98, 202
simplification 13, 165–66, 174–75, 177–78
Skinner, Burrhus Frederic 21, 21n7, 107–8, 155
Smolensky, Paul 153–55, 158
social robotics 56, 58
soul 22, 26, 28, 30, 43, 77, 140–41
speciesism 8, 29–30
specification 109, 112, 124, 126
strong AI 4, 9, 11, 46, 54, 61, 61n1, 62, 67, 71–72, 75, 77, 105, 105n1, 106–8, 110, 113, 116–20
structure-mapping engine 190
symbolic AI 27, 32, 70, 70n4, 155, 183
symptom 70n3
syntactic structure 108–10

temporality 139, 142
testability 184, 201
theory of mind 21n8, 22, 47–48, 50n5, 52, 113, 115
therapy 126, 142
thinking 5, 8–10, 12, 21–23, 25, 25n15, 26–27, 29–31, 39–44, 44n2, 45–50, 50n5, 51–53, 56–58, 62–66, 68, 68n2, 71–72, 74, 74n8, 75, 76n9, 77, 82, 94, 98–99, 101–2, 113, 123, 125, 136, 139, 154, 165, 168, 178–79
thinking, concept of 42, 44–46, 52–53, 64–66, 74n8
thinking machines: *Can machines think?* 9–10, 23, 25, 61–62, 64–67, 70n3, 71, 81
Tractatus Logico Philosophicus (TLP) 3, 3n8, 21, 125, 147, 151, 156, 166–67, 167n2, 168, 168n4, 170, 176
Transformer architecture 11, 105–6, 112
Trust 7n18, 127
Turing, Alan 2, 5, 6n16, 8–9, 17, 17nn1–2, 18–21, 21nn7–8, 22–24, 24n12, 25, 25n15, 26–29, 29n23, 30, 30n26, 31, 31n28, 32, 39–41, 43–44, 44n2, 45–50, 52n7, 53, 54n9, 57, 99, 108, 108n2, 109, 111n3, 115–16, 118, 120, 137–38
Turing/'s test 6n16, 8, 21, 23–25, 30n26, 45–46, 108, 108n2, 115–16, 120
two-way power 93, 96–98

uncanny 107
uncertainty 10, 69, 70nn3–4, 127
understanding 4, 11, 18, 21n7, 22, 24, 26, 42–43, 50–51, 62, 67, 68n2, 89,

100, 107, 110, 112, 116, 128, 146, 149, 155–57, 159–61, 167, 175, 177–78
uniform 14, 65, 165, 172n8, 184, 195–97, 197n3, 198–99, 201–2
uniformity 14, 183–84, 195–97, 197n3, 198–202
universal Turing machine 109

Verbal Behavior 107–8
verification 63–64, 66
von Wright, Georg Henrik 49

weak AI 9–10, 61–62, 67, 71, 115–16
Wittgenstein, Ludwig 1, 1nn1–2, 2, 2nn3, 5, 3, 3nn6, 8, 4–5, 5nn13–14, 6–7, 7nn20–21, 8–14, 17, 17nn1–2, 18–21, 21n7, 22–27, 27n19, 28, 28n21, 29, 29n24, 30–32, 39–44, 44n2, 45–54, 54n9, 55–58, 61, 61n1, 62–68, 68n2, 69–70, 70nn3–4, 71–72, 72n5, 73–76, 76n9, 77, 77n11, 78, 78n12, 79–82, 85–86, 86n3, 87, 87n4, 88–102, 105–20, 123, 123n1, 124, 124n4, 125–142, 145, 145n1, 146–48, 148n7, 149–61, 165, 165n1, 166–68, 168nn3–4, 169–72, 172n8, 173–74, 174n11, 175, 175n12, 176–77, 177n13, 178, 178n15, 179–80, 183–203

Zettel (Z) 26–28, 31

Milton Keynes UK
Ingram Content Group UK Ltd.
UKHW041817041024
449024UK00001B/5